CULTURE AND CONSERVATION:

THE HUMAN DIMENSION IN ENVIRONMENTAL PLANNING

Edited by Jeffrey A. McNeely
& David Pitt

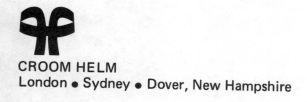

CROOM HELM
London • Sydney • Dover, New Hampshire

© 1985 The International Union for Conservation of
Nature and Natural Resources
Croom Helm Ltd, Provident House, Burrell Row,
Beckenham, Kent BR3 1AT
Croom Helm Australia Pty Ltd, First Floor,
139 King Street, Sydney, NSW 2001, Australia

British Library Cataloguing in Publication Data

Culture and conservation: the human dimension
    in environmental planning.
    1. Nature conservation—Social aspects
    I. McNeely, Jeffrey A.   II. Pitt, David
    639.9   QH75
    ISBN 0-7099-1321-4

Croom Helm, 51 Washington Street,
Dover, New Hampshire, 03820 USA

Library of Congress Cataloging in Publication Data
Main entry under title:

Culture and conservation.

    1. Environmental policy — Social aspects — Case studies.
I. McNeely, Jeffrey A. II. Pitt, David C. III. Inter-
national Union for Conservation of Nature and Natural
Resources.
HC79.E5C85 1984   333.7'1'091724   84-19986
ISBN 0-7099-1321-4

Printed and bound in Great Britain
by Billing & Sons Limited, Worcester.

CONTENTS

7085200

Foreword   vii
Preface   ix
Acknowledgements   xi

INTRODUCTION - Culture: A Missing Element in
               Conservation and Development,
               by Jeffrey A. McNeely and
               Davit Pitt   1

SECTION ONE - RETHINKING CONCEPTS FOR
              CONSERVATION AND INDIGENOUS PEOPLES   11

Chapter 1   Tribal Peoples and Economic
              Development: The Human Ecological
              Dimension, by Robert Goodland   13

Chapter 2   Native Cultures and Protected
              Areas: Management Options,
              by Leslie A. Brownrigg   33

Chapter 3   Conservation and Indigenous
              Peoples: A study of Convergent
              Interests, by James C. Clad   45

SECTION TWO - MANAGEMENT FOR AND WITH PEOPLE   63

Chapter 4   The Lancaster Sound Regional
              Study, by Peter Jacobs   65

Chapter 5   Traditional Land-Use and Nature
              Conservation in Madagascar,
              by Joseph Andriamampianina   81

iii

Chapter 6   Influence of Historical and
               Cultural Differences on the actual
               level of conservation of nature
               between Majorca and Minorca
               Islands, by Miguel Morey   91

SECTION THREE - TRADITIONAL AND INDIGENOUS
               KNOWLEDGE AND PRACTICE   101

Chapter 7   The Andean Native Peoples in the
               Conservation Planning Process,
               by Hernán Torres   103

Chapter 8   The Hema System of Range Reserves
               in the Arabian Peninsula: Its
               Possibilities in Range Improvement
               and Conservation Projects in the
               Near East, by Omar Draz   109

Chapter 9   The Conservation and Management
               of the Jebel Qara Region, by
               H.F. Lamprey   123

Chapter 10   Social Restraints on Resource
               Utilization: The Indian
               Experience, by Madhav Gadgil   135

Chapter 11   Traditional Marine Practices
               in Indonesia and their Bearing on
               Conservation, by Nicholas
               V.C. Polunin   155

Chapter 12   Customary Land Tenure and
               Conservation in Papua New Guinea,
               by Peter Eaton   181

Chapter 13   Traditional Marine Resource
               Management in the Pacific,
               by Gary A. Klee   193

SECTION FOUR - CONSERVATION AND ENVIRONMENTAL
               PLANNING BY THE PEOPLE   203

Chapter 14   People, Trees and Antelopes in
               the Indian Desert, by K.S.
               Sankhala and Peter Jackson   205

iv

Chapter 15   Interactions between People and
              Forests in East Kalimantan,
              by A.P. Vayda, Carol J. Pierce
              Colfer and Mohamad Brotokusumo   211

Chapter 16   Shona People, Totems and
              Wildlife, by Chris Tobayiwa
              and Peter Jackson   229

SECTION FIVE - WHERE WE ARE GOING   237

Chapter 17   Culture and Conservation: Some
              Thoughts for the Future,
              by C. de Klemm   239

Chapter 18   Ethnobotanics and Anthropology
              as Tools for a Cultural
              Conservation Strategy,
              by Enrique Leff   259

Chapter 19   Cultural Ecology and "Management"
              of Natural Resources or Knowing
              when not to Meddle, by P. Nowicki   269

Chapter 20   Towards Ethnoconservation,
              by David Pitt   283

Chapter 21   The Image of Nature in the Urban
              Environment, by F. Terrasson   297

FOREWORD

The mandate of IUCN is to assure that conservation considerations are incorporated into development plans and actions. Sustainable development to be successfully implemented relies as much on people as it does on scientific methods and techniques. Perhaps more so.

If living resource conservation for sustainable development is to be achieved in many areas of the global village, administrators, planners and conservationists must take into account the very large reservoirs of traditional conservation knowledge and experience within local cultures that provide a significant basis for sound management policies and environmental planning actions.

We must provide the means for local people, who maintain ecologically sound practices, to play a primary role in all stages of development in the area they identify with, so that they can participate and benefit directly, in a manner which is consistent with their values, time frames and decision-making processes. By seeking continuous local support in shaping and implementing conservation strategies, the potentials for achieving the goals of the World Conservation Strategy can be increased considerably.

This book is a first attempt to collect a number of case studies of traditional conservation practices. Many of these studies illustrate viable conservation for development practices and all explore critical dimensions of the culture of conservation.

This book is a working document. It is designed to inform and to stimulate the wide network of people and institutions associated with the conservation of living resources. Reactions are cordially invited. The document will be used to support further research into the lifestyles, conservation and development practices of traditional communities and to develop a wide range of action programmes.

Peter Jacobs
Chairman
Commission on Environmental
Planning, IUCN.

Harold Eidsvik
Chairman
Commission on National
Parks and Protected
Areas, IUCN

PREFACE

The essential message of this book is that environmental planning and conservation should pay much closer attention to the cultural context, both popular ideas and grass roots actions.

Traditional or local knowledge has been a greatly neglected resource, especially in poverty situations and fragile ecosystems. Too seldom has environmental planning and conservation involved community and popular participation. All this is especially true of research and action among what the UN calls "tribal and indigenous peoples." Such peoples tend to be the poorest of the poor, and live in the most threatened environments. According to World Bank estimates, they number at least 200 million, forming a sizeable part of the numbers of absolute poor who now number over 800 million worldwide.

The book begins by examining some new models of environmental management that take into account a much closer working relationship with the people themselves. Then there are several examples of the value of traditional knowledge in different ecosystems. Descriptions follow of where conservation has been not just 'with' but by the people. Finally there are commentaries from different disciplines on the state of play and suggestions of how self-reliance and conservation from below can be encouraged.

One final point: Although we have tried in this volume to think in a national context and in terms of concrete cases, we must never forget the socio-economic superstructure and the "one world" environment we all inhabit. International activities then are not just a question of tidying up conflicts on the boundaries or the commonlands, they are very often the key to what happens internally in any nation. So international, intersectoral, planning is of the greatest importance, even if it is often planning without teeth, without the sanctions that make rules stick.

The importance of the total socio-economic structure means the creation of new disciplines which can handle the linkages between the natural and social processes. Of course there are different approaches to this. Our intention is not to come to a judgement on any one appropriate approach - we merely introduce some of the elements for the debate. The rethinking that is going on about culture and conservation needs flowers from many different fields.

ACKNOWLEDGEMENTS

Support for the preparation of papers in this volume was received from a number of sources, especially the United Nations Environment Programme (UNEP) and the Canadian International Development Agency (CIDA). The Editors gratefully acknowledge this support as well as the efforts of the membership of the IUCN Commissions on Environmental Planning (CEP) and on National Parks and Protected Areas (CNPPA) for many comments and encouragements; of the library IUCN/WWF, Gland, for assistance with documentation; of Geneviève Pichard, Sue Rallo, Pamela Grant, Susan Brown, Bonnie Lodevole and Madlen Tschopp for assistance with typing and editing. Pierre Hunkeler, Peter Jacobs and Dan Navid provided invaluable comments and assistance over the long haul while this volume was being prepared.

Introduction

CULTURE: THE MISSING ELEMENT IN CONSERVATION
AND DEVELOPMENT

By

Jeffrey A. McNeely and David Pitt
International Union for Conservation of Nature
and Natural Resources
1196 Gland, Switzerland

THE PURPOSE OF THE BOOK

This book is an attempt to argue for an alternative
or additional cultural, social dimension in environmental planning and management. Put simply, many
of the ideas and values held by ordinary people in
the different cultures around the world often have
a long history coming from times and places where
humans lived in close harmony with their local environment. This perspective is a kind of conservation from below, an attempt to build on indigenous
and traditional knowledge and practice and to ensure
the maximum amount of local direction in environmental and conservational matters.

There has always been something of a love-hate
relationship between man and nature. Man lived off
nature's bounty, but nature also held dangers which
could threaten man's very survival. Through the
years, man adapted to this situation, evolving
social systems, technology and customs which allowed
him to live in a sort of balance with his environment, to make a comfortable accommodation to natural
constraints; because so-called "primitive people"
who are in balance with their environment are able
to live so well on so little, human life at the
Stone Age level has been called "the original
affluent society" (Sahlins, 1972). The people who
continue their existence at traditional levels today
are "ecosystem people" who live within the limits
established by their local environments (Dasmann,
1972).

Once agriculture began to evolve some 10,000
years ago, man's relationship with the land began
to change at an accelerating rate; the ecosystem of
Homo sapiens expanded as man began to control the
forces of nature for the benefit of his expanding

1

population. The most favourable areas soon began to support civilizations which converted natural landscapes into agricultural landscapes; wild species of plants and animals which were adapted to the most fertile soils became extinct, or had to adapt to less favourable habitats.

But even with the coming of agriculture, there was a rich diversity of local cultural adaptations to local conditions and wide areas of natural vegetation remained, especially in the uplands which sometimes served as a "buffer zone" between civilizations. These wildernesses continued to support populations of traditional ecosystem people who maintained their cultural, linguistic and ecological distinctness from the lowland agricultural civilizations. While the area of wilderness was reduced, it was still extensive and much of the natural world was still protected from the most disruptive human influences by cultural/ecological factors such as taboos preventing over-exploitation, tribal warfare which kept wide areas as wilderness "buffer zones" between groups, land ownership by ancestors rather than individuals, and many others (Amaru IV, 1980).

It was the industrial revolution which finally changed things on a global scale. What was once a diverse collection of local ecosystems or river-basin civilizations became a much less diverse and more closely interlinked system which covered the entire world. Ecosystem people became "biosphere people", who drew their support not from any one local ecosystem but from the entire capital of the world's living matter (Dasmann, 1972).

A simplified example will illustrate the point: oil from Saudi Arabia fuels the machines and makes the fertilizers and pesticides which allow marginal land in West Africa to grow a crop of cocoa for Switzerland to make into chocolate which it flys on American-made airplanes to Singapore for distribution in southeast Asia; the profit made by the west African farmer allows him to purchase a Japanese motorcycle, Ethiopian coffee, and Thai rice. The dominance of this all-encompassing ecosystem has placed the human species in a position to destroy many living resources and to disrupt the natural ecological processes which sustain all life. Whereas species and ecosystems were conserved in simpler times by the low level of technology, cultural controls on over-exploitation, and man's relative ecological humbleness, other, more explicit, conservation mechanisms have become necessary as man's technology allows him to exceed natural eco-

logical controls. One mechanism is the establishment of protected areas.

THE IDEA OF PROTECTED AREAS

Early in the industrial revolution, a few individuals of vision saw some of the dangers inherent in
man's increasing impact on nature and promoted the
concept of man's purposeful responsibility for
ensuring the survival of at least representative
portions of natural ecosystems. Following the
establishment of Yellowstone National Park in
Wyoming in 1872, the protected area movement grew
steadily and has now extended over the entire globe.
The International Union for Conservation of Nature
and Natural Resources (IUCN) has provided an
"official" definition of a "national park" (Harroy,
1971), and in 1959 a resolution of the United
Nations Economic and Social Council charged IUCN
with the task of forming and maintaining an up-to-
date list of the world's national parks and equivalent reserves. An international response has been
generated to counter the hazards inherent in the
world ecosystem of modern biosphere man.
     The industrial age today seems to be rapidly
reaching a climax where it will either collapse or
go on to bigger and better riches far beyond human
imagination. Whatever happens, protected areas must
adapt to the changing conditions. Evolving from
the National Park idea of strict protection and
promotion of tourism which had its inception at
Yellowstone over 100 years ago, protected areas now
must be managed consciously to contribute to modern
social, ecological and economic demands (Miller,
1980). At a meeting in Bali in October 1983 experts
from all over the world met to consider the ways and
means for protected areas in different ecosystems
to contribute to human well-being (McNeely and
Miller, 1984).

THE WORLD CONSERVATION STRATEGY

But protected areas are only part of the story. It
is also necessary to have wider programmes for
action. An important step was taken in 1980, with
the publication of the World Conservation Strategy
(IUCN, 1980). This document defined conservation
as "the management of human use of the biosphere so
that it may yield the greatest sustainable benefit

Introduction

to present generations while maintaining its potential to meet the needs and aspirations of future
generations". Living resource conservation under
this definition is seen to have three specific broad
objectives: to maintain essential ecological
processes and life-support systems; to preserve
genetic diversity; and to ensure that utilization
of species and ecosystems is sustainable. Conservation therefore is expected to make important contributions to social and economic development, providing an alternative approach stressing long-term
goals rather than short-term material exploitations.
    Although the World Conservation Strategy has
been very well received and is obviously a most
important document for preserving the natural
heritage, some critics have pointed out that it
says too little about the cultural dimension, about
the value of different ways of life and philosophies
or indeed about popular aspirations. Other international instruments, like the Convention Concerning
the Protection of the World Cultural and Natural
Heritage (1972), interpret culture in a rather
narrow sense and do not really address problems of
living traditional cultures.

CULTURE AND CONSERVATION

However, the 15th session of the General Assembly
of IUCN in Christchurch, New Zealand, in October
1981, recognized the importance of the cultural
heritage of mankind and of the role of cultures -
particularly traditional cultures - in conservation
and the wider processes of development. The Assembly
recommended that heads of governments, ministers,
members of legislatures, administrators, planners
and conservationists:

    a)   take into account the still-existing, very
         large reservoir of traditional knowledge,
         philosophy and experience within local
         cultures which must provide a significant
         basis for the evolution of future manage-
         ment policies and planning actions;
    b)   provide the means for local people who
         maintain ecologically sound practices to
         play a primary role in all stages of
         development in the area they identify
         with, so that they can participate and
         benefit directly, in a manner which is
         consistent with their values, time frames

4

and decision-making processes;

c) seek continuous support of these local people in shaping and implementing conservation strategies, programmes and plans, in order to considerably increase present conservation potentials for achieving the goals of the World Conservation Strategy; and

d) foster further research into traditional lifestyles and human ecology.

As a follow-up to the General Assembly a meeting was convened in Morges in November 1982 by the IUCN Commission on Environmental Planning which had as a major focus the relationships between culture and conservation. It was recognized that cultural data on behaviour and motivation vis-à-vis nature are rarely used, though they often condition the success or failure of conservation projects. Such data as do exist have not been assembled, nor analysed from a conservation perspective.

It was proposed to gather general information on the ways in which behaviour, motivation and cultural patterns function and are transmitted in human societies, to analyse how they relate to nature, to see how they would apply in some specific cases and to identify those which are of a general character and those which are related only to a particular society.

It was suggested that principles for the evaluation and implementation of conservation projects should be developed, to enable the maintenance and reinforcement of positive attitudes towards nature and the modification of those which are less positive. The process of environmental planning must exhibit a sensitivity to the needs and cultures of local populations. In order to achieve this, it is necessary to involve local people in the whole process of development planning. Traditional systems of resource use often, although not always, include elements contributing to environmentally sound and sustainable use of living resources. While current population and other pressures and advances in science and technology may call for drastic changes in traditional systems of resource use, serious attempts need to be made to preserve and incorporate the desirable elements of traditional practices into modern systems. Conservation efforts should preferably be combined with efforts to meet other immediate needs of local populations such as health care, rural development, etc.

Introduction

Finally it was recognized that the most urgent need for research and action related to the so-called tribal and indigenous peoples.

CONTENTS OF THE BOOK

It has already become clear that many of these tasks lie in the future, and one result of the meetings in Bali and Morges has been the preparation of a research action programme. But much knowledge already exists and a wealth of information was brought to both Bali and Morges. In addition there are important materials from the international agencies like the World Bank and other inter-governmental agencies and NGOs who have shown a concern for tribal and indigenous peoples.

This book presents a selection of these papers. It is not intended to be a comprehensive statement, or a state-of-the-art survey but rather a series of arguments and case studies which all point to the importance of conservation from below. We begin with papers which show that the needs and wishes of local people must be taken into account at all times in any management and planning process. We continue with a series of documentation on the value of tra-ditional and indigenous resources, knowledge and practice. Next is a section on the ways in which the people themselves can carry forward conservation and planning processes. Finally, there are sets of papers from the different disciplines and perspec-tives pointing out the lessons we have learned and where we need to go in the future. It is fitting that these future directions should be cast in an interdisciplinary and intersectoral frame. Effective co-operation may well be the key to effective future action, both horizontally between disciplines and sectors and vertically, between the planning and executing agencies and the grass roots itself.

DEFINITIONS

One thing we have tried to avoid is an arid debate over terminology and definition. Accepting that no definitions are perfect, we have worked with the following broad parameters in mind.

When we talk of "culture" (in the singular) longstanding definitions are still acceptable (cf. E.B. Tylor, 1871): "Culture is that complex whole which includes knowledge, belief, art, morals, law, custom, and any other capabilities and habits acquired by man as a member of society." Seen from an evolutionary perspective, culture has given Homo sapiens a significant advantage, providing a form of biological adaptation which is not inherited, but acquired by experience.

When we use "cultures" in the plural, we mean the groups of people who see themselves as having a distinct culture. This definition may well coincide with boundaries and labels that are imposed from outside on what may be called tribes or peoples or sub-nations or sub-cultures or whatever. We recognize that there is a certain fluidity in these boundaries, people moving from one culture to another, either physically, e.g. through migration, or mentally, e.g. through the mass media.

Many cultures in areas of concern to conservationists and a focus of this volume are called tribal and indigenous, and here we use the World Bank's definition (Goodland, this volume). The term "tribal people", often shortened to "tribal" or "tribe", is employed here to characterize a specific type of population typically having stable, low-energy, sustained-yield economic systems. More specifically, the people may be hunter-gatherers, shifting agriculturalists, herders, simple farmers or fisherfolk. The populations included in this terminology exhibit many, if not most, of the following characteristics:

a) geographical isolation or semi-isolation;
b) unacculturated or only partially acculturated into the national society;
c) non-literate, or not possessing a written language;
d) non-monetized, or only partially monetized; largely or entirely independent of the national economic system;
e) ethnic distinctiveness from the national society;
f) linguistic difference from the national society;
g) possessed of a common territory;
h) economic base more tightly dependent on their specific environment;
i) possessing leadership, but no national representation, and few, if any, political rights.

Indigenous peoples are defined as "native" (i.e., birth or origin in the region) and having a long

occupancy of the region. By "traditional" we mean
what the people themselves say or conceive as being
traditional, even if some evidence may suggest
relatively recent introductions.

Some people have rejected terms like "tribal"
because they perceive pejorative connotations, but
it is clear from our message that such terms are
not used in any derogatory sense whatsoever. Quite
the reverse: Our argument is that these cultures
have a validity and vitality which may provide
answers to environmental problems which so-called
developed countries have patently failed to provide.
In addition, the notions of "tribal" and "indigenous" are officially in the UN system and accepted
by the representatives of those peoples, for
example at the UN Working Group on Tribal and
Indigenous Peoples which met in Geneva in August
1983.

The traditional cultures or sub-cultures which
are the focus of this book should be a critical part
of future environmental and development strategies.
The tribal and indigenous peoples have been vari-
ously estimated at between 200 and 300 million
people. They have been called (by the World Bank)
"the poorest of the poor" and have been described
(by the ILO) as the single largest group deprived
of basic needs. Living in fragile ecosystems these
sub-cultures themselves are endangered, sometimes
characterized by dwindling populations nearly always
threatened with one form or other of outside exploitation. It has also been said that the world of
the future must recognize not only the 170 or so
nations but also the thousands of sub-cultures which
are both the heritage of mankind and the living
reality for most ordinary men, women and children.

It is our hope that this volume may contribute
to recognizing the important role that traditional
cultures can play in promoting ecologically and
socially sound development.

REFERENCES

AMARU IV Cooperative. 1980. The Once and Future
    Resource Managers. A report to World Wildlife
    Fund-US, Washington, D.C.
Dasmann, Raymond F. 1972. National parks, nature
    conservation, and future primitive. Ecologist
    6(5):164-167.

Harroy, Jean-Paul. 1971. United Nations List of National Parks and Equivalent Reserves (Second Edition). IUCN, Morges, Switzerland.

IUCN. The World Conservation Strategy. IUCN, Gland (1980).

McNeely, Jeffrey A. and Miller, Kenton R. 1984. National Parks, Conservation, and Development: The role of protected areas in sustaining society. Smithsonian Institution Press, Washington, D.C.

Miller, Kenton R. 1980. Planning National Parks for Ecodevelopment. Center for Strategic Wildland Management Studies, Ann Arbor, Michigan.

Sahlins, Marshall. 1972. Stone Age Economics. Aldine, Chicago.

Tylor, E.B. 1871. Primitive Culture. John Murray, London.

Section One

RETHINKING CONCEPTS FOR CONSERVATION AND
INDIGENOUS PEOPLES

INTRODUCTION

We begin by looking at the way in which "conservation from below" ideas are becoming part of more
appropriate management concepts. The first paper
is in fact taken from a World Bank report co-
ordinated by Robert Goodland which is a pioneer
effort for the international agencies. The point
is made that tribal and indigenous peoples should
figure more prominently in social, economic and
political planning processes and that efforts should
be made to help their cultural and in some cases
physical survival. Brownrigg then presents four
management options in which the argument is to
achieve the maximum benefit from working with the
people themselves. Then Clad asks for a close and
continuing link between what he sees as natural
allies: the conservationists and indigenous peoples.
    There are undoubtedly other management concepts
that need to be put into the pot. One for example
could take Clad's point further and argue for a
greater solidarity than mere alliance, perhaps adding a kind of theory Z[1] to conservation management models. Certainly we have to recognize that
management models are themselves derived from cultural and social contexts. Each social system gen-

---

[1] Theory Z is the brainchild of W.G. Ouchi derived
from the very successful management structures
developed in Japanese business where there is an
exceptional closeness, even kinship, between
managed and managers, with a great deal of power
sharing. Ouchi, W.C. 1982. Theory Z. Avon, New
York.

11

erates its own kind of management, and much of the literature and the examples we present here are derived from the Euro-American context. Other countries have other kinds of socio-cultural systems. For example, different management models are typical of the socialist world (which now includes many third world countries). Here the theory is also populistic in the sense that classes, peasantries or proletariats can take over the management of environmental and other functions and that there is an evolutionary progression[2] toward this end. In the final analysis, most management models are transplanted from one culture to another and must be flexible and receptive to both the broad parameters of culture and the nuances.

2/ For a detailed exposition of this evolutionary theme see Lostakovà, H. 1982. Toward an Evolutionary-Systems Approach to Environmental Conservation and Planning in Different Cultural Settings. Paper presented to the 1982 IUCN/CEP Meeting, Morges.

Chapter One

TRIBAL PEOPLES AND ECONOMIC DEVELOPMENT:
THE HUMAN ECOLOGICAL DIMENSION

By

Robert Goodland
World Bank
1818 H St. N.W.
Washington, D.C. 20433, USA

ABSTRACT

It is estimated that, at present, there are approximately 200 million tribal people, roughly 4% of the
global population. They are found in all regions
of the world and number among the poorest of the
poor. Development projects, assisted by the World
Bank, are increasingly directed to remote, marginal
areas of the rural environment and, without special
precautions, will affect these peoples. It is frequently difficult to anticipate the nature and
dimension of the impact that a development project
may have on tribal people living in these areas,
especially when this is their first contact with
the dominant society. Without precautions, the
ensuing acculturation process proves prejudicial to
such people. Until relatively recently, development
planning had not adequately addressed the human,
economic, and social aspects of the acculturation
process.
    Certain basic needs must be acknowledged and
accommodated if tribal groups are to benefit from -
rather than being harmed by - development projects.
These fundamental needs are equally important, and
each must be met for continued physical, socio-
economic, and cultural survival in the face of development.

INTRODUCTION: FUNDAMENTAL NEEDS

The four fundamental needs of tribal societies
relate to autonomy and participation, to conditions
that will maintain their culture and their ethnic
identity to the extent they desire: (a) recognition
of territorial rights, (b) protection from intro-

duced disease, (c) time to adapt to the national society, and (d) self-determination. Clearly, freedom of choice is worthless without understanding the implications of the given alternatives and the ability to choose between them. That is why tribal people must be allowed time to make their own adjustments at their own pace, and must be given the opportunity to learn about the wider society and to gain a place for themselves within it.

The needs of tribal groups, outlined in this chapter, differ critically from those of other rural and urban populations for whom Bank-assisted projects are usually designed, and from the experience of most development and project planners. Further, social needs differ also among tribal groups themselves as mentioned in Chapter I. For this reason, each project affecting such peoples must be designed to meet the specific needs of the tribal groups within or near the project area.

EFFECTS OF CONTACT

Particular problems occur and needs are evident in cases of uncontacted tribal groups. While there are only a few such groups remaining in the world today, special action is necessary if they are in the area of influence of any project considered by the Bank. These special measures do not apply to the more acculturated peoples who are more frequently affected by development projects. The contacting process, also known euphemistically as "pacification" or "attraction", poses serious risks for the survival of such tribal groups. In some cases, their physical flight from a contact team can so disrupt the normal economic and social life of the group as to leave them underfed, weakened both physically and psychologically, and highly vulnerable to disease particularly when newly introduced to different circumstances. Whether or not actual flight occurs, the risk from introduced disease is common and serious. This is in part because of the special difficulties of implementing preventive or curative health services for a group unaccustomed to such outside attention.

This situation becomes especially critical when the newly contacted group is brought into more or less immediate contact with nationals in addition to the original contact team. Records from various parts of the world document severe and rapid depopulation as an immediate, though not always direct, consequence of contact. Examples of this are the Kreenakrore, Surui, and Parakanan Amerindian groups in Brazil (Dostal, 1972; Seeger, 1981), all contacted in the last twenty years; the Semang and Sakai in Malaysia; the Andaman Islanders and the Todas and Kathodis in India; the Pygmies in Zaire; and the Igorottes in the Philippines. In fact, contact has inevitably resulted in a considerable loss of life among the tribal group involved. A number of precautions must, therefore, be taken if this risk is at least to be held to a minimum and appropriate procedures must be tailored to each specific case.

LAND

The first and fundamental need for tribal survival and cultural viability is continued habitation in and use of the traditional land areas. The tribe's economic resource management, socio-political organization, and belief systems are tightly woven into the particular land areas inhabited and used to obtain and produce all necessities. The members of a tribe are intimately familiar with locations of different game animals and their habits, as well as the vegetation within the traditional range. Maintaining the traditional land-based patterns of environmental adaptation is essential to the perpetuation of most aspects of the tribal way of life.

Large Land Areas
Tribal lands include not only areas which are obviously inhabited at a given time, but others that may be used or occupied only intermittently in supra-annual cycles. Hunter-gatherers - the Kalahari in Southern Africa and Australian Bushmen, for example - range over wide areas and exploit them systematically (Maybury-Lewis, 1968). Pastoralists, such as the Masai in Kenya and Tanzania, the Fulani in Nigeria, the Bedouins of Cyrenaica in north-eastern Libya, the Shah Saran of Iran, and the Gujjars of north-western India, require large areas of land which may seem to the casual visitor to be unoccupied. Shifting agriculturalists, like the Kalinga of the Philippines, also leave large fallow areas to recuperate before replanting.

To the extent that tribal groups inhabit marginal areas, much larger land areas may be required

15

to support the population than would be the case in more fertile regions. When common shifting-agriculture methods are used, new areas are needed for clearance every two to five years when weeds encroach and yields decline. This method of tropical forest land use does not damage the environment when practised by an appropriate number of people, since exhausted soils have time to recuperate while other tracts are planted. The isolation and small size of the cleared areas avoid excessive erosion and accelerate regrowth of forest. Tribal societies practising such systems have traditionally developed population control which enables the society to stay within the techno-environmental carrying capacity of the land.

Tribal people have the knowledge to select more fertile areas and avoid less productive soils. Non-tribal settlers without sophisticated agricultural extension lack such selective ability.

Inter-tribal exchanges are often carried out over long distances. Tribal people may travel weeks or even months on hunting or trading expeditions. Limitations on such routes used for such necessary travel and for transhumance will damage tribal viability.

Modern legal concepts of "private" property are inapplicable to tribal land-use patterns, since land is owned in common and parcels of land are used intermittently. The solution of corporate ownership is outlined later in this chapter. Governments have often acquired lands used by tribal people on the assumption that they were uninhabited wasteland. In the process, they have often disrupted the larger human-land equilibrium systems evolved by the tribal cultures (Bodley, 1975). When land-use patterns are radically altered, traditional tribal economic and social organizations, authority, and belief systems are inevitably impaired.

Symbolic Value of Land

Along with economic significance, the traditional land base holds important symbolic and emotional meaning for tribal people. It is the repository for ancestral remains, group origin sites, and other sacred features closely linked to tribal economic systems.

The Kalinga and Bontoc tribes in the Philippines completely identify with their physical environment. They are part of a complex and well-balanced ecosystem. Their economic and social life is based on the old hand-built rice paddy terraces formed out of the steep mountain slopes along the Chico River. The economic forces tying people to their land also tie them to their traditions because the attachment to the land is more than economic and organizational. The particular land areas were constructed by their ancestors and are, they believe, where the sacred spirits dwell.

The relocation changes that now confront these Philippine tribal people are more devastating than changes in the sixteenth century when nomadic slash-and-burn farmers transformed themselves into settled rice cultivators. Then, they were still able to inhabit lands that were the centre of their life, continuing their self-sufficiency. Now, they are under pressure to relinquish the territorial foundations that have been the basis of their cultural and economic survival (S.E. Asia Resource Center, 1979; Rocamore, 1975).

Similarly in Brazil, attempts by the National Indian Foundation (FUNAI) to transfer the Nambiquara out of the Guapore valley into an inappropriate reserve generally resulted in failure. The Nambiquara refusal to move involved not only the natural resource scarcity in the new area, which was savanna rather than forest, but also the fact that they would lose touch with the land where their dead had been buried (Price, 1977a.)

Legalization of Tribal Land Rights
Land rights, access to traditional lands, and maintenance of transhumant routes are vital to the economic, social, and psychological well-being of individual tribal members, as well as for the maintenance of the group's cultural stability. Those national governments that are signatory to the UN charter and require Bank assistance can be guided by the UN Declaration of Human Rights, 1948 (Annexes 3 and 4) on tribal issues and land title. This is often difficult to accomplish because most tribal peoples hold land in common, demarcated only in the perception of their members. Land is regarded as a common good, to which individuals have rights of use, but which cannot be alienated. The tenure is in the nature of a trust in which all members -

dead, living, and unborn - are co-sharers. Communal title, or group tenure, may need legislative innovation on the part of a nation; such innovations are neither unknown nor especially difficult. The Bank can discuss tribal policies with governments, which would act to implement agreed policies.

In India, the concept of Hindu joint family property, where each male member of a joint family had a fluctuating share in the property (and this included conceived, yet unborn, males) closely approximates the concept of communal tenure. This system has been recognized in law for several centuries and now has been incorporated into "modern" law. In 1946, it was proposed that group tenure in the U.S. Trust Territory of the Pacific Islands be recognized and controlled as a trust, by a Land Control Board. Similarly in Fiji, "native land" has been successfully controlled by the Native Land Trust Board. The exercise has provided a remarkable example of the careful use of tribal lands to promote development. As in the case of communal tenure among other tribal populations, native land in Fiji cannot be alienated; only limited leases can be created with the approval of the Board.

Further, many transhumant migrations are regular, their routes are well-defined and can be demarcated. It should not, therefore, be difficult to grant these tribal people rights of way or easements recognized by law. In most countries, rights of way resulting from continuous use are part of the general law available to all persons. These rights cover both private and public use of lands.

Creation of Reserves

In some cases, the creation of a tribal reserve may be the most feasible means of protecting a tribal group whose culture is endangered by national intrusion, or by a development project, mainly in order to provide time necessary for adaptation. Reserve creation may be vital for tribes in the early first and second phases of integration, and in special cases for societies in the third phase. Such a reserve should function as a secure base, providing the tribe with time and space to make its own adaptations; not a prison in which the tribe is confined. In many cases, land held in reserve status could quite simply be transformed into title held communally by the tribe or, in the early stages of contact, in trust by the national government. Most countries lack such legislative mechanisms, although they are not difficult to draw up. This is the spirit of the Peruvian law of Native Peoples, 1974. Recently contacted tribal groups, when their lands are protected as reserves, can receive some medical attention for introduced disease and some protection against encroachment by outsiders. In Brazil, the living conditions of tribal people on reserves are generally better than among those which have lost their lands. Health benefits, however meagre, derived from the establishment of reserves are critical to the physical well-being of tribal groups (Ramos, 1976a). Although the reserve becomes less necessary as the tribal society becomes able to tolerate or withstand the pressures of the national society, title to their lands remains fundamental.

A major drawback to the establishment of re- serves is tribal exposé to the national authorities who, usually out of ignorance, may encourage or enforce possibly well-intentioned, though often detrimental, modifications to traditional practices. Disruption occurs when a government removes a tribe to a new area in order to resettle it on a reserve and then administers that reserve. The ecological setting is usually quite different on the reser- vation, movement is usually restricted, and nomadic groups are suddenly forced to become sedentary. Religious and cultural practices are usually modi- fied. Even the type of crops planted may be deter- mined before-hand by government representatives. The procedures for involuntary resettlement formu- lated by the Bank will alleviate these problems (see Annex 1).

Enforced "primitivism" is also a disruptive policy occasionally practised on a reservation. This policy is often followed either to promote tourism, since "primitive" costumes, houses, and crafts are tourist attractions, or it is defended as a means of preserving the tribe's cultural ident- ity. However, whereas enforced "primitivism" is always damaging, elective "primitivism" can be ben- eficial as in the case of the unas of Panama. Minority culture has never been a static entity which must be preserved exactly as it is found or as it is believed to have been. Rather it is a dynamic reality that should be provided with con- ditions adequate for development in a natural and progressive manner. Cultural continuity should be encouraged in all spheres, but the choice of whether to continue to modify old ways should be left to the tribal people themselves and not imposed upon them.   Two examples of enforced "primitivism" are:

> On the Matigsalug reservation in the Simod
> area of Bukidnon on Mindanao (Philippines)
> the Monobos are required to wear tribal
> costumes and build tulugan tribal houses
> without the use of nails.
> The Higaunons in the Salug reser-
> vation in Agusan, Mindanao, had to consent
> to the bulldozing of their substantial
> houses, some made of concrete blocks, to
> qualify for assistance from the Office of
> the Presidential Assistant on National
> Minorities (PANAMIN) (Rocamora, 1979).

The reservation system easily accommodates these
practices and systems of exploited labour, as the
reservation is usually located in a remote area and
its inhabitants have little legal recourse or
representation at higher political levels.   The
administration of the reservation represents the
government and enforces government policy; it may
not be inclined, or even able, to respond to the
interests of the inhabitants.   If the tribal group
has no channel through which to articulate its
rights and needs, abuses are likely to occur.   The
major problem with the creation of reserves is
that, as currently practised, control of the tribe
and its lands is transferred to outsiders - be they
government administrators or a specially appointed
group.   The role these administrators generally play
is one of pacification, the resolution of disputes
within the tribe, and the partial prevention of
contact with the national society.   Few administrators have readily moved from a traditional "law
and order" concept of their role to one that is
more development oriented.   In these circumstances,
the socio-economic gap widens between the tribe and
the nationals.   Bank emphasis on strengthening the
tribal agency and tribal administrators in member
governments is more appropriate than for the Bank
to assume a leading role in tribal affairs.
The most successful means by which a reservation could form the basis of tribal development
is, first, and as early as possible, to leave the
governance of the tribe and its resources to the
tribe itself as it was before the reserve was
created.   Second, administrators should act as
facilitators, bringing to the tribe the protection,
benefits, or specially designed education and health
programmes it may request.   Third, the adminis-

trators and eventually the tribal leaders, should
have the power to defend tribal lands against
incursions by outsiders. It is only when tribal
people are accorded equality under the law (either
as individuals, families, or larger groupings -
legal recognition of "pastoralist groups" was deemed
an essential precondition to implementation of Bank-
assisted livestock projects in Chad and Niger) and
have the capability to choose their own destiny that
they can contribute fully to the national society.
All this will be difficult and time-consuming, and
not amenable to acceleration. Tribal representatives
capable of dealing with administrators, nationals,
and the government, as well as with communal title
are pivotal to survival. Though examples are few,
it can be done: the Gavioes in Amazonia (Brazil)
requested the tribal agent to operate only outside
the reservation gates in one year, bought and
managed their own truck the next, and started hir-
ing non-tribal day labourers the following year.

HEALTH

After recognition of title to land, the maintenance
and protection of health standards is the second
fundamental prerequisite to the tribe's survival
(except in the rare cases of "first contact", in
which health measures are initially most urgent).
The process of development can so disrupt life that
new and old health and disease-carrying agents without suffering ill effects. Health is a continuing
property that can be measured by the individual's
ability to rally from a wide range and amplitude of
changes or disruption.
        Indigenous medicine in tribal areas has usually
controlled endemic diseases and met the needs of
the tribal society in its traditional habitat.
Therefore, the object of health measures within the
context of development is to foster existing ther-
apies, to introduce appropriate new repertoires,
and to avoid the introduction of unfamiliar diseases
and conditions that might disrupt existing standards
of health. Three major factors impair indigenous
health: first, transmission of disease; second,
modification of diet and living conditions; and
third, social change and stress. These factors
disrupt the normal levels of community health of the
tribal people compared with neighbouring peasants,
as well as lower resistance and increase vulnerability to disease.

Tribal Peoples and Economic Development

Introduction of Disease

First, health is jeopardized by the introduction, usually accidental, of diseases to which the tribal people have had little or no exposure, either individually or throughout the tribe's genetic history. In such exceptionally homozygous populations, severe and often fatal reactions to pathogens which are innocuous to the national society must be anticipated. The literature on tribal groups is filled with accounts of contracted illnesses and frequent deaths due to contact with outsiders. In fact, the staggering population losses among Amerindians in Brazil after the intrusion of European settlers - from 230 tribes in 1900 to about half that in 1980 - were caused more by disease and starvation, than by conflict.

> In 1500, there were an estimated 6 million to 9 million Amerindians in Brazil. Today barely 200,000 survive - an attrition rate of two million people per century.
> In the 1930s, there were between 2,000 and 3,000 Nambiquara of the Guapore valley in Mato Grosso, Brazil. In the late 1960s, a road (Cuiaba-Porto Velho) cut through their territory and large-scale cattle ranching operations were established. By 1972, more than 20 agribusiness projects were promoted in the region by fiscal incentives from SUDAM (Superintendency for the Development of Amazonia). Diseases almost completely exterminated the Nambiquara to the point that, in two of the Guapore valley groups, the entire population younger than 15 years was killed by influenza and measles (Ramos, 1979; Ribeiro, 1956).

Since disease can be transferred to the tribal group by any interchange with outsiders - such as project labourers and the use of their water, food, supplies, or clothing, or by other tribes who have been exposed to pathogens - protection or isolation is essential until a massive vaccination campaign can be implemented. Medical screening of all project workers is, therefore, imperative.

Alterations in Diet and Living Conditions

Clearly, health is significantly affected by diet and, particularly, by sudden changes in it. Fre-

22

quently, tribal peoples are compelled to adjust to sharp dietary changes. This adaptation is often due to loss of land, with consequent changes in the traditional manner of its exploitation; to relocation to a different environment and, therefore, alterations in food availability; to an increase in wage or debt-bondage labour resulting in inadequate time to work their own lands; or to higher purchases of manufactured or processed foods. The changes are accompanied by malnutrition, dental decay, and lowered resistance to disease (particularly measles, for which no immunity has been developed, and the heightened action of malarial and other parasites). Caries and other dental abnormalities are conspicuously absent or rare among tribal people who have retained traditional diets (Bodley, 1975). Dietary changes also result from the disruption of traditional trade systems and routes.

In the late 1950s and early 1960s, an increase in endemic cretinism, a birth defect, was noted among the people of the Jimi valley in Papua New Guinea. The first cases of endemic cretinism began to appear shortly after contact with government patrols, and the incidence of the disease increased rapidly with more contact.

Investigations revealed that early government patrols rewarded with salt (deficient in elemental iodine) all services rendered by the indigenous inhabitants. The precontact era salt traded into the Jimi valley by neighbouring indigenous groups was a distillate extremely rich in iodine. Contact had disrupted the efficient trading arrangements. The deprivation of a significant iodine supplement manifested itself by the appearance of cases of endemic cretinism.

Contact with dominant groups also results in dietary damage among tribal people who desire to imitate the food habits of the dominant group and, thereby, seek to enhance their own status within the wider society.

Before the dominance of the more Hinduized groups in Nepal, tribal groups like the Kamang, Magar, and Sherpa consumed meat. Today, increasing numbers of these tribes

23

are giving up meat with the result that
their present diets do not provide the
nutritional balance they formerly enjoyed.
Further, as a result of the growing reluctance to slaughter animals, the number of
livestock has far exceeded the carrying
capacity of the land, which is fast deteriorating.

Whether the result of relocation or willing adoption
of new modes of life, sudden change is usually detrimental to health. For example, influenza swept
the Pacific Islands after the islanders were compelled to adopt clothes on the grounds of modesty.
Clothes were worn, but no advice was tendered that
they had to be changed and washed regularly. Colds
and influenza were the consequence. Again, in relocation, tribal houses have been constructed to
provide accommodation only for nuclear families (as
in the unsuccessful attempt to settle the Shah Sevan
of Iran), or they have been constructed of brick and
mortar with galvanized metal roofs, as in Africa.
Many tribal people do not live in nuclear families,
but rather in extended families; and bricks and
mortar do not provide acceptable living conditions.
Breaking up families and providing unacceptable living conditions impair adjustment and lower resistance to disease.
    The diet and health aspects of relocation have
been recognized by the Bank, although until recently
this was limited to involuntary relocation. These
principles are now applied whenever tribal peoples
are affected, whether or not there is relocation
involved. Education in nutrition for both tribal
people and nationals who are in regular contact with
them is desirable.

Social Change
While all change involves some degree of social disruption, rapid change increases social tension and,
ultimately, vulnerability to disease and emotional
disorders, antisocial behaviour, and alcoholism.
While societies are dynamic, the capacity to adapt
to change is not infinite, especially in the case
of tribal populations. The social resources that
help tribal members manage and cope with change are
limited. Unfamiliar concepts, values, and roles
impose additional demands on the coping process of
the tribal society. Unless introduced carefully,
recognizing the absorptive capacity of the popu-

lation, sudden demands decrease the capacity to adapt successfully. Major and rapid social changes are associated with:

a) loss of self-esteem;
b) increase in actual and perceived role conflict and ambiguity; and
c) increase in the perceived gap between aspiration and achievement.

Loss of Self-Esteem

A tribal population confronted with development or modernization often experiences loss of self-esteem; its members feel a deprivation of their sense of personal worth and a devaluation of their social identity. Loss of self-esteem may result from explicit critical or negative evaluations of the tribal culture by the agents of change or members of the dominant society. Belittling the tribal population as ignorant, dirty, or backward is common, and may even be used to encourage the tribal society to change. Development itself may be phrased in terms that implicitly, if not explicitly, devalues the tribal culture and its members. Tribal traditions and knowledge are stigmatized and simply replaced by the dominant culture. Seldom are traditional tribal values acknowledged or are attempts made to perpetuate them.

Increased Role Conflict and Ambiguity

Rapid social change introduces new individual or group roles and modifies old ones. These modifications increase role conflict and ambiguity, which further erode the self-esteem and social identity of an individual or group. For example, people in a hunting and gathering society are trained to be independent and opportunistic, and to use initiative. These qualities become disadvantages when such people are forced to offer themselves as dependent and obedient wage or debt-bondage labourers. Tribal leaders suddenly find that their value has been downgraded and their power is usurped by the arrival of an appointed official or by the appointment of a new non-traditional tribal leader by nationals. From the position of managers, leaders are reduced to servants. This is traumatic for them personally but even more so for the people who benefited from or depended on their leadership. Even such fundamental matters as the relationship between the sexes may be radically altered.

The Nivakle in the Paraguayan Chaco
adapted to settler intrusion into their
traditional lands by raising their own
herds of cattle, sheep, and goats.
Mennonite settlers in the Central Chaco
discouraged the Nivakle from maintaining
these flocks, which were difficult to keep
off the Mennonite farms. The Nivakle
were, therefore, forced to rely on the
Mennonites for wage labour, of which there
was not enough for all. Meanwhile, the
patriarchal Mennonites dealt only with
male Nivakle and paid only the men, damaging what had traditionally been a very
egalitarian relationship between men and
women in Nivakle society.

The Nivakle had traditionally spaced
their children through the practice of
abortion. They also believed that a nurs-
ing mother who had sexual intercourse
would harm the soul and, therefore,
cripple the body of her baby. Mothers
nursed as long as they had milk and
refrained from sexual intercourse. Their
husbands were expected to share sex with
other women who were not bound by the same
retribution. The Mennonites vigorously
opposed these customs, moving to stamp out
abortion and to promote sexual fidelity
between husband and wife. This resulted
in a population increase among Nivakle and
considerable anxiety as to the fate of
their children, reared under conditions
that threatened both their souls and their
bodies.

In 1962, there was a severe drought
in the Chaco. The Mennonite settlers felt
obliged to retrench and to lay off many
of their Nivakle labourers. But many were
now totally dependent on working for the
Mennonites. In the case of the Nivakle,
they had lost their livestock and had
acquired a larger number of mouths to feed
(Loewen, 1964).

Increase in the Aspiration-Achievement Gap

Rapid social change widens the gap between the aspirations of an individual or group and the ability

to achieve new goals, particularly since traditional ways to achieve goals are often disrupted. During disruption due to development, the normal resources for the support and maintenance of institutions with the tribal group cannot operate effectively, because the entire population must meet added demands for adjustment. At the same time, the social and maintenance mechanisms of the dominant society are largely inappropriate for the tribe's needs. Encouragement of achievements or goals that are unrealistic or unattainable within the traditional value system will further widen this aspiration-achievement gap.

CULTURAL AUTONOMY

The prerequisite for successful survival of a tribal group as an ethnic minority is the retention of autonomy: cultural, social, economic. This freedom of choice involves continued control by the tribal people over their own institutions: tribal customs, beliefs, language, and means of subsistence or production.

Economic development has often been promoted at the expense of tribal institutions. Development strategies often tacitly assumed that there were no viable institutions or practices existing in the tribal culture that could be used to foster development. This "vacuum ideology" has led to the large-scale transfer of national structures or practices to tribal cultures that were little understood (Colletta, 1977). The primary example of this is the spread of Western technology and schooling throughout the non-Western world by colonial warders. While contact with nationals will inevitably bring some change in tribal practices and attitudes, prevailing basic customs and traditions need not be drastically altered or eliminated. Furthermore, the tribe alone should choose which traditions should be altered. Retention of tribal customs enhances maintenance of ethnic identity, stability as a productive unit, and, more importantly, successful adaptation to new circumstances. One reason, for instance, why the Balinese have been relatively impervious to outside influence is that they have maintained their cultural integrity, will not admit non-Balinese as members of their communities, and have adopted changes that reinforce their culture.

Tribal Peoples and Economic Development

Policy of Cultural Autonomy
The policies usually adopted concerning the degree
of social change that is to occur within tribal
groups range widely. The two extremes are: total
enforced isolation of the tribal groups allowing no
change, on the one hand, all the way through rapid
and complete assimilation resulting in the loss of
the tribe's identity, on the other. Isolation
should be rejected as impossible: a zoo-like ar-
rangement of an enforced primitive state. Complete
assimilation into the national society denies, then
extinguishes, ethnic diversity. Furthermore, as
noted earlier, rapid change can separate tribal
people from their cultural identity: a form of
extinction.
   An intermediate policy adopted by the Bank
under the projects it finances is more humane,
prudent and productive. This allows the retention
of a large measure of tribal autonomy and cultural
choice. Such a policy of self-determination emphasizes the choice of tribal groups to their own way
of life and seeks, therefore, to minimize the imposition of different social or economic systems until
such time as the tribal society is sufficiently
robust and resilient to tolerate people so that they
themselves can manage the pace and style of their
own involvement with the national society. The
following conditions are essential if this intermediate policy is to succeed:

   a) National governments and international
      organizations must support rights to land
      used or occupied by tribal people, to
      their ethnic identity, and to cultural
      autonomy.
   b) The tribe must be provided with interim
      safeguards that enable it to deal with un-
      welcome outside influences on its own land
      until the tribe adapts sufficiently.
   c) Neither the nation nor the non-tribal
      neighbours should compete with the tribal
      society on its own lands for its resources.

The Bank adopts this intermediate policy, where
appropriate, in order to assist these beleaguered
societies. When these conditions are observed, not
only does tribal culture survive, but the tribe
becomes a productive contributor to the nation,
rather than a ward of the state.
   Cultural autonomy differs from the integration-
ist approach in several respects. First, cultural

28

autonomy stresses the value of the tribal culture and the desirability of maintaining the culture rather than replacing it as quickly as possible with the customs and values of the dominant society. Second, cultural autonomy recognizes the potentially harmful effects of unrestrained contact between dominant culture and tribal culture, and seeks to moderate them. Third, cultural autonomy creates conditions under which the tribal members themselves control the pace and manner of their adjustment to national society and culture. Finally, cultural autonomy does not preclude the training of selected tribal representatives in the dominant culture and their role as mediators with the latter - provided controls by the tribe are designed to prevent abuse of authority by the dominant society.

Desired Outcome
Action to guarantee the physical survival of tribal populations and encourage freedom of cultural choice is directed towards the following outcome:

a) a tribal population that forms a rec-
    ognized and accepted ethnic minority - one
    component of an ethnically pluralistic
    national society;
b) as such, this ethnic minority maintains
    its traditional way of life, more or less
    modified in accordance with the preferences
    of the tribal population itself;
c) the tribal economic system progressively
    evolves from "precontact" subsistence to a
    sustained-yield agro-ecosystem with the
    production of a surplus on occasion.

Immediate integration of tribal populations can only swell the numbers of the rural and urban poor. Since developing countries already face enormous problems in their attempts to eliminate poverty, adding to the numbers of the poor by dispossessing tribal societies only worsens their situation. This is ameliorated by maintaining ethnic minorities as viable and productive societies, and by retaining their cultural autonomy. This policy will be fa-cilitated by recognizing the need for a pluralistic view of national identity and an understanding that cultural or ethnic diversity is desirable. Then, tribal peoples will belong to societies as fully participatory and productive components.
    Given the fundamental importance of economic

patterns in all cultures, and considering the extreme contrasts between tribal and national economies, the economic interaction of tribal cultures
with the national market economies is a critical
one.
    A tribal culture may surrender part of its
political autonomy, but can still continue to be
ethnically distinct if it is allowed to retain its
economy and if it remains unexploited by outsiders
(Bodley, 1975).

REFERENCES

Bodley, J. 1975. Victims of Progress. Cummings,
    Menlo Park.
Colletta, N.J. 1977. Folk Culture and Development.
    International Journal of Adult Education
    10·(2).
Dostal, W. (Ed). 1972. The Situation of the Indian
    in South America. World Council of Churches,
    Geneva.
Maybury, Lewis D. 1968. The Savage and the Innocent.
    Beacon, Boston.
Price, D. 1977. Acculturation, Social Assistance and
    Political Context Proceedings, 42nd Inter-
    national Congress of Americanists (603-9).
Rocamora, J. 1975. Rural Development Strategies.
    Ateneo de Manila University, Institute of
    Philippine Culture.
Rocamora, J. 1979. The Political Uses of PANAMIN.
    S.E. Asia Chronicle 6-7: (11-21).
Seeger, A. 1981. Nature and Society in Central
    Brazil. Harvard University Press, Cambridge.
South East Asia Resource Center. 1979. Tribal People
    and the Marcos Regime. Berkeley, California.

These extracts appeared originally in the World
Bank's Report (Tribal Peoples and Economic Development, pp. 16-29, 1982) and are reprinted with the
kind permission of the World Bank.

ANNEX 1

THE WORLD BANK AND INVOLUNTARY RESETTLEMENT

The Bank tries to avoid involuntary resettlement whenever feasible. Where relocation is unavoidable (for instance, in the case of large construction projects, such as dams, irrigation schemes, ports and airports, new towns and highways), a well-prepared resettlement plan should be drawn up in accordance with principles that leave room for considerable flexibility in the solutions and implementation that are most suitable in any particular case. Where only a few people are to be relocated, appropriate compensation for assets, coupled with arrangements for removal and a relocation grant may suffice. In the case of large numbers of people, or whole communities, the resettlement plan would include compensation as one principal element, as well as relocation and establishment in a new area, or integration with existing communities in an already settled area. The major objective is to ensure that settlers are afforded opportunities to become established and economically self-sustaining in the shortest possible period at living standards that match those before resettlement; that the settlers' social and cultural institutions are supported and their own initiative is encouraged; and that the new areas should be one in which the skills and aptitudes of the involuntary settlers can be readily employed. Important considerations include access to land, markets, employment and the provision of needed services and infrastructure in the new area. Careful preparatory work with the involuntary settlers, the host community, and their respective leaders prior to the move is of primary importance.

Chapter Two

NATIVE CULTURES AND PROTECTED AREAS:
MANAGEMENT OPTIONS

By

Dr Leslie A. Brownrigg
AMARU IV
57155 East End Station
Washington D.C. 20037, USA

ABSTRACT

On their own lands, the culturally native populations of Latin America protect large areas in
natural ecosystems and achieve a renewable resource
of a living environment. This relation can be reinforced by each of the four management options for
the formal designation and organization of protected
areas which are outlined in this paper: native owned
lands, where the protection of the area is by native
peoples; reserves, where a protected natural area
corresponds with the territory of a particular
native population; buffer zones, where a protected
area serves as a physical or ecological barrier
between native lands and the lands of others; and
research stations, where certain areas under native
management are organized as agricultural or ecological research stations.

INTRODUCTION

On their own lands the culturally native populations
of Latin America protect large areas in natural ecosystems and achieve a renewable use of the living
environment. This relation can be reinforced by
each of the four management options for the formal
designation and organization of protected areas
which are outlined in this paper.
    Native populations and national resource man-
agers are appropriate allies. For both, the need
to reach a mutual understanding is urgent. From the
history and situation of native peoples, resource
managers can understand more fully the problems of
protected areas. Native peoples now inhabit extensive areas of Latin America which may be developed

33

in ways which disregard both them and the natural environment, but the management options presented here would benefit both native peoples and the nation.

There are problems at both the local and the national level in the protection of an area, whether it be a biological reserve, a national forest or the communal lands or territory of a native population (World Bank, 1981). At the local level, resident native peoples maintain resource use within ecological limits. The social and behavioural patterns of native populations have been integrated with natural environment variables in a way which usually, though not always, results in ecologically sound long-term use of an area. Native peoples have usually defended their territories from invaders; whole cultures have perished in the attempt. Frontiers between societies have tended to be lawless. Native American ethnic groups faced frontier situations long before the arrival of Europeans and multinational corporations. Forest and desert groups faced the expansionism of ancient Andean and Mesoamerican states, and small tribal groups have ebbed and flowed across the landscape. Groups defending their territories are denounced as savages for the methods they employ, though the more brutal invasion methods used by the mainstream culture are not denounced in similar terms. Spontaneous, unplanned penetrations by lumbermen, commercial hunters, and unauthorized expeditions have also caused problems.

At the national level, the problem of protecting an area requires the clear legal designation of its function, supported by administrative and institutional structures. Once an area has been identified, placed under protective status, and provided with personnel and an operating budget, its perpetuity must be assured through constant vigilance.

Since earliest colonial times, native populations have sought perpetuity, yet have endured a history of expropriations. They have faced changes in political regimes or policies, administrative inconsistencies, and the distribution of rights over aspects of the indivisible ecosystem to different bureaucracies which are separately empowered to govern different natural resources (land, water, forests, fish) and different human activities (mining, transportation, colonization, defence). One agency may control mining, another plan external use for water while a third, evoking eminent domain or national interests, may seize a part or all of a

tribal territory for roads, reservoirs or colonization.

The problem of national level legal rights
differs for groups which have title for their land
and those which do not. Native peoples who do not
have titles are more vulnerable, because their very
existence and occupancy can be easily ignored.
"Negative certificates" have been issued stating
their land is vacant; when inhabitants are discovered, they are evicted even though their tribe
may have lived in the area for centuries.

The most important aspect of native Americans'
land-use practices for administrators, policy-
makers, planners and developers is their inclusion
of 1) reserve areas in natural or second growth
fallow and 2) common lands governed by strict codes
to perpetuate their usefulness for generations yet
unborn. These unique aspects of native American
land tenure are the spatial and social manifestation
of their conservationism. The entire movement to
create protected areas and natural reserves is re-
inventing at the level of the nation-state the con-
figuration that native populations have traditionally used within their territories.

Natural lands are important because all native
cultures use wild plants and animals and vary only
in the degree of their dependence (Levi-Strauss,
1950). For native cultures, the requirement for
reserve areas of natural or fallow vegetation is
integral to their agro-ecosystems. Native systems
of agriculture involve a great variety of species
and modes of production to diversify their economic
base and to minimize risks.

Fallow areas are also important. Unstressed
native agricultural practices are clearly designed
for either low or high impact on the environment,
though both levels of impact may be observed among
areas of the same ethno-linguistic groups or within
a single village system. The low impact design
requires long fallows during which the natural pasture or forest ecosystems can recover from a few
years of isolated, cyclical, rotated or itinerant
use. Fallow use cycles are long, averaging 6 years
fallow per each year of use in high pastures to
25:1 in tropical lowlands. Such areas are sustained
over centuries of light exploitation. Fallow systems
require only moderate man/land ratios and the availability of land in natural vegetation (Budowski,
1960; Ruddle, 1974).

The high impact pattern transforms the natural
environment by constructing land forms which serve

as man-made and man-maintained niches for intensive agriculture. Among the land forms, a scale of productivity and permanence can be distinguished. Some forms are flexible or temporary and can be renovated with minimal new inputs of labour or abandoned to fallow. The more permanent and productive land forms require high labour and resource investment for their initial construction and long-term maintenance. These forms both support and require more dense human populations, but because investments are made at optimal sites, surrounding areas may be left in natural ecosystems or used for other practices based on fallow regeneration. Many areas under intensive production have complex ecological dependencies upon the wild or fallow areas, and for this reason, such areas are protected by the native populations.

Given this history and pattern, and the close union of the goals of native people to preserve the environment in perpetuity with the goals of the advocates of protected areas, alliance is a logical step. As local residents, native peoples clearly have an advantage as the local level protectors, while the resource managers have some advantages in the national political process; national-level resource managers have much to learn from native peoples (Table 2.1).

OPTIONS FOR MANAGEMENT

The options outlined below give guidelines for four possible forms of co-operation, each of which would require rather different administrative structures. The options have in common a redundancy of functions, designed to strengthen the protection of an area. The options are based on actual and proposed examples, reflecting legal and political realities and problems which have occurred in implementation. The options can be called:

a) native-owned lands, where the protection of the area is by native peoples;

b) reserves, where a protected natural area corresponds with the territory of a particular native population;

c) buffer zones, where a protected area serves as a physical or ecological barrier between native lands and the lands of others; and

d) <u>research stations</u>, where certain areas under native management are organized as agricultural or ecological research stations.

Option 1:   Native Owned Lands

For those native populations with formal communal titles to their land, or where native people are members of such legal corporations as co-operatives, <u>ejidos</u>, <u>comunas</u> or formally designated native reserves, certain parts of their titled lands can be designated as areas formally protected by them (see Table 2.1).

Examples of the uses of native peoples' technology for management of resources and the environment above, the ecology of many native populations requires that certain areas be maintained in a natural ecosystem, either for light use by itinerant horticulture, gathering, fishing, or subsistence hunting, or that broad areas be rested during long fallow cycles. Recognizing the native communities as the official protectors of such areas may also enhance their legal position.

Not all titled native communities still have such reserve areas, and if they do, in many cases the areas have been historically reduced in size and so degraded by overuse. Where the phenomenon of small settlements amidst large territories (low native population/land area ratios) still exists, it should be reinforced with a recognition of the responsibilities which the native peoples have undertaken.

To develop this option, natural resource managers can assist native peoples by scientifically documenting the merits of the native systems of management. Since even titled native communities are facing pressures to change their production practices, such recognition may enhance their security of tenure, while simultaneously creating protected areas within a domain beyond systems of national parks.

For some native populations without titles to their land as corporate groups - a situation which exists both for ethnic groups in remote regions without cadastral registries and for ethnic groups where only individual members hold titles - the option of organizing part of their territory as a protected commons represents a variation of the native lands/native protected option.

Native Cultures and Protected Areas

Table 2.1

Management Consideration	Example
Crop types preserved	Centres for study and breeding potatoes, palms, etc.
Transfer of soil conservation techniques	Terracing, irrigation
National, international agencies seek alternatives to environmentally and financially costly development	Appropriate technology
Alternative models of agricultural development	Development of terraces instead of lowland colonization
Erosion control	Terracing
Drainage	Raised fields and platform fields (revival of ancient systems or expansion of currently rare systems)
Soil fertility maintenance	Knowledge of when to rest or fallow fields or change crops
Land capability determinations	Knowledge of indicator species
Pest and disease management	Crop combinations and rotations (polycultural practices) crop selection
Fisheries management	Native fishing technologies
Wildlife management	Native hunting technologies

Option 2: Reserves

This option combines the formal designation of a protected area within the territory occupied by a native ethnic group. It requires that the traditional residents are given both the authority and a suitable communications technology to oversee the activities of their own group and to expel any unauthorized invaders. In this option, the conservation agency at the national level is the official administrator of the area, with the official managers working closely with their associates, the resident native population.

Certain basic rules, derived from experience, will need to be observed to achieve positive results. The first basic rule follows the fifth recommendation of IUCN's 1975 General Assembly (Kinshasa, Zaire), that resettlement of native peoples be avoided. A native culture will remain intact only in its home territory, where the productive capacity of the environment is intimately understood.

A second basic rule is that the protected area be sufficiently large to accommodate its dual function. The creation of reduced reserves serves only a symbolic end and begins a process of cultural devolution and ecological degradation. To combine the functions of a reserve for nature with a reserve for native populations, the ecological necessities and resource requirements of each human ecosystem must be understood on a culture by culture, area by area basis.

The third basic rule is that protected areas planning must also anticipate population increases and culture change. It is unrealistic to expect a group to atrophy, or worse, to "return" to some traditional technology long ago discarded in favour of a more modern alternative. Proper discharge of their new role as the local guardians of protected areas will bring whole groups into increased contact with representatives of the national agency which formally administers the area. The national conservation agency must take on special responsibilities in guiding the contact, but not to limit cultural changes which contact of this type will inspire.

Another basic rule is that the entire population of the traditional residents must be made official park guards. The threat to the integrity of a protected area originates largely from the outside. If reserve administrators expend their expectably meagre resources controlling the native residents, they will have neither sufficient force nor

the peoples' good will to expel outsiders. If the
native residents' movements in their territory is
unduly restricted, they will lose their effectiveness as guards of the entire area.

These rules all require the participation of
the native population in the planning and implementation of the reserve. The underlying problem in
the several attempts to implement this option have
involved an absence of good communications between
reserve planners and the native peoples. There are
examples from Latin America of planning such reserves without any basic facts about the resident
groups - where they were located or what language
they spoke, let alone how their settlement patterns
fit into their total ecological adaptation to the
environment.

This model is attractive for those native populations which do not have formal rights to their
land, nor an avenue to pursue land titles within
the jural structure of their country. It also has
certain merit for some smaller, rarely contacted
groups, which are not capable of pursuing the involved legal struggles to obtain rights to their own
land.

Option 3: Buffer Zones
The creation of a buffer zone as a natural protected
area formally administered by a national conservation agency and located between the territory of
a native group and the lands exploited by others can
also help achieve a margin of security and protection for native populations. The mutual benefit of
this plan is the compatibility of the land-use patterns of neighbours, or mutual buffering. A national
park or forest can serve as a physical barrier
against diseases for which less-contacted native
groups have little immunity and against the movement
of settlers toward the native lands and peoples.

This model is the principle of two parks currently proposed: Yanachanga National Park above
Amuesha territory in the eastern flank of the Andes
and the mosaic of special purpose parks and reserves
in Yanomamo territory in the northern Amazon basin.

The proposed Yanachanga National Park is promoted by the Amuesha people. The proposed location
is a mountain chain north of Oxapampa in Peru, the
most easterly of the Andean cordillera. Yanachanga's
forested crests retain waters which eventually flow
into the basin of Palcazu, land of the Amuesha. At
the eastern border of the proposed national park,

proprietary communal forest reserves are suggested, where the Amuesha can gather and hunt primary natural resources. These would in turn adjoin the cultivation and pasture areas of the Amuesha communities proper (Smith, 1981).

There are several versions of the mosaic of parks and reserves among the Yanomamo; the buffer model underlies some of these proposals. The establishment of this reserve mosaic is complicated by administrative interest groups in two countries and the very large area where the Yanomamo are dispersed in settlements of moderate permanence. The notion of a mosaic of reserves appeals to administrative interests, and the buffers would be administered by entities separate from the authorities of Yanomamo reserves.

Implementation of the buffer zone option requires good planning and co-ordination, including prior recognition, titling of native lands, and an identification of the critical zones for the native human ecology and settlement. The option is not appropriate for densely populated areas, but can be implemented in a variety of low density settings: puna, islands, tropical forest and deserts. Selection among potential protected areas in these habitats might include the conscious intention of also buffering lands of native people.

Option 4: Research Station

The final option proposed is to place under protection as research stations certain lands managed in a traditional way by native populations; this option may be included as part of any of the first three options. It is based on a recognition of the value of the agricultural and environmental knowledge of the native cultures, and recognizes that without a special context the valuable knowledge of native peoples may soon be lost.

To counteract the net loss of biological varieties of our earth, we must recognize that among the most threatened varieties are those which are domesticated, which cannot survive as ferals, and which only a limited number of native people know how to cultivate. This cultural heritage and economic good deserves special protection. At present, the monuments and dead cities of the ancient American civilizations are protected as national archaeological parks, while the key data concerning the agricultural systems and natural resource management which produced sufficient surplus to support their construction are being lost. Much of the agriculture, horticulture, herding and managed harvest of wild species now labelled "subsistence" is exactly the same which, with access to a larger resource base and in other economic systems, produced a surplus for non-agrarian urban populations of considerable wealth.

Native peoples possess an exact knowledge of their environments, including the species and ecological relations among them. Hunting, gathering and fishing under native regimes apply knowledge of the natural history of each species to sustain yields through managed harvesting. This managed harvesting led to the domestication of plants and animals quite independent of the similar developments in the Old World; the Andes, Mesoamerica and the Amazon basin are three of the most important global hearths of domestication. While only a narrow spectrum of the species domesticated and still cultivated by native peoples in Latin America have ever diffused beyond their own lands, those that have diffused have revitalized the nutritional base of the world; potatoes and maize, for example, helped fuel the industrial revolution in Europe.

Today, native peoples' crop inventories are more important than ever, since once discovered, modern techniques are available to fix, reproduce and disseminate the varieties.

There are methods to transfer native knowledge to Western science. What little is recorded in majority languages from native ethnoscience has been transferred by ethnobotanists, farm system agronomists, anthropologists and linguists who perform field research. Recently, a formal proposal was presented to establish agricultural stations to study the cultivation of endemic varieties, to learn how distinctive genotypes are modified by field practices and microenvironments (Brush, 1980).

The special advantage of a protected area in native management as an agricultural or resource management research station is the potential economic value of the cultigens and technologies which can be discovered. Native systems may require temporary insulation from the relative devaluation of their crop and stock inventories in certain transitory commercial conditions. The primary purpose of protecting such areas would be to provide a setting where researchers and students from the national cultures can undertake an apprenticeship with native peoples.

CONCLUSION

Each option of relations between native cultures and protected areas will fit only in certain circumstances. The appropriateness of a particular option and its details must be determined on a case by case basis, and certain elements from different options can be combined to form new models.

Appropriate planning will require the participation of the native peoples themselves, through interpreters if necessary. Professionals with considerable experience among native peoples and with the particular ecological zones must also enter the planning, such as farm system agronomists, anthropologists, botanists, ecologists, foresters, zoologists and others. Their skill will be necessary to interpret the full traditional patterns of land use, basic resource areas and needs.

For resource managers, the benefits of working with native peoples include gaining an additional constituency, recruiting personnel with profound knowledge of local areas and learning about long-term resource strategies which have proven their adaptability for thousands of years. For native peoples, the benefits include legal recognition of ecologically-sound traditional land-use practices, appropriate employment on their traditional lands, and new advocates at the national level.

As Simeon Jimenez Turon, a member of the Ye'cuana tribe of Venezuela, has said:

> Understand learned one that there can be no intermediary who understands our region better than we do, or who knows us better than we know ourselves. Those who want to learn from us may do so, but you must also teach us the laws and useful means to pursue our goals and petitions before the official authorities. Insofar as you help us, we will help you.

ACKNOWLEDGEMENTS

This paper is based on research presented in The Once and Future Resource Managers, a report by AMARU IV Co-operative, published jointly by the World Wildlife Fund-US and AMARU IV. Readers are directed to that study for details and additional references. Steven A. Romanoff, co-author, has reviewed this paper. This paper was prepared for

Native Cultures and Protected Areas

IUCN's Commission on National Parks and Protected Areas in co-operation with the United Nations Environment Programme.

REFERENCES

Brush, 1980.
Budowski, Gerardo. 1960. Tropical savannas, a sequence of forest felling and repeated burnings. Boletín del Museo de Ciencias Naturales 6/7 (1-4): 63-87.
Lévi-Strauss, Claude. 1950. The use of wild plants in tropical South America. In J. Steward (ed.), Handbook of South American Indians. Bureau of American Ethnology Bulletin No. 143. Washington, D.C.: Smithsonian Institution.
Ruddle, Kenneth. 1974. The Yukpa cultivation system: a study of shifting cultivation in Colombia and Venezuela. University of California Press, Berkeley.
Smith, J.L.D. and Mishra, H.R. 1981. Management Recommendations for the Chitwan Tiger Population. The Parsa - Extension and the Bara Hunting Reserve. Smithsonian Institution/World Wildlife Fund Project 1051.
World Bank, 1981.

Chapter Three

CONSERVATION AND INDIGENOUS PEOPLES:
A STUDY OF CONVERGENT INTERESTS

By

James C. Clad
91 Ellice Street
Mt. Victoria
Wellington, New Zealand

ABSTRACT

This paper describes the way that indigenous peoples
and conservationists can work together to attain
their common objectives. These can be approached
in three main ways: through quasi-legal efforts to
protect and enhance the welfare of indigenous
peoples; how to use legal instruments in the best
ways (the choice of tactics); and how to enlist new
allies and leverage. The argument that indigenous
peoples and conservationists are natural allies is
made with particular force when strategies to preserve tropical forests are discussed. An example
based on New Zealand's experience is given, providing a number of guidelines on how to bring benefits
to the local indigenous population.

INTRODUCTION

The prevailing temperament in the world today of
"development at all costs" requires advocates of
indigenous peoples' welfare - particularly of the
integrity of isolated tribal groups - to marshal
arguments available to best effect and to choose
both remedies and advocates with care.

The renewed political assertiveness by (and on
behalf of) the world's estimated 200 million indigenous peoples has three broad dimensions[1].
The first concerns itself with "remedies", with
quasi-legal efforts to protect and enhance the welfare of indigenous peoples. Both international law
and national law remedies fall into the first category. The second dimension follows from the first:
how best to use these (often quite insubstantial)
remedies to best effort - in other words, the choice

of "tactics". The final dimension develops from the first two: a search for new allies and leverage.

A crucial issue before tribal societies (at the national political level) and lobbyists on their behalf (at the level of international pressure and advocacy) is therefore to find strategies that will enlist the energies of others to act on their behalf. This task involves a search for convergent interests, for pairing indigenous objectives with other matters on the international agenda. Many sympathetic human rights groups at the international level have begun to lobby for better aboriginal entitlement, and in other political struggles arising out of resource exploitation projects, national linguistic policies, mass tourism proposals or improved social services, there is also much interest and relevance to the movement for improved aboriginal entitlement.

Of all these concerns, none approaches as close a coincidence of interests as the conservation movement.

In common with much of the environmental lobby, indigenous or tribal peoples have battled to overcome the lack of receptive constituencies - either within or outside the home country - that are capable of exerting pressure (financial, electoral or moral) on decision-makers. Indigenous peoples not only lack this basic political capital, but they also (unlike conservationists) have the misfortune of carrying demands - e.g. calls for greater self-determination - that run counter to the mainstream of political development for the last 30 years, a period witnessing a trebling of nation-states, each jealous of its prerogatives.

"Self-determination", "inviolability of indigenous territory" or "freedom to the use of mother tongues": these and other demands represent an attack on the prevailing political consensus, all the more so in countries where loyalties are uncertain and governments promote assimilationist nationalisms. Moreover, because many issues crucial to indigenous peoples arise from large-scale economic activities (e.g. resource exploitation and extraction, hydro-power schemes or transportation improvements), governments see indigenous resistance as obduracy - or worse, as a challenge to the very legitimacy of economic development fostered under government patronage.

The coincidence of interests characterizing the indigenous peoples' movement and the international lobby for better management of natural resources has been apparent for some time. Since 1975, for example, the International Union for Conservation of Nature and Natural Resources (IUCN) has had a "Task Force on Traditional Lifestyles" examining the interplay of traditional peoples and the natural environment. For the purposes of the Task Force, "traditional lifestyles" have been defined as:

> The ways of life (cultures) of indigenous people which have evolved locally and are based on sustainable use of local eco-systems; such lifestyles are often at subsistence levels of production and are seldom a part of the mainstream culture of their country, though they do contribute to its cultural wealth.

One of the best recent formulations of this convergence of objectives appears in a paper entitled "Native Cultures and Protected Areas: Management Options" (Brownrigg, 1981). "Native populations and national resource managers are appropriate allies," Brownrigg writes, "Given ... the close union of the goals of native people to preserve the environment in perpetuity with the goals of the advocates of protected areas, alliance is a logical step."

In the same paper, Brownrigg delineates the common goals more explicitly:

> For resource managers, the benefits of working with native peoples include gaining an additional constituency, recruiting personnel with profound knowledge of local areas and learning about long-term resource strategies which have proven their adaptability for thousands of years. For native peoples, the benefits include legal recognition of ecologically-sound traditional land-use practices, appropriate employment of their traditional lands, and new advocates at the national level.

The argument that indigenous peoples and conservationists are "natural allies" is made with particular force when strategies to preserve tropical forests (traditional homeland to a variety of isolated forest-dwellers) are discussed. The clash between what might be called the "resource-extractive dynamic" and hitherto isolated or uncontacted peoples seems most acute in regions of dwindling tropical forest cover. The January 1980 issue of

The Ecologist, for example, argued that, "... maintenance of primary forest and its use in traditional
ways preserving it for millenia in balance with indigenous lifestyles might well be consistent with
the local people's aspirations for an improved
subsistence lifestyle based firmly on their own
culture, their own society and on local self-
determination".
   This is not the only area where co-operative
possibilities between conservationists and indigenous peoples exist: similar management objectives
for mangrove forests, coral atolls or upriver water-
shed protection may be better served by links with
appropriate indigenes²/.
   The remaining pages of this paper examine these
propositions, looking at obstacles impeding a genuine working alliance, either internationally (as a
coalition of compatible viewpoints) or nationally
(as a concerted response to particular development
issues).

INDIGENOUS LIFESTYLES OR INDIGENOUS PEOPLES?

If one merely asserts that certain indigenous ways
of living deal more gently with an ecosystem's
carrying capacity than resource-extractive policies,
then the point is unexceptional. Indeed, one writer
states that the conservation movement can only "deal
with traditional lifestyles and patterns, rather
than with traditionally living peoples" (emphasis
added) (Schultze-Westrum M.S.). If nothing more than
"lifestyle patterns" or "practices" disassociated
from living cultures receive conservationist en-
dorsement, the convergence of indigenous peoples'
and conservationists' interests will remain at the
level of principle only. If mutual support in the
field is the objective, however, the "natural alliance" posited above needs to be looked at more
closely.
   The proposition that both movements gain by co-
operation stands or falls on their compatibility of
views. In a number of respects they differ markedly.
   One perspective (the indigenes') sees unceasing
encroachment penetrating inwards to the core of
separate cultures. Danger resides in a restive
external dynamic that deliberately (or even with
the best of intentions) administers the fatal elixir
to the aboriginal status. The other view (that of
the conservationists) sees an agrandissement rolling
outwards from the metropoles in which they most

often reside, a complex combination of "development", land hunger and movement in commodity markets that threatens generic diversity and specific species. Conservationists therefore seek local indigenous support for (or, at the very least, acquiescence in) protection of remaining wild lands. Indigenes seek relief from encroachment, either by a lessening of external pressure or by a strengthening of tribal position vis-à-vis national authorities.

In principle, a comfortable convergence exists. Pragmatically, however, considerable difficulties belie an easy assumption that interests are automatically shared. The following pages focus on what may be the blind spots in this argument and suggest ways to marshal conservation's "natural constituency" to better effect.

The key principles of the conservation movement originate (as a recent IUCN working group paper notes) "from the urban society of highly developed countries". These principles promote "a system of mainly restrictive control patterns upon the ecosystems that are set up by national governments". The paper also notes that "correlations with traditional cultures that inhabit resource management areas" have not been well studied (Schultze-Westrum, 1980).

Any restriction on the use of territory has as its essence the principle of exclusion. To protect, one must exclude certain categories of outsiders or specific activities judged to be harmful. Because the power to exclude is so inescapably political, national governments not surprisingly reserve this power for themselves. Indigenous peoples almost never initiate this exclusion (legitimized by the national authorities on grounds of "national development", "national security" or "resource conservation".

To this extent, therefore, protected areas (of whatever description and for whatever purpose) continue to be, for indigenes, paternalistically devolved and implemented. Precisely for this reason, a national park in areas of traditional settlement is more likely to be feared as "taking something away" rather than welcomed for the protection it bestows. Useful contrasts between indigene reactions to national park creation in Canada, the USA and Australia have been described recently (Gardner and Nelson, 1981), and it appears that even active involvement of indigenous peoples in protected area planning and administration yields uneven results, largely because most resource management agencies are still perceived as "taking something away" - if only in an intangible sense. A history of unequal dealing with dominant "settler cultures" supports indigenes' suspicions. In those areas where indigenous peoples have become politicized and seek self-determination, the "foreclosure of opportunity" effected by prohibition of development within indigene territory may be deeply resented. Development per se is not always resisted by indigenes; what troubles (and rallies) them is their powerlessness vis-à-vis the outsider.

Just as indigenes misunderstand conservation trade-offs, so also may conservation planners misjudge the extent to which aboriginal groups living within or adjacent to proposed protected areas actually wish to work for (or guard) the attainment of conservation objectives. For example, assumptions that traditional lifestyles practised by the indigenes necessarily complement conservation objectives often turn out to be wide of the mark. Some commentators acknowledge this; for example, Brownrigg (1981) writes that, "the social and behavioural patterns of native population have been integrated with natural environment variables in a way which usually, though not always, results in ecologically sound long-term use of an area (emphasis added)".

To illustrate how choice of new technology poses awkward problems to conservationists, the following indicative examples might be noted:

- Some Inuit whale hunters now favour using explosive harpoons and other contemporary technology.
- Petrol-powered chain saws accelerate land clearing by slash and burn agriculturalists.
- Occasionally explosives are used to stun-kill fish in traditional Maori hunting and fishing areas of New Zealand.

These examples suggest that some contemporary manifestations of traditional "lifestyles" can no longer be assumed to conform to a harmonious prototype.

In part, many of these misapprehensions result from protestations from the fledgling international indigenous peoples movement which attributes all the disruptive ecological consequences of possessive individualism to western colonizers. The following extract from a report to the International NGO Conference on Indigenous Peoples and the Land, held from 15-18 September 1981 in Geneva, illustrates the point:

> In the world of today there are two systems, two different irreconcilable "ways of life". The Indian world - collective, communal, human, respectful of nature and wise - and the western world - greedy, destructive, individualist, and enemy of mother nature.

Similar views embellish pronouncements from the World Council of Indigenous Peoples. While the sincerity of such statements cannot be disputed, the likelihood of their being true is open to question. Such formulations by the indigenes themselves consolidate the view that indigenous lifestyles are, almost by definition, compatible with conservationist goals. Such statements not only ignore past adoption of biologically disruptive technology by aboriginal peoples but also in a curious way buttress the fallacy of the "noble savage", a uniquely European conceit.

The same misconception lies buried in the automatic assumption that indigenous peoples will accept or even welcome cultural status as a condition of their involvement in conservation management. The specialist literature shows many examples of national parks or protected reserves having, as one objective of a multiple-use design, the goal of retaining traditional technologies, settlement patterns and food gathering. While this is a worthy objective, incorporation of endangered tribal cultures into conservation areas must be subject to the caveat that these peoples may maintain their isolation only for as long as they desire to do so.

The World Bank makes a similar point:

> Enforced "primitivism" is a disruptive policy occasionally practised on a reservation. This policy is often followed either to promote tourism ... or it is defended as a means of preserving the tribe's cultural identity. However, whereas enforced "primitivism" is always damaging, elective "primitivism" can be beneficial as in the case of the Cunas of Panama. Minority culture never has been a static entity which must be preserved exactly as it is found or as it is believed to have been. Rather it is a dy-

51

namic reality which should be provided
with conditions adequate for development
in a natural and progressive manner.
Cultural continuity should be encouraged
in all spheres, but the choice of whether
to continue to modify old ways should be
left to the tribal people themselves and
not imposed upon them (IBRD, 1980).

To act otherwise leads to results as coercive and
contrived as the disruptive development which
"anthropological reserves" are designed to prevent.
During their occupation of Taiwan, for example, the
Japanese turned the small island of Lan Yu (ancestral home to the Yami people) into a private botan-
ical/anthropological museum with living exhibits and
severely limited admission. Until defeated in 1945,
Japan restricted access into Lan Yu to officials and
anthropologists, making no effort to raise material
living standards or to intervene with medical or
educational services. This achievement was as pa-
ternalist as the imposition of government-initiated
economic development in tribal territories.

While the idea of creating coterminous nature/
anthropological reserves is not new, the concept
has gained renewed support in recent years. In
June 1979, for example, a group of Brazilian and
foreign anthropologists formally urged the Federal
Government in Brasilia to create a national park
for the Yanomamo Indians, an indigenous group of
around 20,000 persons living in north-western Brazil
and Venezuela. The proposal's sponsors fear that
Brazil's readiness to allow mining concessions in
Yanomamo territory will lead to cultural extinction.
One sponsor - the London-based Survival International group - reports that twenty-six distinct
tribes have been culturally destroyed in Brazil
during the past decade. The "ethnocide" has been
accompanied by extensive disruption to local ecosystems from mining, forestry or land settlement
projects.

Dasmann (1975), Jungius (1976), Gardner and
Nelson (1981), Gorio (1978) and many others have
written about protecting indigenes' habitat and
local ecosystems by creating multi-purpose national
parks. The countries choosing to do so are as dis-
parate as the Congo (Odzala National Park), Botswana
(Kalahari Reserves), Peru (Manu Park), USA (Gates
of the Arctic Monument), Canada (the Yukon's Kluane
Park), Australia (Kakadu National Park in the
Northern Territory), Papua New Guinea (Varirata

National Park) and Honduras (Rio Platano Biosphere Reserve). Other examples include a proposed reserve at Siberut (an Indonesian island near Sumatra where traditional Mentawai lifestyles are threatened by timber concessions), Tanzania's Ngorogoro Crater (where the Masai have the right to graze their cattle), the Ghin forest reserve in India (which permits traditional gathering by the Maldhari people), and several of Sweden's National Parks (where the Laps still graze reindeer). Nearly all of these areas have been established in the last decade (the list above is indicative only).

At the levels of principle and practice, therefore, conservationists have become increasingly aware of the "close interrelationship between ecological factors, rural traditions ... and cultural patterns (like sustained selfreliant land-use, intimate knowledge and adaptation, self-restriction and conservation) that offers tangible direct benefits, including reserve guardianship and ranger functions, field knowledge of local fauna and flora and long-term resource strategies which have proven their adaptability for thousands of years" (Dasmann, 1975). What is needed is a more balanced view of the opportunities present in this co-operation.

INDIGENOUS PEOPLE AND CONSERVATION AREAS:
SOME LESSER OPTIONS

While attention focuses primarily on national parks as safe havens for endangered cultures (or, vice versa, on tribal lifestyles as intrinsically supportive of conservationist ethic), one should not assume that the convergence of interests starts and ends there. Indeed, just as IUCN (1978) acknowledges that "the National Park can be complemented by other distinct categories which ... can provide land managers and decision-makers with a broad set of legal and managerial options for conservation land management", so too is there an intermediate range of options available to indigenous groups and resource managers desirous of collaboration. In other words, the territory inhabited by indigenous peoples need not be co-extensive with the protected conservation area. Just as there is a recognition that hitherto neglected parts of the human habitat (which traditionally have not been included in national park activities) now need urgent attention, so also is there a significant range of opportunities to involve indigenous peoples at any place along the "spectrum" of acculturation to the national society - from the virtually uncontacted to the almost entirely acculturated. The World Bank for example, distinguishes four successive phases of acculturation or integration into the national society: completely uncontacted tribes; semi-isolated groups in intermittent contact; groups in permanent contact; and integrated groups retaining a residual sense of tribal identification (IBRD, 1981).

Indeed there may be good reasons why tribal groups (or national governments) do not welcome tribal incorporation into entirely "conservation-specific" entities like national parks: tribes find this may compromise their land claims to the same or adjacent areas; inclusion in a park may constrict customary livelihood activity; or the park design may restrict too severely the territory's future resource-extraction possibilities. In addition, national governments may not welcome parks with an "anthropological" element because inclusion of affected tribes in park planning may "tribalize" them (i.e. politicize them to the extent their tribal solidarity is enhanced by reaction to outside pressure).

At this juncture it might be salient to explore New Zealand's experience in developing "half-way house" possibilities, which (although they fall well short of creating extensive nature/anthropological reserves or parks) illustrate a variety of collaborative possibilities with indigenous peoples.

New Zealand protects over 2.6 million hectares of national parks and special purpose reserves, much of it gifted directly to the nation by Maori tribes. For example, elders of the Ngati Tuwharetoa gave land for the country's first national park at Tongariro in 1889; other examples include the gifting of scenic reserves at Lakes Rotoiti and Okataina to the nation and more recently a grant of land at Taranaki to comprise Egmont National Park.

New Zealand's legislation (the National Park Act 1952 and the Reserves Act 1977) now promotes gifting of land for conservation purposes, and the management of "multiple use reserves" (which includes indigenous use) permits interesting alternatives to public ownership of land. Some of the indigenous uses which reserves and national parks in New Zealand quietly accommodate include food and herb gathering (usually done on horseback) in the North Island's Urerewa National Park, mutton-bird hunting on Kaitoreti Spit and active assertion of traditional fishing rights on Lake Waikeremoana by the local tribe (which also rents the lake to the surrounding national park).

Conservation objectives are also being enlisted to deal with difficulties inherent in the Maoris' communal tenure. Although 75% of New Zealand's 300,000 Maoris (approximately 10% of the total population) now live in urban areas, 1.3 million hectares of rural Maori land remain. By custom, Maori communal landowners share the land in equal portion with all progeny so that each generation tends to add to the total number of owners of each communally-held block. This leads to two difficulties; the land is not able to support all the owners, and special arrangements are necessary to enable landowners to make binding decisions about future land use. Up to now, Maori land has been leased - often to European New Zealanders - but new responses to indigenous tenure have evolved. One quarter of Maori land is unoccupied, and considerable areas are still in primary or secondary bush. Much of this is administered as Maori Reserve Land under the relevant legislation, and one option being investigated by the New Zealand Government is the creation - with full tribal support - of "tribal reserves", entry to which will be restricted to owners whose usage will conform to specific conservation objectives.

Some of this experience has guided New Zealand's assistance to the fledgling Sagarmatha National Park in Nepal. Some 2,500 of Nepal's estimated 20,000 Sherpa people live in the 124,000 hectares of the Park (which also includes the Khumbu area, famous for Mount Everest).

The treks and mountaineering following the opening of the area to outsiders in 1950 has led to worrying changes in traditional Sherpa life, associated with the depletion of manpower (for porters) and firewood (it is estimated that each mountaineering expedition needs 30,000 kilogrammes of wood for fuel).

In association with New Zealand rangers, the Park's managers have determined upon the following objectives, directed specifically at the inclusion of the indigenous Sherpas in the Park's activities:

- <u>constant liaison</u> with monastery lamas;
- <u>restoration</u> of religious structures within the Park;
- <u>retention and protection</u> of all monastery buildings;
- <u>maintenance</u> of traditional village water supply schemes;

- <u>active encouragement</u> of the traditional character and architectural styles of villages within the Park;
- <u>prohibition</u> of all trekking within sacred areas (including whole mountains) where guardian spirits reside;
- <u>employment</u> of Sherpas as rangers on a preferential basis;
- <u>retention</u> as far as possible of firewood as the Sherpas' fuel (rather than displacement by kerosene or other new - and imported - fuel technology);
- <u>internal modification</u> where possible of traditional Sherpa houses to minimize heat losses and consequently reduce firewood consumption; and
- <u>revival</u> of Sherpas' traditional forest-use control system, i.e. the <u>Shing-i Nawas</u> ("protectors of the forests") who were empowered to allocate wood for families.

These objectives demonstrate an active involvement of a partially-acculturated indigenous people in a Park which is <u>not</u> co-extensive with the indigene territory. Briefly, the conservation objectives of Sagarmatha are to arrest a situation where over half of the forest cover within the park territory has disappeared and to revive, within a system catering also to outsiders' mountaineering expeditions, a pattern of traditional usage in which prior to the influx of tourism and mountaineering, the Sherpas were managing a partly modified landscape under a system of social and community controls which ensured wisest use of forest resources and minimized long-term forest degradation.

CONCLUSIONS

The launching in March 1981 of the <u>World Conservation Strategy</u> (IUCN; 1980) brought the convergence of indigene and conservation interests into sharp focus: the strategy deals with global problems such as deforestation, desertification, depletion of fisheries, soil erosion and misuse of crop lands - all matters of direct concern to aboriginal populations. The logic behind this compatibility of interests has already occurred to the World Council of Indigenous Peoples which was invited by the United Nations Environment Programme in 1980 to prepare a study on "environmental degradation in indigenous areas". The WCIP is following closely the operation of the international agreements such as the 1972 Convention for the Protection of World Cultural and Natural Heritage. This Convention was followed by the Man and the Biosphere Programme, resulting in a number of "biosphere reserves" created in various parts of the world, many with a direct effect on the indigenous peoples *in situ*. The Rio Platano Biosphere Reserve in Honduras is a case in point; the reserve is designed, *inter alia*, to protect two indigenous tribes.

As suggested above, outright conflict between conservationist and indigenous objectives has occurred in the past. Tribes have been expelled from national parks or denied the use of resources within the Park: e.g. the Shakilla were driven from Lake Rukana Park in Kenya and the Ik expelled from Kidepo National Park in Uganda. Understanding of conservation objectives by aboriginal peoples remains low (battles erupt in Ethiopia's Simien Park over woodcutting rights, for example). Some conflict even has an international dimension; enforcing the Migratory Birds Convention and accommodating native Indian demands have caused headaches for governments in Canada and the USA. Another example: International Whaling Commission sessions grapple with Inuits who oppose bow-head whale-hunting prohibitions, and argument still revolves around Inuit rights to use modern whaling technology.

Several commentators have advanced suggestions for successful involvement of indigenous groups with an interest in territories in which restrictive land-use policies are tied to conservation objectives. Brownrigg (1980) offers four management options for resource managers contemplating co-operation with indigenes:

a) *reserves*, where a protected natural area corresponds with the territory of a particular native population;

b) *native-owned lands*, where the protection of the area is by native peoples;

c) *buffer zones*, where a protected area serves as a physical or ecological barrier between native lands and the lands of others; and

d) *research stations*, where certain areas under native management are organized as agricultural or ecological research stations.

Brownrigg concludes that, "Each option of relations between native cultures and protected areas will fit only in certain circumstances. The appropriateness of a particular option and its details must be determined on a case by case basis, and certain elements for different options can be combined to form new models."

Discussing Peru's Manu Park, Jungius (1976) urges incorporation of indigene-inhabited territories into a national park and creation of a buffer zone. Indigenes are to practise traditional hunting patterns, except where species are endangered. The objective is to provide for "gradual social and economic development on the basis of (the peoples') own culture and traditions".

Dasmann (1975) argues that national parks should "permit indigenous people to maintain their isolation for as long as they wish to do so", and to allow them "to become the protectors of the parks, to receive a share of park receipts and in other ways to be brought to appreciate its value".

Gardner and Nelson (1981) analyse national park agencies, paying close attention to institutional character, extent of management control, extent of indigenous or park agency control of land and links between the agencies and indigenes in three parks in the USA, Canada and Australia respectively. They find that the best indigene/conservationist relations occur when:

- indigenes see national parks as assisting to maintain their culture (and to provide employment);
- indigenous organizations have strong bargaining positions (related to unambiguous title to their lands); and
- permitted land use in the Park is well-defined.

In addition to these guidelines, the following issues should be addressed by conservationists:

- the suspicions of indigenous peoples (many of whom - such as New Zealand's Maoris - are substantially acculturated into the national society) need to be directly countered with arguments that demonstrate clear advantages from supporting conservation aims;
- national parks, reserves or even restrictive land-use policies in general should not be seen as foreclosing indigenous economic or

self-development opportunities. Indeed, in some parts of the world, argument often centres on the "retention of resource-extraction possibilities" by indigenous populations - e.g., the Inuits in Canada's Northwest Territory - who prefer to exploit their own natural resources, albeit at a different pace;

- Conservation areas of whatever description should not be seen as pre-determining title to the lands in question; however, the creation of conservation reserves co-extensive with areas inhabited by indigenous peoples can be a first step towards acknowledgement of native title to the area in question; i.e., there are "gifting back" possibilities (available, for example, in New Zealand where the Crown may return lands to Maori tenure with conservation-inspired restrictive land-use covenants).

- Whatever indigene/conservation deal is struck, the terms of the agreement should be beyond reach of upset by other, separately empowered bureaucracies of the national authority (e.g., tax agencies or defence authorities).

- If fully restrictive nature/anthropological reserves are created (or established in all but name) some hard decisions must be faced. Intrusions by census-takers, missionaries, tourists, security forces or even medical personnel must be kept to a minimum if the integrity of the reserve is to last.

At the country or field level, conservation lobbies (particularly at the international pressure-group level) should become conversant with the following areas of direct concern to threatened indigenes:

a) The economics of import-dependent agricultural projects, extractive silviculture or mass resettlement schemes (such as Amazonian small holdings or Indonesia's "transmigration" programmes). These endeavours are often poorly reasoned. By analogy to well-founded second thoughts about the advantages of mass tourism, opportunities exist to take pressure off non-renewable resources (and the indigenes who may live among them) especially if feasible alternatives in the form of intensive/

improved productivity techniques (such as new rubber-tapping methods or quicker re-generation of exotic trees) can be offered to national planners.

b) The creative use of existing legal remedies. For example, recognition by national authorities of indigenes' animist religions can yield unexpected results; in most states, places of religious significance invariably enjoy legal protection from all development. Australian aboriginals, for example, have large tracts of land declared reserves because they are sacred sites.

c) Intimate local knowledge of local fauna and flora is frequently acknowledged but inventories of such knowledge (e.g., pharmaceutical benefits from tropical biota) are lacking. The material advantages of such knowledge (which in the dominant national societies is protected by copyright or other "intellectual property" statutes) wait to be quantified.

d) Tribal lands include not only those areas inhabited at any given time, but other tracts which are used only intermittently. There are two possibilities here: first, many countries permit acquisition of rights to land by prescription, i.e. continuous and uncontested use of the land for a determined number of years. A wider definition of particular indigene land "uses" can lead to successful tribal land claims (and therefore to more lands put outside the reach of "development"). The second possibility concerns the systematic, non-damaging land use practised by intermittent users such as hunter-gatherers (the Kalahari or Australian bushmen) or pastoralists (Fulani or Masai of Africa, the Gujjars of India or the Bedouins). The advantages of these practices need to be demonstrated quantitatively to national authorities.

Together with a summary of some other analyses of convergent indigene/conservation interests, I have tried to suggest guidelines and areas of further research that should make genuine collaboration more likely at the national, or "field", level as well as at the level of principle. The essence of the task seems to be in the choice of strategies to enlist the support of indigenous peoples themselves for conservation objectives (whether in the form of reserves or mere practices) while retaining the confidence of the national authorities. Tribal peoples have suffered for centuries under the impact of exogenous expansion into areas that once supported greatly larger numbers of indigenes, and the process has led to decimation and even extinction of many tribal populations. Some indigenes have proved to be demographically resilient, retaining tribal identities while acculturating to the national (or "settler") society. Some - the Surui or Parakanans in Brazil, the Andaman islanders, the Semang and Sakai in Malaysia, the Todas in India or the Mbuti in Zaire - live precariously close to cultural or even physical extinction. The starting point, it seems to me, for co-operation with tribal peoples or their advocates is to recognize that national society and the indigenes need to be persuaded that conservation objectives can be married to the quest for better aboriginal entitlement, to the lasting benefit of all parties. It is not an easy task but it is one worth doing, and worth doing well.

NOTES

1. It is estimated that nearly 4% of the world's population are "tribal peoples" (IBRD, 1981). The term "indigenous peoples" is applied to a wider population; the World Council of Indigenous Peoples uses the following definition:

> The term indigenous people refers to people living in countries which have a population composed of differing ethnic or racial groups who are descendants of the earliest populations living in the area and who do not, as a group, control the national government of the countries within which they live.

A Sub-Commission of the UN Human Rights Commission has commissioned a report which adopts the following "working definition" of the term "indigenous peoples":

> ... the existing descendants of the people who inhabited the present territory of a country wholly or partially at the time

when persons of a different culture or
ethnic origin arrived from other parts of
the world, overcame them and, by conquest,
settlement or other means reduced them to
a non-dominant or colonial condition; who
today live more in conformity with their
particular social, economic and cultural
customs or traditions than with the
institutions of the country of which they
now form part, under a State structure
which incorporates mainly the national,
social and cultural characteristics of
other segments of the populations which
are predominant.

In a paper entitled "Law, Politics and Indigenous
Peoples: A Study of Convergent Interests" (prepared
for Cultural Survival Inc., Cambridge, Mass (1981),
the author reviewed historical and contemporary
doctrines of international law as they apply to the
status of indigenous peoples, including international conventions and declaratory pronouncements
with direct or tangential bearing on the protection
of indigenous peoples and national laws in various
countries where indigenous questions, mostly concerning land disputes, are being litigated.
    2. The potential for liaising with indigenous
peoples in island, estuary or tidal flats environments is often neglected. Traditional fisheries and
marine lifestyles depend closely on the retention
of basic character of these particular ecosystems;
and co-operative possibilities between indigenes
and conservation managers exist. See, for example,
an IUCN paper prepared for the Second Regional South
Pacific Symposium on the Conservation of Nature by
G. Carleton Ray (SPC-IUCN/2 RSCN/WP.5: 1975) which
envisages incorporating traditional usages into the
management of marine reserves. See also: Auburn,
F.M., "Convention for the Preservation of Man's
Cultural Heritage in the Ocean," Science, 185 (4153)
1974, and Kearney, R.E., "Some Problems of Developing and Managing Fisheries in Small Island States",
in Island States of the Pacific and Indian Oceans
(edited by R. Shand), Australian National University, 1980.

This paper was prepared for IUCN's Commission on
National Parks and Protected Areas in co-operation
with the United Nations Environment Programme.

Section Two

MANAGEMENT FOR AND WITH PEOPLE

INTRODUCTION

An important element in the new management concepts
we have talked about is not only that the ultimate
aim should be _for_ the people, but that there should
be a maximum effort to work _with_ the people. There
is a need to respect their value systems and traditional practices. There is a need to understand
their history, both its broad parameters and its
nuances. There is a need to work with grass roots
social organizations. This section contains papers
concerned with these themes in different cultures,
different social-economic situations and different
ecosystems. One point coming from the papers is
that in protecting the environment through national
parks or protected areas, the indigenous people
should be involved as fully as possible - the maximum of utilization by local people for their own
benefit is the goal. There is often a special
relationship between local indigenous peoples and
their environment which is not well understood by
outsiders, even those who prepare conservation
plans. To understand this relationship, to have a
meaningful dialogue, to be able to reach an agreement on what should be done to ensure that local
interests are not compromised or the long-term
environmental future threatened, it is necessary to
move much closer to the people themselves.

Chapter Four

THE LANCASTER SOUND REGIONAL STUDY

By

Peter Jacobs
Faculté de l'Aménagement
Université de Montréal
5620 Darlington
Montréal, Québec H3T 1T2
Canada

ABSTRACT

The paper describes a pioneer environmental planning
exercise by the Government of Canada in the northern
Arctic region. The Inuit participated in the public
reviews and presented a clearly articulated position. The paper emphasizes the need to take into
account these alternative cultural positions.

The Lancaster Sound Regional Study is the first
attempt by the Government of Canada to initiate a
process of environmental planning in the northern
Arctic region of Canada. The first phase was designed to define the goals and objectives of the
study, to collect and analyse information about the
region, to identify conflicts and compatibilities
of existing and potential activities, and alternative strategies or options for the use and management of the region.

The second phase focused on a comprehensive
public discussion and review of the Preliminary
Green Paper produced at the end of Phase I. This
phase included three inter-related activities:
review by the four communities of the Lancaster
Sound Region, a northern workshop held in Resolute
Bay, and a southern workshop held at Carleton University in Ottawa that included Inuit, conservationists, industrialists and representatives of
the federal and territorial governments.

The Minister of the Department of Indian and
Northern Affairs, the Honourable Mr John Munro,
responsible for the Lancaster Sound Region study,
noted that "planning for Lancaster Sound's abundant
and varied resources is a crucial and complex issue
that demands the fullest possible public input. We

need the special knowledge of the people of the region as well as the considered advice of people in government, industry and academic institutions and the concerned general public".

The Department of Indian and Northern Affairs is to be congratulated for its initiative in encouraging public review of the Lancaster Sound Regional Study. Praise is warranted for at least two important reasons. Firstly, the issues at stake in "opening-up" the northern frontier of Canada affect northern residents and the Inuit in particular far more directly and far more immediately than those who live in the south. Not to involve those most directly affected would flaunt the most elementary principles of social justice. Secondly, and as a result of recognizing this principle, the Department encouraged and supported public review with transparent good will to an extent that is without precedent in the Lancaster Sound Region of northern Canada. A continuing series of community visits was organized, virtually from the start of the study, to inform the residents of the four communities most directly affected as to the nature, extent and consequences of the future development scenarios that might affect the region. Background papers, preliminary and final drafts of policy papers, and an extensive data atlas were reviewed at northern and southern workshop on two different occasions by all interest groups concerned with the future of the Lancaster Sound Region. The Department engaged independent chairmen for the public review sessions to assure that they received as objective and unbiased a report of public views as was possible. In this and all other aspects the Department respected its commitment to public review to the fullest extent.

Five major issues were raised during initial public review. These included:

1. the need to more fully analyse future options for the Lancaster Sound Region and, in particular, to outline the benefits and inconveniences of each option for northern residents;
2. the need to negotiate land claims;
3. the need to fully develop a possible future scenario based on the sustaining use of the living resources of the region;
4. the need to integrate a conservation component into all of the proposed options for the use and management or the region;

and finally
5. the need to evolve a northern land-use planning process.

Many of the Inuit have expressed a strong preference for a renewable resource based economy as they perceive this option as the most directly related to their needs, the most compatible with their perception of a viable life style, in short the most beneficial of the options proposed for the future use and management of the Lancaster Sound Region.

The support of a growing and increasingly healthy, young Inuit population strictly on the basis of a renewable resource based economy has been challenged by industry and questioned by the Inuit themselves, both during the last round of community visits held early in 1983, and at the public workshop held later in the same year.

In this regard, it is essential that studies be initiated that will clarify the relationship of population projections in the northern communities coupled with immigration that can be anticipated from growth and industrial development to the projected sustainable yield of living resources in the region.

If the maximum sustainable yield is equal to or greater than the needs of the projected population, then a renewable resource base economy is a viable although not necessarily exclusive option for the Lancaster Sound Region. If the yield is less than the needs of the projected population then an option based exclusively on harvesting renewable resources is not viable and additional sources of employment would have to be developed and supported. These studies would form an essential and early part of the projected planning process and would be based, for the most part, on existing data acquired during the initial phases of the Lancaster Sound Regional Study.

The Lancaster Sound Regional Study can be viewed as a coherent attempt to deal with Canada's own north-south dialogue. Balancing the national and regional interest across two cultures is a challenge of national and even global importance and one that will be closely monitored. Appropriate attention and more detailed analysis must be devoted to a clear projection of the economic, social and ecological benefits that might reasonably be derived by the resident of the Lancaster Sound Region from each of the six options for use of the region proposed by the Federal Government.

Lancaster Sound Regional Study

"The Lancaster Sound Region: 1980-2000" was released in July 1982. The report postulates six options for future use of the Lancaster Sound Region and, for each option, the basic premise, rational, description of activities and implications are outlined.

The titles of the six options for future use are:

1. No New Development;
2. Environmental Protection;
3. Renewable Resource Economy;
4. Northwest Passage Shipping;
5. Balanced Development; and
6. Non-renewable Resource Economy.

Upon release, the Minister, the Honourable John Munro, indicated that "balanced development of renewable and non-renewable resources..." has been the policy of the Federal Government now and for perhaps as much as a decade.

There remains, however, substantial disagreement as to the definition, interpretation and application of this policy position. In particular, balanced development means something quite different to the Inuit than it does to industry, and neither of these groups in anywhere near as homogeneous an expression of interest as may have been assumed.

The debate on definition of balanced development and the implementation of a conservation strategy in northern Canada has tended towards defining diametrically opposed positions. Conservation of natural environments is contested not so much in terms of location and extent as it is in terms of the timing of implementation. The Inuit clearly wish to conserve first and develop later.

Both the mining and gas and oil industries are loath to eliminate any significant regions from potential development activities. The Federal Government would seem to be posed to reserve certain areas of the North for conservation purposes in advance of industrial development.

In fact the concept of "conservation for development" is the underlying position of the World Conservation Strategy. The report People, Resources and Environment stressed the need to incorporate a conservation strategy into each of the options presented. Should the regional planning process focus on alternative rates, scales and means of achieving balanced development in the Lancaster Sound Region, then a conservation strategy would

68

presumably be an integral part of each development scenario as would development be an integral part of each conservation scenario.

Furthermore, it is reasonably clear that the six options are not mutually exclusive and that a sequential implementation of these options might have generated a more broadly based support. In fact, the Canadian Arctic Resources Committee suggested that given the declaration by the Minister in favour of the balanced development option that it would have been a good deal more productive to present a set of options that outlined different rates and scales of development. Granted that the Green Paper as published is not structured in this manner, subsequent activity within the proposed regional planning process can and should avoid reproducing policy, scenarios, strategies, plans or any combination of these elements in formats where one or another of the key actors in the planning process must lose in order that another might win.

Similarly, the presumed opposition of conservation and development options is a perceived opposition that is not necessarily an inherent characteristic of "balanced development" which by some definitions, if not most definitions, would include both conservation and development objectives.

As Justice Berger so eloquently stated in his report of the MacKenzie Valley Pipeline Inquiry (Berger, 1977a):

> The issues we face are profound ones, going beyond the ideological conflicts that have occupied the world for so long, conflicts over who should run the industrial machine and who should reap the benefits. Now we are being asked: How much energy does it take to run the industrial machine? Where is the machine going? And what happens to the people who live in the path of the machine?

Clearly, one of the dominant themes addressed during the public review of the draft Green Paper focused on Canada's own north-south dialogue. To what extent are the potential benefits of northern development directed towards southern residents? The social costs associated with northern development were clearly perceived to be born primarily, if not exclusively, by residents of the region, and more specifically by the Inuit.

There is an overriding concern amongst the

Inuit that we lack an adequate understanding of the full implications of future development in the North. There is fear and concern that culture, life style, economy and ultimately the environment of the North will be destroyed. "In our minds we are concerned that the technology that is available today is inadequate to mitigate any foreseeable disaster in the Arctic waters."

A variety of perspectives as to the future uses of the Lancaster Sound Region were expressed during public review. Irrespective of the perspective held, however, virtually all participants agreed on the urgent need for a planning process for the high Arctic, in general, and the Lancaster Sound Region, in particular. Consensus on the need for a planning framework as a means of managing future uses in the region was one of the clearest and most convincing reactions to the Lancaster Sound Regional Study derived from the public review process.

A discussion paper developed by the Federal Government noted that "the past decade has seen an increasing frequency of conflicting demands for use of land in the North, generated by competition among industrial, conservation and native interest".

The report concluded that "to meet this challenge a Northern Land Use Planning Policy and a Northern Land Use Planning Process are required to:

- ensure orderly and planned development compatible with environmental objectives, the national interest, and the social and economic well-being of native people and other residents of the territories;
- improve co-ordination among departments and agencies with respect to northern land and resource use;
- establish a system for determining the allocation of lands to various uses based on the lands composite values and for guiding the application of land and related resource regulatory systems;
- provide a public consultation process and forum for assessing and proposing solutions to land use conflicts arising among the government, natives and private sector bodies concerned with northern development and conservation activities; and
- make recommendations on changes in policy and programmes necessary to achieve co-ordinated and comprehensive land-use planning and management of territorial lands".

In January of 1983, the Department of Indian and Northern Affairs released a draft proposal entitled "Land-Use Planning in Northern Canada". The proposal defined northern land-use planning as "an organized process for determining the uses of land and related resources based upon co-operative decision-making by governments, groups and individuals".

The Department proposal states that the primary responsibility for preparing northern land-use plans will rest with northerners, that public involvement will be encouraged and will be included in the land-use planning process, and that northern land-use plans will be prepared on a regional or land-use planning area basis.

There is, however, a tendency to focus on existing institutional structures and frameworks to develop important new conservation and planning initiatives. This tendency if continued and expanded acts counter to all the productive input achieved during public review. The proposed northern land-use planning structure shows little evidence or recognition of the important role that the public can play prior to reviewing "acceptable" plans developed by planning commissions. As currently constituted, a director of land use planning prepared northern plans in Yellowknife under the direction of the Planning Commission. The tendency to centralize the planning process effectively eliminates any opportunity to develop local or even regional planning expertise or to develop local and regional planning institutions. This, coupled with an apparent absence of public input in the acquisition of data, the organization of studies, the synthesis of these studies into planning strategies, renders the proposed planning process more and more distant from those who so strongly support the need for planning in the region.

To whom will the "acceptable plans" be acceptable if participation in their preparation is constrained to a few people working in Yellowknife? The Lancaster Sound Regional Study and the experience derived from it indicates that the proposed planning process will either be boycotted or recycled, with the inevitable delays that will result, to include people from the region concerned.

The Department is urged to reconsider the proposed structure and form of the northern land-use planning process to incorporate local and regional public participation and review during all phases of the planning process. The process of public review launched during the Lancaster Sound Regional

Study is quite probably irreversible. Potential benefits in support of this strategy include a local understanding and commitment to the planning process as well as an active and informed citizenry.

Inuit and Indian associations' reaction to the federal planning initiative focused on a joint statement of principles to guide the land-use planning process in the Northwest Territories that includes the following eight points:

1. Man is a functional part of a dynamic bio-physical environment and land use cannot be planned and managed without reference to the human community. Accordingly, social, cultural and economic endeavours of the human community must be central to land-use planning and implementation.

2. The primary purpose for land-use planning in the Northwest Territories must be to protect and promote the existing and future well being of the permanent residents and communities of the Northwest Territories taking into account the interests of all Canadians. Special attention shall be devoted to protecting and promoting the existing and future well being of the aboriginal peoples and their land interests as they define them.

3. The planning process must ensure land-use plans reflect the priorities and values of the residents of the planning regions.

4. The plans will provide for the conservation, development and utilization of land, resources inland waters and the offshore.

5. To be effective the public planning process must provide an opportunity for the active and informed participation and support of the residents affected by the plan. Such participation will be promoted through means including: ready access to all relevant information, widespread dissemination of relevant materials, appropriate and realistic schedule, recruitment and training of local residents to participate in comprehensive land-use planning.

6. The planning process must be systematic and must be integrated with all other planning processes and operations.

7. It is acknowledged that an effective land planning process requires the active par-

ticipation of the Government of Canada, the Government of the Northwest Territories, and regional and territorial organizations representing aboriginal people.

8. It is recognized that the funding and other resources shall be made available for the system and be provided equitably to allow each of the major participants referred to in paragraph 7 to participate effectively.

These general principles have been accepted with only very minor modifications by the Federal Government and by the Government of the Northwest Territories. In addition, negotiations are proceeding apace to achieve agreement on the definition and purpose of land-use planning in the North, on the operational principle that will govern the process, on the structures and process of land-use planning, and on the roles and responsibilities of the Government of Canada and the Government of the Northwest Territories.

In the final chapter of People, Resources and the Environment that reported on the public review phase of the Lancaster Sound Regional Study a challenge was issued to government, to industry and to northern residents. The challenge articulated was to move beyond a planning scenario based on the perceptions of the southern culture of Canada towards a thoroughly considered adaptable future for the Lancaster Sound Region. The report noted that "to do so will require imagination and patience; coherent policy and planning guidelines agreed to by those who have concerns in the region; pilot projects for transportation, research, education and training to test our ideas, most important we need the will to persevere in developing an innovative planning and management process. Industry, government and northern residents will have to forego adversary roles and efficiency may have to yield to effectiveness so that we may ensure the cultural differences and heritage of the people who will be most influenced by this growth".

The report noted that "the application of planning methods and techniques derived from southern Canadian experience may well aggravate rather than alleviate problems related to the future use and management of the North". The report noted further that while "northern and southern peoples and traditions are neither inferior nor superior, they are different. If we plan we must do so with as full an understanding of these differences as possible and with an astute sensitivity to the range of values that underlie these differences".

To a large extent the challenge expressed in People, Resources and the North has not been accepted. To do so, the report suggested, would require "coherent policy and planning guidelines, pilot projects in training and education amongst other concerns, and that all actors forego adversarial roles".

The process will require a good deal more than statements of principle such as those developed by CARC and modified by public workshops two years ago and those developed subsequently by native organizations related to land-use planning. The process requires a strong conceptual basis, an appropriate form and structure, and an operational basis that allows real input from those affected by proposals for growth, development and the changes associated with both.

One glaring example of a weak conceptual planning base is most evident in the draft policy - the bio-physical realm is rather brutally disassociated from social, cultural and economic considerations. This flaw is so critical as to suggest that the entire public review process was either totally misunderstood, ignored, or both. Clearly everything that emerged from the transcripts of the public workshops over a two-year period, as well as from written statements from native organizations and from community meetings, was that the North is a whole and cannot be neatly sliced apart into clean independent sectors. This, more than anything else, is at the core of public review and reaction to the Lancaster Sound Regional Study. The land, water, ice; the animals, birds, fish; the people; all form one indivisible whole. Any planning process that disassociates socio-economic and cultural factors from their bio-physical context is suspect, a process that does so in the North is bound to be rejected. This, at the very least, is the message inherent in the negotiated set of principles proposed by native organizations.

During the public workshops the Department noted that a policy for land use in the North "is being developed by the Department to try to devise a system by which the type of conflicts that develop for use of a given area can be attacked or considered right at the start, and not wait until conflicts develop".

A great deal of support for a truly northern

land-use planning process was expressed during the public review phase of the Lancaster Sound Regional Study. The Department of Indian and Northern Affairs was clearly anxious to proceed in this direction, and the Canadian Arctic Resources Committee had sponsored a workshop in 1979 that had established seven key principles for the development and protection of Lancaster Sound. During the workshops, participants strongly supported their inclusion as part of the proposed planning process.

The report People, Resources and the Environment noted that "Adoption of the principle that guidelines for the management of Lancaster Sound was virtually unanimous during public review. However, the brief submitted by the Department of Fisheries and Oceans noted that the real challenge with these principles will lie in their implementation". The report recommended that the final Green Paper incorporate aspects of the policy paper released in July 1981, and illustrate its application to the Lancaster Sound Region. The report noted that "insofar as only the skeleton framework of a northern land-use planning process can be developed in a policy paper, much work remains before a viable planning process can be established on an ongoing and operational basis". Not the least of the questions that must be addressed is "How shall we plan?"

It is not at all evident that consensus to embark on a regional planning exercise for the high Arctic will a priori result in innovative and appropriate policy, strategy and tactics for the use and management of the high Arctic or for any region of the high Arctic such as Lancaster Sound. In fact, the application of planning methods and techniques derived from southern Canadian experiences may well aggravate rather than alleviate problems related to the future use and management of the North. My intention of this final section is not to dampen enthusiastic support for a regional planning process north of 60°, but rather to suggest that such a venture must be truly adapted to the people and the place for which it is intended.

One issue at stake is the design of institutions and decision-making processes that might illustrate Canadian recognition of our own and distinct north-south dialogue. In order that our responses to this challenge be meaningful and appropriate, we must be innovative. We cannot rely on the theory that those formulae developed in one context will necessarily be suitable in a context that is distinctly different and unique.

A southern, paternalistic planning approach with regard to the North would be one of the clearest signs that we are unwilling to learn and that we are dealing from a position of superior knowledge. Our southern and northern peoples and traditions are neither inferior nor superior; they are, however, different. If we plan, we must do so with as full an understanding of these differences as possible and with an acquite sensitivity to the range of values which underlie these differences.

One of the most fundamental characteristics of planning is the intellectual and cultural setting which supports the process. Whereas the Inuit seek consensus on those issues that affect them most profoundly, we are accustomed to debating public issues that are terminated and resolved by majority votes, frequently by elected representatives. Decisions based on adversary positions are distinctly different from those based on consensus. The process requires more time, is highly participatory, and directly involves those responsible for implementing a decision and those who will be directly affected by such a decision. Not surprisingly, a significant distinction between the North and the South is our understanding of time.

Time
Industry - and to a large extent the Federal Government - is concerned that expeditious decisions are required if Canadians are to achieve energy self-sufficiency, a favourable standing in the world market place and the perception of competent management of our own affairs. The Inuit move to a different rhythm. "It takes people time to change their living habits", time to adapt to the rapid rate of change in the North, time to acquire the necessary training and education required to participate fully in the future development of their homeland.

Time is also essential if we are to understand the concerns of the Inuit, if we are to perfect the technology necessary to support our development proposals and to safeguard the environment of the North. Southern time is linear and sequential, northern time is cyclic and repetitive. Can we design a planning process capable of accommodating both? Must one concept of time dominate the other? Do we really believe that we have run out of southern time, or do we too have time to deal with this fundamental dimension of the planning process rooted in cultural perceptions?

Space

Our concept of space is equally bound by our cultural heritage. In the South, space has been divided and subdivided since the first military engineers from Europe set foot on North American soil over 400 years ago. Land surveying and land division is a normal part of our view of the space that we inhabit. Land-use planning history and theory relies heavily on the premise that different spaces can and should be used for different activities. Allocating exclusive uses to specific spaces is a familiar part of our Canadian urban experience. Occasionally, as in older western cultures, multiple-use areas have been designated for a combination of typical urban functions such as commerce, housing and on occasion small industries. Restricted use of space has been introduced in the urban fringe and in southern resource management areas to allow a range of compatible, but limited uses to occur in the same place at the same time.

How applicable are these concepts of spatial division and the subsequent allocation of designated uses to the high Arctic where space has not been characterized by its divisibility, but rather by its extent and continuity? How much more difficult is it to trace lines on a territory where the distinction between land and water varies so radically from winter to summer? How much more difficult when we know that spatial segregations of northern and southern waters are predominately vertical and not necessarily horizontal in shape and form? Can we design appropriate planning methods and techniques - indeed a planning philosophy - to accommodate cultural and technical variance in our southern perception of space?

Appropriate Technology

Energy self-sufficiency in Canada is a stated national goal. To the South, the phrase implies secure sources of oil, gas, hydro-electricity, some marginal use of nuclear energy and other "alternative energy" sources.

How appropriate is this vision for the North? Can we develop a planning process wherein the issues of energy self-sufficiency, shelter and travel, to name only a few, are appropriate to the context of Canada's high Arctic?

Appropriate technology, in short, is culturally based. It is not necessarily appropriate to all contexts at all times (western technology), but is by definition appropriate to a specific context during a particular period of time. When we speak of technology to assure that oil spills can be contained or that the weather can be properly monitored, or that biological populations can be properly accounted for, we speak of only one of a number of technologies. As suggested earlier in this report, solutions to some problems perceived in one cultural setting such as the "need to hunt" cannot necessarily be resolved with reference to the technology of another cultural setting that has created a constraint on the first by its "need to ship".

The Form of Information
The very manner by which we deal with information is also culturally bound. The acquisition of data, its treatment and the conclusions which we reach on the basis of this data are unlikely to be universally accepted. The problem is compounded when various departments of government or people with northern experience state quite openly that there are important gaps in our understanding even within carefully defined sectors of scientific enquiry. The issues are compounded when we attempt to integrate these sectors and to understand the dynamics of the ecosystems of the high Arctic. We have a tendency, if not a scientific ideology, to disaggregate complex systems in order to better understand them. It is unlikely that the system of Inuit knowledge and understanding follows the same paths of enquiry. To what extent have we tried to incorporate, let alone understand, centuries of Inuit observation of nature in our description and understanding of the high Arctic?

Can the incomplete basis upon which we propose to erect a regional planning process afford to ignore, or to treat as marginal, the knowledge-base that has served a culture for thousands of years; a culture that lives at peace with itself and its surroundings?

Planning for Change
Throughout this report, and particularly in the latter sections, stress has been placed on the need for a coherent policy framework and guidelines within which the proposed regional planning process

might function with due regard to our national interest. The Inuit participants throughout the public review process have articulated a clear and direct goal: the maintenance of life style options. National goals include energy self-sufficiency, those outlined in Canada's North: 1970-1980; and goals articulated in a document entitled "Departmental Direction Plan for the 1980s", developed by the Department of Indian and Northern Affairs. To what extent can we design a viable planning process north of 60° which will accommodate and necessarily reinforce the realization of these sets of goals? Can we stretch beyond the simple maintenance of life style options towards the qualitative and quantitative improvement of these options?

Planning deals necessarily with a future state, and the changes which will occur between a given condition and a set of possible future conditions. Within a range of possible futures some are more probable than others. Many of the issues raised in this paper can be considered as a set of performance criteria against which our efforts to develop a planning process north of 60° may well be judged. These criteria are by no means exhaustive. They do indicate some of the conditions and issues which must be incorporated into a viable planning process for the North. Failure to do so will undoubtedly lead to a certain and predictable future based on the goals, objectives, issues and perceptions of the dominant southern culture of Canada.

The challenge we face is to move beyond this scenario towards a more thoroughly considered, adaptable future for the Lancaster Sound Region. To do so will require imagination and patience.

The Inuit who participated in the public review were most eloquent in defining one of their essential goals for the future: the maintenance of life style options. Key strategies in achieving this objective focus on full participation in the planning, management and decision-making processes that will directly affect those who live within the region.

The Department has launched an important study in northern Canada, a study that from the start included an important component devoted to public review of the study, its findings and the recommendations that derived from both. Clearly, the locus of concern must shift to the northern land-use planning process proposed by the Department of Indian and Northern Affairs. A creative and dynamic land-use planning process in the North can succeed in structuring viable paths towards achieving "balanced development" but only if such a process is creative and truly reflective of northern conditions and perceptions.

Chapter Five

TRADITIONAL LAND-USE AND NATURE CONSERVATION IN MADAGASCAR

By

Joseph Andriamampianina, Département des Forêts
Etablissement d'Enseignement Supérieur
  des Sciences Agronomiques
Université de Madagascar
B.P. 175, Antananarivo, Madagascar

ABSTRACT

Although the population of Madagascar is just 9 million for a country of almost 600,000 sq km, there is still a serious lack of productive agricultural soils. This paper discusses the original vegetation of Madagascar, the changes in land-use that have taken place over time, and the traditional conservation measures that have been developed. As many of these traditional conservation methods are becoming weaker with increasing land hunger, the Government has stepped in with a conservation programme which includes the establishment of protected areas, public education, and international co-operation.

THE LAND DEVELOPMENT PROBLEM IN MADAGASCAR

In Madagascar, it has always been difficult to solve land development problems. In spite of its extensive area (590,000 square kilometres) for a population of 9 million, this agriculture-oriented country has but little fertile and easy-to-cultivate plots. This can be understood through the analysis of the key factors having an impact on the development of agriculture: the climate, the soil, and the distribution of the human population.

The Climate
Madagascar has the typical climate of subtropical countries which means that water is the main problem for agriculture. Water resources are unevenly distributed depending on the geography and seasons. In the arid south-western part, precipitation amounts to about 350 mm annually whereas rainfall

reaches more than 3,000 mm in the eastern part and comes to 1,500 mm in the centre (where rain only falls during 4 to 5 months a year).

The Soil

However fertile the soil might be, the land is difficult to cultivate due to the very rugged landscape. Volcanism and geological phenomena have played an important part in the shaping of the island and furthermore, the soil is, by its very nature, very sensitive to erosion. Most of the island is covered with a reddish ferruginous soil, the result of the modifications which have taken place in the underlying bed. Thus, wherever the vegetation cover has been unable to protect the soil from run-off waters, intensive erosion has formed ravines and caused land slides, giving this bumpy look to the landscape.

The Population

On Madagascar, there is a problem of population distribution: a density of more than 60 per square kilometre on the central highlands and along the eastern coast more than 100, falling down to 5 or less on the western coast. The raw figure compared to the total area does not account for the pressure placed upon some areas. The island having, as we said, a very rugged landscape, it is estimated that agricultural land does not exceed 15% of the total. This inevitably leads to the deforestation of land unsuitable for agriculture, to the degradation of forests and consequently to the loss of wild flora and fauna habitats.

LAND-USE

Most probably, long ago the forest covered the main part of the island. Today it only covers 10% of the total area due to the impact of different land-uses and to centuries-old traditions that we will discuss later.

Different Land-Uses

Central Madagascar. According to botanists, long ago, the central highlands were covered, up to 1,500 to 1,800 m, with mountain forest with herbaceous undergrowth and from 1,800 m up with a thick bush composed of lichen and moss-covered bushes. Apart from some isolated woodlands at the top of the mountains, all the forest vegetation highly sensitive to fire has been destroyed by man. Among the common land-uses are the flooded rice fields on the lowlands and other crops (such as manioc) on the deforested hills and most of all, burning for grazing lands. Every year, fire destroys vast grazing or even reforestation areas. In this way, people hope that old dry and hard grass will burn to be replaced by tender shoots, and that ashes will fertilize the soil. But this is merely an illusion for not only is selection taking place the wrong way, eliminating fragile plants, but this practice enhances desertification and helps destroy the biological and cultural heritage. However, this is nothing compared to what happens in the west and south.

<u>Southern and Eastern Madagascar</u>. In the west, the tradition is more pastoral than agricultural and to expand their grazing lands, the people choose the easiest way: burning down the forest. Savannah has replaced the forest and as it has little nutritious value, more and more land had to be burned. Pastoralists have thus created vast grasslands which extend over most of the western part of the island. The situation is even more critical in the south, where large herds are left to graze overnight. Lands are burned for grazing and little room is left for some meagre food crops.

<u>Eastern Madagascar</u>. Here people are more dedicated to agriculture than in the south and west. They have adopted another burning method called "tavy". It consists of burning the forest after it has been cut down for temporary crops (mainly mountain rice), the land being abandoned to natural vegetation once it is impoverished. In Madagascar, about 200,000 hectares are cultivated in this way every year and abandoned after 2 or 3 years. Under the alternate action of the sun and the rain, the barren soil, fragile by nature, is rapidly degraded.

Psycho-sociological Analysis of Traditions

<u>Burning practices</u>. One could wonder why people of Madagascar are so keen on burning practices. There

must be reasons for this long-lived habit. It seems to start with the fact that farmers do not yet realize the disadvantages of burning practices. They cannot understand why the forest, which does not bring them any advantage and appears only as an obstacle to agriculture and grazing cattle, should be protected. They think that a few hectares of deforestation does no harm as nature seems so vast and infinite. A local saying even compares all that is endless to the eastern forests. Moreover, the tavy and the fires are ancestral practices and for the farmers they are easy and simple techniques from which their ancestors always benefited. The country has always been burned; why then should they change their methods? It is hot, everything dries up, grass burns, trees are bent and consumed by fire: they think it is the way it has to be and that no one can fight Nature's will without risks. So one wonders. Is it man's ancient fatalism in front of nature's forces, or do technicians make a mistake when they worry about burning practices and deforestation? The debate seems to be without end, for in Madagascar, people may think fire is evil but a necessary evil.

Part played by the cattle in people's life. For many, Malagasy cattle are status symbols, the number of which are more important than their quality. In the west and the south - where fires destroy large areas - people raise huge herds mostly for celebrations and especially for funerals which must be magnificent. Fear and the cult of the dead are important in Madagascar; ritual sacrifices require impressive slaughters. Thus people must own many heads of cattle and this leads to the unwise practice of burning.

Good influence of some creeds. There are, however, some creeds and superstitions which advocate forest protection. They concern mountain forests, the protection of which is linked to the awe people have of mountains. Even the many small pitons scattered all over the island are often taboo: they are believed to be the cemetery of the souls of the dead. Nobody would dare set fire to them. Therefore the natural reserves created mainly in the highest areas of the country are being conserved partly because of those creeds and partly because it is too difficult to cultivate their steep slopes. But we will see that these creeds and superstitions tend to disappear and that forests which have been conserved until now are threatened.

Consequences

It is not necessary to give all the consequences of this form of agriculture and cattle breeding based on burning practices. On the other hand, the extinction of a unique flora and fauna (resulting from the fact that the country has been isolated since ancient geological periods) should be underlined. Madagascar has an exceptional number of ecosystems, many endemic animal and plant species, some of which are extremely old while others have quickly evolved to occupy the many available ecological niches. The loss of these species would not only affect Madagascar but also the whole of mankind.

GOVERNMENT MEASURES: PROTECTED AREAS

First of all it should be said that it has been a long time since action for nature protection started in Madagascar. Already under the Ancient Malagasy Kingdom the "305 Articles Code" condemned those who were convicted of deforestation to be chained. During the French occupation of the island, the authorities became aware of the progressive extinction of natural flora and fauna and of its consequences. Several measures were enforced, most of which still apply or have been updated or appended since independence. Many legal texts have been published including rules on burning practices and deforestation, on protected species, reforestation, soil conservation, etc. This document will deal mostly with protected areas and the steps taken to conserve them.

The Different Categories of Protected Areas of Madagascar

Strict Nature Reserves. Madagascar now has eleven strict nature reserves, nine of which were created in 1927 (there were ten of them but one was downgraded in 1964), one was created in 1939 and another one in 1952. These reserves were established with the aim of preserving different types of fauna and flora on the island and thus are sanctuaries forbidden to all human activity and even to the circulation of the people from nearby villages, according to the 1968 African Convention on the Conservation of Nature and Natural Resources. The sites have been selected in order to provide a sample as representative as possible of the many features of the island and are situated, unless impossible, in scarcely populated or mountainous areas, so that they would be protected from the population always in search of new agricultural lands (see paragraph "Good influence of some creeds").

National Parks. Madagascar has two national parks which were created in 1958 and in 1962 to complement the samples of nature protected in the strict nature reserves. Their Statutes are based on the afore-mentioned 1968 Convention.

Special Reserves. This concept applies to parts of forests where any kind of exploitation or land-use is prohibited. There are now 23 special reserves in Madagascar and they aim mainly at the conservation of some plant and animal species. The reserves created after independence were established in 1962, 1964, 1965, 1970 and 1982.

People's Approach to Protected Areas
We said that Malagasy people had a strong respect for traditions. However, they accepted the taboos imposed by their kings and masters on certain areas; they also accepted the reserves created by the French administration. The word "Reserve" and especially "Nature Reserve" implied a measure of respect and of fear of the unknown dangers concealed by the sites situated in the high mountains. People understood the necessity of preserving memories of the past as well as the surroundings in which their ancestors lived. Thus the reserve concept was fitting well in their customs and did not hurt their feelings. But this attitude tends to disappear due to wrong interpretations of the steps taken during the colonial era, to education which tends to banish creeds and pagan superstitions, to a population increase leading to fear of lack of space for agriculture, and to an unwise step of the government which downgraded one of the first ten strict nature reserves in 1964. Fortunately, through education efforts made by the authorities, in spite of their limited means, most of the people living close to

the reserves are aware of the necessity to conserve these territories.

Protected Areas Management

Staff. The Administration Forestière is in charge of Protected Areas management. Unfortunately, there is not enough monitoring staff. For a total area of 700,000 hectares, the 13 strict nature reserves and national parks only have one agent each, most of the time isolated in the wilds without a vehicle and thus unable to fulfil their missions. Only two of the special reserves have one agent each.

Funds. No funds are allocated to protected areas maintenance; the funds allocated by the Administration Forestière are mainly used for activities concentrating particularly on development which is still the main priority area.

INTERNATIONAL HELP

We already mentioned that Madagascar had no adequate means to protect its parks and reserves but this does not mean that the government did not make a move. Aware of the seriousness of the degradation of Nature in the country and of the difficulty in handling daily problems raised by protection of Nature in general and of protected areas in particular, the authorities have asked international agencies for help.

The Contribution of IUCN and WWF

Madagascar is a member of IUCN. Since the first days of independence (1961) Madagascar became a member of IUCN, and was the first French-speaking African country to do so.

Conference on Nature Conservation. IUCN greatly helped the government in organizing the Conference on Conservation and Rational Use of Nature in Antananarivo, October 1970. Attended by Malagasy officials and several scientists from many countries, the conference can be considered as an important step towards the protection of Malagasy parks and reserves. It helped make people aware of the exceptional part played in the world by Madagascar's protected areas because of the value of its natural resources; it promoted understanding of the degradation threat which, as everywhere else and perhaps more than anywhere else, grows with development. IUCN launched a real SOS to help the Government of Madagascar in its protection effort and several recommendations were issued related to protection of certain wetland habitat of threatened birds, and related legal measures followed.

Different forms of help. It is next to impossible to go into details about the sort and amount of help WWF/IUCN rendered to the Malagasy Government since 1960, for protection of reserves and parks as well as for staff equipment. We will simply underline that two years ago, five new projects were handed over to WWF/IUCN by the Government, were accepted by that organization, and are now being completed. The projects concern protection of three reserves, working equipment and vehicles for the managers of the reserves, audio-visual equipment for promotion of conservation and environmental education.

Establishment of a WWF agency. In 1979, the government issued a decree allowing WWF/IUCN to create an agency in Antananarivo. This WWF/IUCN move is very important for it makes it possible to obtain international funds. Moreover, through the WWF/IUCN agency, better monitoring is assured and projects can be dealt with according to their priority.

GENERAL PRINCIPLES

Staff Training

There are not enough personnel in the protected areas, partly due to the fact that their activities are slightly different from those of the forestry staff. To ensure the monitoring and conservation of protected areas is an essential task but it is by no means the only one. The study of plants and animals of the areas is the main activity of the monitoring agents. They must therefore take an interest in nature, have good observation capacity, be sociable but severe. Such staff must be trained.

Autonomous Management

Although it seems quite logical to place parks and reserves management under the authority of the Administration Forestière, they need a measure of independence since the staff needs to be specialized and therefore is not interchangeable without good reasons. Most of the time they acquire necessary knowledge only in the course of their career. Furthermore, being autonomous, they could obtain funds to be used exclusively for protection.

Education

Conservation of Parks and Reserves must not only be brought about through legislation. Enforced legislation should be complemented - and it is an essential requirement - by education or re-education of tne people. No-one can blame the man who deforests part of a reserve if he has not been told that it is part of a unique national heritage. Much remains to be done in this field and today education is the main activity of the monitoring staff.

CONCLUSION

The main hope for the protection of Malagasy parks and reserves is the noticeable awakening of a national awareness. Nowadays, a strong current tends to underline Madagascar's uniqueness. The island's natural heritage is being promoted, as well as its historical, literary and artistic wealth. In the meantime an international current supports national efforts. In that sense, the WWF/IUCN agency will contribute a lot to these efforts which aim at transmitting the Malagasy heritage to future generations.

Chapter Six

INFLUENCE OF HISTORICAL AND CULTURAL DIFFERENCES
ON THE ACTUAL LEVEL OF CONSERVATION OF NATURE
BETWEEN MAJORCA AND MINORCA ISLANDS
(BALEARIC ISLANDS, SPAIN)

By

Miguel Morey, Depto. de Ecología
Facultad de Ciencias, Ctra. de Valldemosa Km 7,5
Palma de Mallorca, Spain

ABSTRACT

The paper argues that social and cultural systems
can lead to critical ecological differences even in
very similar environments. The example of Minorca
and Majorca is used to demonstrate this point.
Minorca has had a relatively slow process of economic growth based on sound commercial principles and
a relatively liberal political and social environment, with tourist numbers also growing gradually.
Majorca by contrast, depressed economically due to
land fragmentation and a stratified society, was
also subject to a massive post-war tourist influx,
which led to much more environmental degradation
than in Minorca.

The state of conservation is the result of the
interaction between the natural characteristics of
the territory and the culture developed historically
by the people living there. The interaction occurs
in both directions, the physical environment influences the type of culture developed (agriculture,
cattle raising, industry, commerce, etc.) and the
culture developed (depending in part on religion,
ethics, etc.) modifies the environment.

In this paper I want to emphasize the importance of the apparently small historical differences
between people to produce different culture models
and to achieve actually a very different level of
conservation. This is the case in the west Mediterranean Spanish Islands, Majorca and Minorca. After
successive occupations since ancient times, Majorca
was conquered by the Catalonian army in 1229 and
from this date almost everybody was and spoke
Catalonian. The conquest of Minorca by the

Catalonian army was achieved 57 years later and this difference in time affected patterns of rural inheritance. However, the most important cultural differences between both islands arose during the 18th century in three successive periods of British domination of Minorca (1708-1756, 1763-1781, and 1798-1802). The rural properties passed from the nobility to the bourgeoisie with a concomitant change of economy and to semi-extensive cattle commercial raising, giving a higher standard of living than Majorca, which remained underdeveloped. With the advent of mass tourism in the 1950s the economic and social structure of both islands was very different. In Majorca "minifundism" dominated in rural areas making difficult the development of a prosperous agriculture and economy; Minorca has modern farming and industrialization. Majorcan society is forced to promote a mass tourism that gives an easy wealth but spoils the environment, whilst in Minorca it is possible to delay the beginning of touristic development, slowly increasing the number of tourists and developing a rational tourism without spoiling nature. The negative type of tourist development of Majorca (and also of Ibiza) has received internationally the name of "balearización".

Both islands belong to the same administrative province of Spain, have the same laws and local government but have been able to develop different environmental policies. This emphasizes the importance of cultural influences on environmental planning.

In many countries there has not been conscious environmental planning for conservation. Some western countries have very recently developed and applied a set of laws for conservation and sustained development, but generally only when there has been much environmental degradation. Because of lack of planning, the actual level of conservation depends in most cases on the interaction between the natural characteristics of the territory and the cultural background of the people that live in the region. The first steps in environmental planning must begin with an accurate analysis of the status of conservation and historical research.

Different cultures produce different types of conservation approaches. For example, even if a generalization, eastern cultures emphasize conservation whilst the western cultures tend to be exploitive. It is, however, necessary to be very careful in making generalizations, because sometimes

Culture and Conservation in Balearic Islands

very small historical and cultural differences between two very near and similar countries or territories have produced completely different types of
conservation.

The Majorcan and Minorcan Islands are situated
in the middle of the west Mediterranean Sea, separated only by 20 nautical miles (36 km). Majorca is
more than five times bigger than Minorca and its
population in 1960 (before the tourist boom) was
eight times bigger. As a consequence of their pro-
ximity, the physical and geographical characteristics are very similar. They are very similar in
flora, fauna and types of communities and ecosystems. The most important differences are due to
the presence in Majorca of a northern mountain ridge
that is absent in Minorca and from the presence of
a siliceous lithological substrate in Minorca, and
on the other hand to the historical and cultural
differences that we will analyse in this paper
(Table 6.1 summarizes the main types of environment).

Both islands have had a very similar historical
development, suffering since ancient times invasions
by different ethnic and cultural groups (religion,
language, etc.) until the 13th century. Majorca
was conquered by James I in 1229 and Minorca by
Alfonso II, 57 years after. In both cases the old
inhabitants (of Arab origin and language and
Mahomdan religion) were almost completely eliminated
from the islands, which were populated by Catalonian
Christians speaking Catalonian. This difference of
57 years affected the rural transmission of noble
properties but more important effects were due to
the conquest and occupation of Minorca by the
British. Though the British occupation was only
for 60 years, Minorca really had a British model of
development for almost a century (1708-1802).
Whilst Minorca developed a commercial agricultural
system and a liberal political system, Majorca
remained linked to Spain and medieval models of
society. At the beginning of the British domination,
Minorca was divided into a few noble properties,
totally lacking in Majorca. During the century of
British domination almost all the noble properties
were bought by the middle class. The exploitation
systems of the nobility were substituted by dynamic
capitalist-type systems with development of manufac-
turing of agricultural products and commerce. Poor
dry cereal crops were replaced by improved semi-
extensive pastures for sheep and cattle as in Great
Britain. This kind of land management is only

93

Table 6.1 - Main Environments

Type of Environment

Mountain (mountain type plants and animals, with a high proportion of endemic types)

Evergreen oak forest (climax vegetation)

Pine forest (forest of Pinus halepensis with developed shrub layer)

"Marina" (shrub community with Olea, Erica, Pistacia, Rosmarinus and pine)

Marshes (brackish zones with Pragmites, Thypha Artrocnemum and aquatic avifauna)

Coastal dunes (mobile sand dunes and fixed dunes by shrubs and pine)

Coastal cliffs

Semi-extensive pastures (without irrigation, for cows and sheep)

Irrigated forage (stabulated cattle)

Cereal crops with scattered trees

---

possible when the land is divided into big properties, but not when the size of property is too small. Properties therefore were not divided between all the sons of every owner and they have remained relatively large averaging 43.15 ha in 1972. On the other hand the medieval management of land in Majorca continued almost until the beginning of the 20th century, when the rural nobility became in Majorca and Minorca Islands

Majorca	Minorca
Serra de Tramuntana	-
Wet parts of the low mountains	Scattered in the island especially in the centre
Arid zones of low mountains	Very scarce. Scattered in the island
Proximity of the coast, except parts of the north	Proximity of the coast. Sometimes penetrating far inland
Albuferas in the north and south. Menaced	Albufera in the north. Menaced
Palma Bay (destroyed). Alcudia Bay (half destroyed) and big system of Campos (virgin but menaced)	On the southern coast
Almost all the coast	Almost all the coast
-	Very widespread in the centre and north
Plain zones near Palma, La Puebla and Campo	Only on a few protected areas of the south
All the plains and low parts of mountains	-

impoverished and had, of necessity, to sell the properties in little parcels of land producing "minifundism" (the average size of rural properties in Majorca in 1970 was only 7.91 ha) (GALMES and SALVA, 1982). The larger properties, with cattle, permitted in Minorca the development of industries derived from the products of cattle (cheese, butter, leather, shoes, etc.).

Another cultural effect of the British domination (and of the French too, in spite of this occupation being even shorter) was the improvement of schools and the creation of cultural institutions many years before these appeared in Majorca.

When mass tourism started in 1950 there was "minifundism" in Majorca in the agriculturally richest areas, with very old-fashioned systems of exploitation and commerce, and almost without industrialization or hotels. At the same time in Minorca there were improved pastures with the introduction of new well-adapted forage species like Hedisarum coronarium, (ALENYAR et al. 1982) which was very widespread from 1870 (BOLOS et al., 1970) as well as Trifolium alexandrinum, Medicago arborea, Vicia sativa, etc.

In these circumstances it is natural that when mass tourism came the people of Majorca accepted this as the only way of improving the level of living. There was a massive social, economic and environmental transformation after the construction of hotels first and then flats and chalets. On the other hand, Minorcans preferred a slow development of tourism without negative impacts not only on the landscape, but also on rangeland. To give some idea of the increase in tourism in Majorca, the case of the little village of Calvia (about 120 km) at the western part of the Bay of Palma may be cited. Calvia, from having an almost nil tourist capacity in 1950 had 35,519 beds in hotels, 46,909 beds in bungalows and 9,324 beds in chalets in 1975 (BISSON, 1977; Consel General Interinsular, 1982). These 91,752 beds for tourists represent more than the total number of beds in Tunisia, 50% of those of Rumania, 25% of those of Greece and 15% of those of Yugoslavia. In Minorca there is not anything like Calvia, but in Majorca there are many other very similar cases like El Arenal of Palma and Llucmajor and the Bays of Alcusia and Son Servera. The data on the Balearic Islands reflect very closely those of Majorca, from about 4,054 beds for tourists in 1950, to 222,680 in 1975. Tourist growth increased enormously, 125,000 visited in 1950, 400,000 in 1960 and 3,573,000 in 1973 (ALENYAR et al., 1982). Since then there has been slow growth as is seen in both periods.

These facts have produced in Majorca very important changes on the economy, sociology, commerce, agriculture, industry and conservation. The "per capita" rent has increased from 100,000 pesetas in 1960 to 270,000 pesetas in 1973 (ALENYAR et al.,

1982). This fact has produced drastic social changes. Traditional agriculture had been abandoned and only in a few parts of the island has it been substituted by more modern systems of culture and commerce. During this same period employment has passed from an agricultural situation in 1960 (34% working in the primary sector, 31% in the secondary and 35% in the tertiary sector) to an unbalanced proportion in 1973 with more than half of the population working in the tertiary sector (13% in the primary sector, 34% in the secondary and 53% in the tertiary sector) (Atlas des Iles Baléares, 1979). This represents a change in 13 years from a rural society to a commercial one without passing through an industrial phase. Imports passed from 400,000 Tm in 1960 (200,000 Tm of exports) to more than 2,000,000 Tm in 1973 (300,000 Tm exports).

Another consequence has been an increase in immigration to Majorca especially by people from the south and centre of Spain (a positive immigrant balance of 75,000 immigrants in Majorca from 1960 to 1975, and only 5,000 in the same period in Minorca) (Atlas des Iles Baléares, 1979). This high proportion of immigrants produced the most important cultural changes in Majorca since the Conquest of the 13th century because of the different languages of the immigrants (Castilian Spanish, not Catalonian), cultural levels and customs. The impact of all these changes on the environment has been very big in Majorca. The consciousness of the necessity for the protection of nature in Majorca began approximately in 1965. The main law regulating the occupation and transformation of land up to 1973 was the "Ley del Suelo" (Law of the Ground) that did not take into account conservation. In 1973, the Provincial Environmental Plan for the Balearic Islands ("Plan Provincial de Ordenación de Baleares") was promulgated, but was insufficient and inadequate for the protection of nature. The destruction of nature did not increase too much because of the energy and economic crisis of the European countries, not because of the restraints derived from the new law. In 1975 there was a political change in Spain with the inauguration of a democratic monarchy and there were changes in environmental planning, reflected in 1978/79 in a new improved provincial law, "Plan Director Territorial de Baleares", which is still too general and has great difficulties of application in practice. In fact, in spite of this law, some important environments are still threatened in

Majorca, especially the last near virgin brackish marshes and the coastal dunes system of the island (in the village of Campos in the south), some little islands like Dragonera and some near little virgin coves. There are great difficulties also in obtaining the status of "Natural Park" for the North Mountain Ridge ("Serra de Tramuntana") and for the Islands of Cavrera with very clean waters and rich fauna to the south of Majorca. From the study of the evolution of culture and conservation of nature during the history of these two Mediterranean islands some conclusions can be drawn:

1. Small cultural differences over a period of time can produce very big differences in the status and perspectives of conservation.
2. Insularity produces cultural systems especially conservative, but subjected to successive drastic changes by military or pacific invasions.
3. New cultural influences come erratically but interrupt normal evolutionary processes rather like catastrophic natural events such as fires.
4. When there is more wealth there is a better possibility of coping with such potentially-destructive invasions.
5. The quick increase of the economic level, in the Majorcan case, too rapid economic (tourist) development, overloaded a system ill prepared and unbalanced economically.
6. Because of isolation, every island of an archipelago, in spite of having very similar physical and human characteristics, has its cultural peculiarities and must be the subject of particular and differentiated environmental planning. In the case of Balearic Islands there is a completely different environmental and development problem for Majorca and Minorca (and also for Ibiza).

REFERENCES

Alenyar, M., Barcelo, B. and Arnaiz, P.C. Evolución Económica. In SA NOSTRA. Cien anos de la Historia de Baleares. Ed. Salvat. Barcelona.
Atlas des Iles Baléares, Geográfic. Economic. Históric. 1979. Ed. Diáfora Barcelona.

Culture and Conservation in Balearic Islands

Bisson, J. 1977. La Terre et l'Homme aux Iles
    Baléares. Edisud.
Bolos, O., Molinier, R. and Montserrat, P. 1970.
    Observations phytosociologiques dans l'Ile de
    Minorque. Acta Geobotánica Barcinonensis, 5:
    1-150.
Calmes, J. and Salva, P. Agricultura y Ganderia. In
    SA NOSTRA. Cien años de la Historia de
    Baleares. Ed. Salvat. Barcelona.
El Turismo en las Baleares. 1981. Consel General
    Interinsular. Palma de Mallorca.
El Urbanismo y el Medio Ambiente en las Baleares.
    1982. Consell General Interinsular. Palma de
    Mallorca.

Section Three

THE VALUE OF CULTURAL, TRADITIONAL AND
INDIGENOUS RESOURCE KNOWLEDGE AND PRACTICE

INTRODUCTION

One of the premises for a management approach based
on an increased degree of co-operation with local
indigenous people is that there is much more to
traditional knowledge, philosophies and practices
than environmental managers have realized. The
collection, collation, evaluation and discussion of
these materials is an urgent task but we already
have some materials and a selection of these is
presented here. One point to emerge clearly is
that these valuable, and usually environmentally
sound, knowledge systems are disappearing and often
disappearing rapidly. There is an African saying,
that "when a knowledgeable old person dies a whole
library disappears".

As significantly, outside attractions are pulling
local people away from their home environments to
the cities, and encouraging them to spend their
time on other things, even if they stay at home.
The traditional knowledge system is often then
destroyed even if there is not the colonial regime
that Gadgil talks about in India. Many of the
papers in this section point to the environmental
problems that arise with the disappearance of the
traditional cultural base.

Chapter Seven

THE ANDEAN NATIVE PEOPLES IN THE CONSERVATION
PLANNING PROCESS

By

Hernán Torres
Corporación Nacional Forestal
Chile

ABSTRACT

It is argued that traditional societies in the Andes
region have a right to preserve their cultures,
whilst at the same time they are entitled to benefits from outside. Many development projects have
not included the local people or their cultures and
they have suffered for this reason. What is needed
are both national and local policies ensuring such
participation.

INTRODUCTION

In the Andes there are traditional societies with
economies based on llama and alpaca and subsistence
cultivation. Their survival today is threatened by
land degradation as well as economic and cultural
pressures from the surrounding regions. To protect
these native peoples, decision makers and planners
must help them by acknowledging their right to a
separate existence as well as their rights to the
lands where they have traditionally lived, whilst
permitting them to attain benefits from outside,
such as education and health.
    Isolation in the modern world is in fact almost
impossible and hence some degree of cultural assimilation cannot be avoided. Such an evolution may be
beneficial if there is not to be massive damage to
the culture and if poverty is to be avoided. Participation in planning is part of this communication
process. But many development projects which have
been carried out in the Andean region of Peru,
Chile, Bolivia and Ecuador, have unfortunately not
included the active participation of the Andean
peoples in the planning process and have suffered

for this reason.

In spite of the demographic and cultural shock of the Spanish conquest and the economic domination of the central Andes by a small outside elite, the hispanic system of multiple ecology is still a predominant pattern from Ecuador to Bolivia (Brush, 1982). The system involves agriculture at varying altitudes between 3,200 and 4,600 m. Due to a 50% inclination in the terrace level, the communities practise a varied agriculture based on native potatoes, barley, maize - an agricultural system which has existed for thousands of years. Each species is planted in accordance with a system of fallowing in which a parcel of land rests from one to five years. Natural fertilizers such as the manure of cameloids are applied. This traditional technology is menaced by pressures to plant other, more marketable products, as is happening in most of the central highlands of Peru. The native knowledge about the ecosystems, plants, weather prediction, and the rotation system which has served efficiently for land use over many centuries, is in danger of extinction.

Frost is frequent at higher levels in the Andes, so that herding in these regions is more important than agriculture. Most of these areas are moderately to severely overgrazed. The excessive number of animals causes a major problem for native pastureland. The use of these lands for grazing could be optimized for a good yield of meat, milk, or wool per hectare, yet carefully controlled to conserve the natural resources.

At present, many Andean peoples do not regulate or rotate grazing activities. The shepherds are usually untrained women and children, and most of the animals are of mixed breed and the introduction of exotic animals like sheep, horses, cattle, etc. is still occurring in a random fashion. In summary, bad exploitation of the land has, in some areas, produced extensive destruction of natural resources.

PLANNING ALTERNATIVES

A conservation planning process conceived in terms of benefits to the native peoples demands two carefully defined levels of participation for national action and a native peoples' action. Native peoples have to participate in the planning process voluntarily. Maximum attention should be given to the viewpoints of these populations and the conservation plans must include the needs and aspirations that are felt in the native communities.

Essential also when formulating plans to preserve the environment and to help the Andean population is equitable access to, and rights in, land. In some cases, it should be possible to implement new regulations on tenancy of the land which will allow for greater popular participation in the conservation planning process.

Brownrigg (1981) has suggested some achievable forms of participation which seem feasible to both planners and native peoples. Two proposals are appropriate for the region:

a) In a Protected Area, where a protected natural area corresponds with the territory of a particular native population.

b) In Native-Owned Lands, where the protection of the area is by native peoples.

In a Protected Area

In this alternative the government agency at the national level is the administrating authority and the official planner/manager has to work in close relationship with the resident native peoples. The protected area must be sufficiently large to permit the accomplishment of the two functions - preserving the environment and protecting their native culture. Both cultural changes and population increases have to be anticipated. Planners/managers should not expect the local people not to make progress or worse, to return to some traditional technology when there is a more modern alternative.

The integration of natives as park rangers would improve the communication between natives and manager, and also this utilization of natives would improve the control of the protected area, as has occurred in Lauca National Park in Chile and Pampa Galeras National Reserve in Peru.

In Native-Owned Lands

In this alternative resource, planners and managers can assist native peoples by technically documenting the advantages of the native systems of resource management. To the native peoples, who are facing pressures to change their production practices, such recognition may enhance their security of tenure, while simultaneously creating protected areas within a domain beyond the systems of national parks. If changes in the law allow the recognition of the native peoples and their communities as the official protectors of the areas where they live, this may enhance their legal position.

CONCLUSION

The participation of the Andean native peoples in conservation planning, as well as motivation and interest, will only be possible if they exercise direct influence on the administration and utilization of the natural resources. Obviously, the latter cannot not be achieved if there is not a national policy allowing a gradual participation of these groups in these activities which lead to a harmonious and balanced economic development of rural areas.

Successful planning will require the participation of the native peoples themselves, using interpreters where necessary. Also, this planning process will require the entry of professionals with considerable experience among native peoples and in specific ecological zones.

Working with native peoples, planners and managers will obtain benefits, because natives become strong supporters of conservation policies. Also, planners and managers will obtain benefits by recruiting native personnel with profound knowledge of local areas and learning about long-term resource strategies which have proven their adaptability over thousands of years. On the other hand native peoples will obtain benefits by the legal recognition of their traditional land-use practices, appropriate employment on their traditional lands, and new and more support at the national level.

REFERENCES

Brownrigg, Leslie. 1981. Native cultures and protected areas: management options. In Proceedings of the 18th Working Session of IUCN's Commission on National Parks and Protected Areas. Lima, Peru.
Brush, Stephen. 1980. The environment and Native Andean agriculture. In Symposium on Environmental Problems of Development in Latin America, San Francisco, California. The Natural and Human Environment of the Central Andes.

Mountain Research and Development, Vol. 2, No 1, pp. 19-38.

Lanino, Italo. 1977. Antecendentes de las explotaciones ganaderas en Isluga, altiplano de Iquique, Chile Universidad del Norte.

Torres, Hernán. 1981. Some considerations about the rights of primitive peoples in the areas of forest development. Paper presented at the International Seminar on Forest, Environment and People in the Third World. ENDA - United Nations, Madras, India.

Chapter Eight

THE HEMA SYSTEM OF RANGE RESERVES
IN THE ARABIAN PENINSULA

Its Possibilities in Range Improvement and
Conservation Projects in the Near East[1]/

By

Omar Draz, Desert Institute Council
Matarieh, Cairo, Egypt

ABSTRACT

The Hema system, once common in the Arabian Peninsula, was based on a philosophy of protection and
improvement instead of exploitation. Basically the
Hema provided a fodder reserve for nomadic populations, and controlled grazing, protecting certain
species. The paper asks for a reintroduction of
the Hema system as a means of range improvement and
stopping the present destructive grazing and uncontrolled tree and scrub cutting.

INTRODUCTION

The Arabian hema grazing system is probably the
world's oldest effective range conservation programme. It can be controlled for use by individuals,
by tribes or by government. A survey in Saudi Arabia
(1962-66) of historic ahmia, such as Hema Hail,
Hema al Hourma and Hema Al Ra'bza (rainfall under
150 mm), formerly administered by the Government,
showed that these lands were opened to free grazing
by Decree in 1953. Today it is difficult to see any
difference in the vegetation on these government
reserves and adjoining lands because of destructive
grazing and uncontrolled tree and scrub cutting.
The tragic story of loss of fertility, aridity and
transformation to man-made desert, the fate of
millions of acres in the Near East, has thus been
repeated. In contrast, tribal or personal ahmias,

1/   First published in 1969 as FAO/PL:PFC/13.11 and
since revised.

which have been properly managed, show the suit-
ability of this system to the local environment.

This paper will discuss the hema system of
range reserves in the Arabian Peninsula and possibilities of reintroduction in the Near East as a
means of range improvement and for soil and water
conservation purposes.

HEMA IN ISLAM

The Prophet Mohammed was concerned with fodder
reserves because they preserved the strength of the
Islamic nation. He protected Hema Alnaquia (a wadi
near Medina), which was used mainly by animals, to
defend the cause of Islam. The prophet is known to
have said: "Hema is only for God and His Prophet".
Evidently this saying has been interpreted that a
governor or an Islamic state is allowed to protect
the ahmia in the best interests of the community.

Al-Iman Al Shafi's (ninth century) stated that
during pre-Islamic days, a Sharif-al-Koom (influen-
tial person), upon arriving in a village, would mark
the boundary of his grazing land by the distance one
could hear a dog bark. In addition to this area for
his personal use, he also enjoyed the privilege of
the surrounding lands grazed by others.

This extremely unfair practice, according to
Al-Imam Al-Shafi'y, was the system practised by the
Jahilia (pre-Islamic or unenlightened people). It
was subsequently corrected in accordance with the
saying of the prophet, "Muslim people are partners
in water, fire and ephemeral range".

The Hema Al-Rabza, near Dari'ya in Saudi
Arabia, is the pasture reserve once protected by
Omar Ibn-El-Khattab, the second caliph. The length
of the hema was about 250 km. A geographic Arabic
dictionary "Mo'gam Ma Ista'gam", revealed that
during the time of Othman, the third caliph, this
hema was expanded and the number of grazing animals
(mainly camels and horses) increased to 40,000.

Omar Ibn Abdul Aziz (seventh century), one of
the most capable caliphs of the early Islam days,
is known to have been very strict in keeping the
hema protected. Cutting of even a single branch
from such a reserve warranted a severe beating.

The Holy Quran is a proponent of conservation
and forbids the unnecessary cutting down of trees,
destruction of crops or any wanton destruction
whatsoever in war or in peace. Both law and the
Islamic concept are against such destruction.

TYPES OF HEMA

The ahmia may be classified, according to the types of protection, as those where:

a) animal grazing is prohibited. Cutting of grasses is, however, permissible during specified periods and droughts. The head of the tribe grants special privileges for a limited number of needy people to use the reserved range. A specified number of each family are allowed to cut mature grass during the season, either for storage or for direct use;

b) grazing and/or cutting is permitted, but restricted to certain seasons of the year, as in Hema Elazahra and Hema Hameed around Belgurashi in Saudi Arabia;

c) grazing is allowed all the year round. The kind and number of animals permitted for grazing are specified. Most of the ahmia around Taif are in this category, and grazing is restricted to cattle and donkeys. There is, however, no restriction on hay cutting after grass matures;

d) the reserve is kept for beekeeping. There is a limited number of these ahmia and grazing restrictions are relaxed after the flowering season;

e) the reserve aims to protect forest trees such as juniper, acacia or ghada (Haloxylon persicum). These ahmia are usually the common property of a village or a tribe. Cutting of trees is prohibited except in great emergencies or needs, such as rebuilding a house destroyed by a calamity or for building a mosque or school. Sometimes the wood is sold to raise funds for the benefit of the village or tribe.

Some ahmia are reserved for a particular tribe, one village or more. The tribal or village head manages the utilization of such reserves. However, comparatively smaller units are kept close to terraces or cultivated wadi beds for the use of local residents.

RIGHTS OF OWNERSHIP OR USE

Rights of ownership or use are determined as follows:

111

a) those who possess documentary evidence of hereditary ownership of rights of use;
b) those without documentary evidence, but who maintain control of ahmia because of long-term possession and use.

Some difficulty is, however, experienced in Saudi Arabia in protecting the hema, because of people who misunderstand the 1953 Decree.

Through the local tradition "ourf", such rights are maintained. Trespassers are penalized by chiefs of tribes or villages. A person committing offence for the first time usually pays a fine of a sheep or its equivalent. The fine, in certain cases, contributes to the welfare of the tribe or community, instead of being paid to the owner of the hema.

During a drought year, when there is a great scarcity of fodder, a calamity-stricken tribe may request permission to graze animals on the hema. The owner of the hema generally permits grazing but places a limit on the number of animals and specifies the period of grazing. This restriction is a protection against overgrazing.

HEMA SYSTEM IN SAUDI ARABIA

Ahmia in the Taif area of Saudi Arabia were studied to determine boundaries, location, method of upkeep, ownership, grazing rights and presence of old water and soil conservation works. A total of 30 ahmia were located and investigation showed that 18 were well looked after and kept under proper control, while 12 were open to unrestricted grazing. The Hema Beni Sarr in the Higaz mountains was selected for a special study.

The range has long been protected and its history can be traced back some 50 years, to the reign of Sharif Hussein of Mecca. Two tribes, Beni Sarr and Beni Hassan, quarrelled over its control, but Sharif Heidera, a judge of Sharif Hussein's reign, gave his verdict in favour of Beni Sarr and conferred upon this tribe the rights of custody and use. The Hema Beni Sarr has been kept under protection since that time.

This pasture, with a total surface area of about 800-1,200 ha is located north of Belgurashi at about 2,000 m above sea level. Yearly average rainfall is between 400 and 500 mm.

Soil profiles observed along road cuts showed substantial accumulations of good soil under the grass cover. This soil has retained its fertility and has the capacity to produce abundant forage. Increased growth of choice grazing plants has reduced the growth of undesirable vegetation, and high producing grasses now dominate the landscape. The grass cover is mainly composed of Themeda triandra, Aristida sp, Andropogon sp and Stipa spp. Localized patches of Cymbopogon sp and Polygala sp were also found, together with some Olea chrysophylla and Juniperus procera. The plant cover of the areas outside the hema is composed of heavily grazed grasses and large numbers of non-palatable shrubs. Dodonea viscosa, Olea chrysophylla and Juniperus procera are also present in fair numbers.

The right of use of this hema is strictly limited to the Beni Sarr tribesmen. No year-long grazing is allowed but cutting of grasses is permissible during periods of scarcity or late in the summer season when the grass is mature.

Permits for cutting or collection of grass are granted by the tribal head. No more than a specified number of persons of each family are allowed to cut mature grass and only on certain days of the week.

Although no reliable data are available on the numbers of animals for which this range is kept as a reserve, it is evident that an equilibrium between vegetation and animals has always been maintained. The perennial vegetative cover of palatable grasses within the hema, as compared with the surrounding areas, could support this assumption.

Hema Hureimla, 80 km north of Riyadh, with under 80 mm of rainfall, is another good example of the effect of protection and conservation on the regeneration of plant cover. Comparison of parts of the protected wadi against the non-protected parts shows a contrast; Draz has counted 28,000 Acacia sp. in an area 4 x 1 km along the protected area, against nil along the upper or lower parts of the same wadi. A small dike outside the hema did not have any appreciable effect on the perennial vegetative cover compared with that growing under hema protection.

Hema Oneiza, in the heart of Najd plateaux, has the unique objective of protecting Haloxylon persicum trees for effective stabilization of moving sand dunes adjacent to Oneiza along a 70 km by 40 km area.

"Ghidal" is another type of hema once common in Maghreb, Algeria and Tunisia. Only few examples are left in these countries.

The total number of existing ahmia in Saudi
Arabia has recently been reported to be not less
than 3,000.

THE MAHMIA OR MARAH, AND THE KOZE SYSTEM IN SYRIA

A reference to hema practised in the Sweida mohafazat rangelands is made by Shibly Al-Aisamy and co-
workers (1962) who, while describing the troubles
which occurred late in the 19th century, reported
the following:

> ... the harsh injustice, which had been
> described clearly and in detail by the
> folkloric poet (Shibly El-Atrash), created
> a new widescale revolution in 1897. Among
> the direct reasons mentioned for this
> revolution was that one of the guards of
> the hema of Urman (close to El-Qrayé,
> rainfall about 300 mm) quarrelled with a
> bedouin who trespassed this hema. Upon
> the complaint made by the bedouin to
> Mandouh Parsha (the Military Governor) in
> Sweida, 30 soldiers were sent to Umran
> under the pretext of arresting the guards
> and punishing them; yet the real reason
> had been to arrest representatives of this
> village who previously met secretly with
> representatives of neighbouring villages
> to protest the Turks' injustice...

The previous presence of hema in this region has
also been confirmed by several old Sheiks of the
Drouz during personal discussions (Draz)[2].
Investigations in Syria revealed the presence
of a large number of hema-like reservations, maintained at present in groups. The local name for
these is mahmia (plural mahmiat) derived, like
ahmia, from the Arabian word for protection. The
termmarah or mahmia is used along the Syrian-
Lebanese border, while koze is Kurd for hema.
The reserves along the Syrian-Lebanese borders

---

[2]   A unique type of hema existed close to Damascus
for about five centuries up to 1930 where (according
to government documents), a 100 ha area had been
maintained as pastureland for aged or unfit horses
until the end of their lives.

(rainfall about 300 mm) are maintained chiefly for winter grazing of goats. The 1958 Forest Protection Act was designed to stop goat grazing in the forest areas and provided for confiscation or slaughter of goats found grazing in public lands including most of the mountainous areas of Syria. However, the Government has not enforced the Act and perhaps the only place where goats are still grazed with no interference from forest guards can be found within these marah. Other mahmiat within the same area that were formerly managed by Syrians (about 30) have all been abandoned or confiscated under the same Act. Observations indicate that adverse results have followed enforcement of the Act because of inadequate control. Cutting of the edible sindyan tree (Quercus sp.) for firewood or charcoal production has gone faster than expected, leaving behind denuded hills and mountains subject to the effect of wind and water erosion. The protected mahmiat did not suffer the same fate, as they have been carefully managed and grazed to maintain a good tree, shrub and grass cover.

A mahmia studied in more detail was found to have a vegetative cover mainly composed of sindyan trees, za'rur (Crataegus sp), Phyllyrea media, and a comparatively small number of the prickly shrubby billan (Poterium spinosum). A rich understorey of clovers, vetches and a large number of annual and perennial grasses at an early stage of development were present. About 50 goats were grazing this 50 ha reserve.

The vegetative cover in the surrounding areas was greatly deteriorated. The shrubby billan was the dominant plant species, indicating previous forest cover. Remnants of the heavily grazed and cut sindyan trees are scattered over the area. The Mukhtar of the nearby Elhawi village stated that these trees were cut down within a few years after the 1958 Forest Protection Act. The only remaining mahmiat are the trees within the village cemetery.

These findings indicate that probably man rather than goats is responsible for the destruction of the forests. Elimination of goats has not proved to be the answer but rather has aggravated the situation. As demonstrated in the protected mahmiat, a system of grazing management with the correct numbers of goats and sheep has proved its efficiency. These systems, whether named hema, mahmia, or marah, have been developed by the local people over countless decades and could not successfully be replaced by systems planned for different

115

environmental and sociological conditions. In Syria, the result has been nearly complete denudation of its highly productive range and/or forest lands and a loss of about one million goats.

A mahmia system of grazing, called koze, has been traced along the Syrian-Turkish-Iraqi borders. Various kozat in the area between Kamishly, Makekizeh, Ein Diwar and Tell Kotchek (rainfall 400-500 mm) were visited. In principle, there appears to be no difference in the methods of maintenance and/or utilization of such reserves. Tribal tradition is adequate for controlling rights and responsibilities.

Usually the local people are reluctant to give information about the kozat, fearing that they may lose their right of use because of government intervention. Inspection of a reserve south-east of Ein Diwar, close to the Iraqi frontiers, showed the plant cover to consist mainly of <u>Chrysopogon gryllus</u> (shafer), <u>Phalaris tuberosa</u> (giachon) and <u>Hordeum bulbosum</u> (korram). Shafer is highly rated by the local shepherds, owing to its high palatability and long season of growth, especially during the drier season of the year. Its voluminous deep root system also has great value as a soil binder.

Tribal tradition allows most of these reserves to be grazed only during the winter season, between mid-December and the end of March. Areas where shafer and/or giachon constitute most of the plant cover may, however, be grazed in the summer season.

There is evidence that a number of native and/or exotic perennial plants which have proved successful at Himo Experiment Station (Kamishly) could be tried for reseeding and expanding programmes of the kozat system of grazing in this and adjacent regions in Turkey, Iraq and Iran.

Another type of hema has also been observed in the Hassia-Breig region, located south of Homs between the main roads to Damascus and the Lebanese borders. This unique range reserve, which covers a surface area of about 40,000 ha of rough poor soils, was, up to 1958, a part of a feudal system of land tenure that came to an end through the enforcement of the Ayrian Land Reform Act. The system of grazing in this vast hema had been organized through permits for grazing rights to be given to the shepherds belonging to the adjacent villages, against a fixed rental value of about S£1 per goat or sheep per season (i.e. about US$1 per four animals). As this hema is considered to be potential forest or subforest land, it was confiscated by the

Government and has been transferred to the Forest Department. Practically the same system of grazing management has been maintained, except that about 600 ha are now completely protected from grazing to allow for natural forest regeneration (Zweitina area). The rest of the area is now grazed only by flocks of sheep while previously it was grazed mainly by goats. It seems that a smaller number of animals are now being grazed through the year, as against a much larger number during the winter season only[3].

In the higher altitude of the hema (Zweitina area) at 800 to 900 m, where grazing has completely stopped (since August 1972), regeneration of <u>Pistacia palaestina</u>, <u>Pyrus syriaca</u> and <u>Amygdalus orientalis</u> has been satisfactory. Otherwise, all over the hema, <u>Artemisia herba alba</u> and <u>Salsola vermiculata</u> form the main vegetative cover, indicating that annual precipitation might be between 200 to 250 mm.

In a few villages south of the Hassia-Breig region, smaller mahmiat are managed as range reserves for the benefit of village flocks. Both ourf and government orders support efficient control of these reserves.

The possibility of application and utilization of the same system of grazing in adjacent areas and under similar conditions appears encouraging.

NEGLECT OF THE HEMA AND ITS CONSEQUENCES

In Saudi Arabia, marked denudation of plant cover occurred in most of the previously protected ahmia as a result of free grazing of these reserves which took place through misunderstanding of the 1953 Decree. While this Decree was meant to replace the grazing rights of ahmia only so long as they were protected by the local Amirs in different regions with grazing animals owned by the Government, the decree was interpreted by the different authorities as withdrawal of all controlled grazing measures, thus allowing free grazing. Resultant denudation of the plant cover in these range reserves led to serious soil erosion associated with frequent destructive floods. Consequently, most of the ancient dams and water conservation systems which previously

---

[3] This hema has been developed to become the Hassia government range and sheep centre.

worked efficiently under the prevailing climate conditions and protective measures of the hema system,
failed to withstand the flooding and siltation that
occurred when protective vegetative cover was destroyed.

Meanwhile, large amounts of runoff water have
created another serious problem. The flood water
after any appreciable rain storm soon collects in
the wadi beds, to disappear into the sea, salty
depressions or into nearby sand dunes. The scarcity
of plant cover and destruction of water conservation
works have thus become major factors inhibiting
percolation of rainwater. The decreased water percolation in most areas has in turn reduced the flow
of spring water. A survey showed that the old dams
constructed in pre-Islamic times are now useless.
Samalagee Dam, situated below Hema Thumula and 400
m wide, can store no water because the spillway was
destroyed by floods. The construction of this gigan-
tic dam proves that ancient peoples had a keen
interest in water conservation works - present
residents of the area lack even the ability to restore the damaged spillway. Five more dams, or
"sad", close to Hema Nageeb, have met a similar
fate and about ten surrounding villages have been
adversely affected. Wells have almost dried up,
and villages are continuously asking for help.
Altogether the number of ruined dams in the area
are 20 sad and about 40 smaller sad known as "stony
okad".

Sad Saisad is an example of another neglected
dam, which was constructed probably by Moawia, the
fifth Islamic caliph, who succeeded Mohammed the
Prophet 13 centuries ago. The Ministry of Agriculture of Saudi Arabia has lately authorized the
development of a soil, water and vegetation plan in
the Sad Saisad area to include a part of the adjacent abandoned Hema Saisad, thus reviving its protection.

The only two springs (gheil), which kept flowing after a long period of drought, have their main
rainfall catchment areas along two well-protected
ahmia, i.e. Hema al Nomoor (the largest hema in the
Taif area) and Hema al Machada.

Recharging of the groundwater table by reconstruction of the ancient dams and water-works, and
revegetation of the ahmia, would greatly increase
water supplies for the Taif deficient area.

HEMA IN THE RANGE IMPROVEMENT AND
CONSERVATION PROGRAMMES IN THE NEAR EAST

The hema system was once common in parts of the Arabian Peninsula and is still used in parts of Saudi Arabia, Yemen, Oman and Syria. It originated in the Near East and is suitable as a means for controlled grazing in selected areas in arid, semi-arid and mountain ranges, where nomadic grazing is the only system practised. Carefully protected ahmia would furnish fodder reserves essential for stability of nomadic grazing. They would also change the attitude of the people towards the range, introducing the philosophy of protection and improvement instead of exploitation.

Ahmia, moreover, give the range manager an insight into the potential forage productivity of range sites and indicate how much improvement can be expected when large areas of run-down ranges are upgraded and given prudent care. Although soil and water conservation programmes might include several physical or mechanical methods, in most cases there is no substitute for revegetation for which the hema system has proved its efficiency.

Introduction of the system to new areas in this region, or to localities where it has previously been practised, might require different techniques from one country to another. In most cases, however, this has to be a gradual rather than an abrupt change.

In Saudi Arabia, concepts have lately been changed to support ahmia. The Royal Decree of 1953 which allowed for free grazing of the historical ahmia, has been clarified so as to exclude tribal or personal ahmia. To demonstrate the role and importance of the system, part of Hema Saisad (one of the abandoned historic ahmia) east of Taif, was put under protection in 1965. Plans have been made by the Government to establish a range experiment station within this hema.

During 1968 the Syrian Arab Republic approved the execution of a World Food Programme/FAO assisted project, in which range and forest potentialities of the Gebel Abou Rejmaine, north of Palmyra, would be managed as a hema within a project for stabilization and development of nomadic sheep husbandry. The Al Ommor tribe, supported by governmental and WFP assistance, has become responsible for protection, development and use of this mountainous area. The successful introduction of hema in the form of range co-operatives has encouraged expansion of the pioneer work. The number of hema co-operatives has now increased to 46 (1979), covering around 4 million ha. The recent discovery that ahmia do exist in a number of localities in Syria, indicating previous existence in similar areas, might allow for expanded application of this system. It could also be integrated within pilot agricultural development programmes.

In certain cases, minor changes in Forestry, Land Tenure and/or Range Protection Acts legalize these reserves. The system could also be integrated within a grazing act suitable for many parts of the Near East countries.

Groups of people meeting in the various countries where hema has been maintained, are of the opinion that if previously practised rights of usufruct were restored or allowed to be given, subject to fulfilment of certain requirements, regeneration of vast areas of range or forest land could be achieved.

REFERENCES

Abu Obaid Abdullah Ben Abdul Aziz el Bakree el Andalosse (about 1000). A dictionary of the unknown names of towns and places. Four volumes revised and explained by Mustafa El Saqqa. Committee for Writing Translation and Publishing Press, Cairo, Egypt, 1949. (In Arabic).
Arram Assalami. (about 1000). Mountains of Tihama and Hijaz, their inhabitants, villages, water resources and names of their trees. Revised by Zainal and Nassif, Jedda, Saudi Arabia, 1953. (In Arabic).
Brockelmann, C. 1949. History of the Islamic peoples. Routledge and Kegan Paul, London.
El Hamadanee. 960. Description of the Arab island. Revised and published to the satisfaction of the historian Mohammed Ben Abdullah Den Belheed El Najdee, Saadah Press, Egypt, 1953.
FAO. 1953. Report to the Government of Saudi Arabia on agricultural development. J.D. Tothill. Rome. ETAP Report 76.
Fitzgerald, D.F. 1955. Vesey. Vegetation of the Red Sea coast south of Jedda. S. Afr. J. Ecol (43).
Fitzgerald, D.F. 1957. Vesey. Vegetation of the Red Sea coast north of Jedda. S. Afr. J. Ecol., July.
Philby, H.St.J.B. 1952. Arabian highlands. Cornell University Press, New York.

Samhoodee Al Medani. 1367 Higri calendar (1947). Kholaset el Wafa Biachbar Dar Al Mostafa, Issa A. El Halaby Printing House, Cairo, Egypt. (In Arabic).

Shibly Al-Aisamy and co-workers. 1962. Sweida mohafazat. Ministry of Culture and National Guidance. (In Arabic).

Yacoot El Hamawee. A dictionary of towns. Dar Sader and Dar Beirut, Beirut. (In Arabic).

Chapter Nine

THE CONSERVATION AND MANAGEMENT
OF THE JEBEL QARA REGION

By

H.F. Lamprey[1]/
Project Co-ordinator
Unesco/UNEP Arid Lands Project
Nairobi, Kenya

ABSTRACT

The management of Jebel Qara Region depends, it is argued, on the preservation of the traditional Jebali economy, including the indigenous cattle breed, forest reserves, national parks, etc. A Conservation and Management Authority is proposed, including both government departments and the people.

INTRODUCTION

Mr R.H. Daly, Government Adviser on the Preservation of the Environment in rural Oman, asked the author to visit the Jebel Qara plateau in South Oman with a view to furnishing advice on measures necessary to ensure the conservation and rational development of the area. This mission was also undertaken because it was apparent that the unusual state of preservation of the Jebel Qara ecosystem might present valuable clues to indicate how the processes of ecological degradation and desert encroachment can be avoided through appropriate land-use practices.

During his visit to Salalah, capital of the southern region of Oman, the author was privileged to have an audience with His Majesty, Qaboos bin Said, the Sultan, in company with Mr Daly and Dr M. Woodford, FAO Veterinarian. His Majesty listened to a brief account of the recommendations for the

---

[1]/ Report prepared for H.M. Sultan Qaboos bin Said and reproduced herewith by his kind permission.

123

conservation and management of the Jebel Qara. After expressing his great concern for the conservation of the Jebel, His Majesty requested a written report. This has been prepared in response to his request.

BACKGROUND INFORMATION

The Jebel Qara is a long, narrow plateau approximately 2,000 km^2 in area, with an average height of 700 m above sea level, lying roughly parallel to the south-facing coastline of the southern region of Oman. The plateau, which is some 100 km long and 20 km wide and is somewhat irregular in outline, lies about 20 km from the sea from which it is separated by an arid coastal plain. Inland from the plateau is the great expanse of the Arabian Desert. The Jebel is remarkable for the richness of its vegetation, its undulating surface being covered by tall grass and its valleys and the seaward slopes by moderate to dense broad-leaved woodlands. It is inhabited by the Jebali people whose population is estimated at between 15,000 and 20,000, and whose economy is based upon their unique breed of small cattle (estimated at between 40,000 and 100,000).

The Jebel is the only extensive area of Arabian indigenous vegetation which has survived in a virtually undamaged state. Unlike the greater part of the Arabian Peninsula, which is degraded to varying degrees, most of it being reduced to total desert, the Jebel Qara remains as a productive and beautiful region, probably little changed in several thousand years. The possible reasons for its preservation are discussed below.

Until very recently there was no technological development of the area. In recent years development has been confined to the building of a major road across the plateau (with a small number of tributary roads and tracks) and the provision of six "Civil Aid Centres" served by bore-holes. Economic exploitation of the Jebel Qara has so far been minimal, consisting of the removal of some bull calves for fattening and a beef production centre near Salalah. However, general proposals have been made for the further economic development of the region, through an expansion of the beef production scheme, through tourism, and through the extension of civil aid facilities for the Jebali people. The siting of a residential town on the Jebel Qara has also been suggested.

Experience elsewhere in the arid and semi-arid zones has shown that there are considerable dangers inherent in the economic development of rural economies based upon fragile ecosystems if the development is not guided by the application of certain fundamental ecological principles. There can be little doubt that the grasslands and woodlands of the Jebel Qara are vulnerable to ecological degradation through excessive or inappropriate land-use methods. The equilibrium which has, until now, existed between the Jebali people and their resources, resulting in the preservation of their habitat, will inevitably be threatened by almost any form of development. It is of the greatest importance that the future management of the Jebel Qara should be directed towards its conservation; firstly as the home and source of subsistence of the Jebali people; secondly as a productive ecosystem capable of contributing indefinitely to the economy of Oman; thirdly as an area of outstanding natural beauty and scientific interest and fourthly as a major water catchment area serving the town of Salalah and the agriculture of the coastal plain.

With its very low rainfall, the capacity of the Jebel Qara to gather water from the hill mists carried in by the southerly monsoon depends mainly on the presence of the natural vegetation, as has been demonstrated by the experiments of Dr Fallon, rangeland ecologist. The protection of the water catchment is, in itself, sufficient justification for the maintenance of the present vegetative cover of the Jebel Qara.

In the absence of a well planned and executed management policy in which all aspects of the development of the Jebel are integrated, hurried, piecemeal and inappropriate development of the region could result in the irreversible destruction of the vegetation and its loss as a productive region.

Further to the west, and separated from the Jebel Qara by 50 km of arid country, lies the Jebel Qamr, a mountainous ridge rising steeply from the sea to over 1,200 m. The seaward slopes of this ridge support luxuriant vegetation, watered by the monsoon mists, characteristic of the sub-humid tropics. The area is of exceptional beauty and scientific interest, especially as the habitat of a rich and varied bird fauna. It supports a small population of Jebali people.

The Jebel Qamr is similarly vulnerable to inappropriate management and could become ecologically degraded in the same way as the Mediterranean coasts of southern Europe, parts of which it resembles. Thus the proper management of the Jebel Qamr, while not as urgently needed, will become a matter of concern over the next decade.

The wild animals of the region have become rare and extremely shy. Although several mammal species are known to live in the Jebel Qara and Jebel Qamr areas they are rarely seen. Those known to occur in the hills, are the ibex, the red fox and the wolf and, in the foot hills and the adjacent desert plains, the Arabian gazelle and the hyaena. In recent times the Arabian oryx is thought to have been exterminated in the desert areas of Oman as has the Arabian ostrich. There is the strong possibility that the declaration and protection of national parks and nature reserves in the Jebel Qara and Jebel Qamr Regions would permit the re-establishment of populations of indigenous wildlife.

CONTRIBUTORY FACTORS IN THE PRESERVATION OF THE JEBEL QARA AND JEBEL QAMR

The present well-preserved state of indigenous vegetation of the Jebel Qara and Jebel Qamr is due primarily to the favourable geographical coincidence of the moisture-bearing southerly monsoon winds striking the south-facing slopes of the Jebel. Since most of the water gathered appears to be condensed from mists, rather than as rainfall, the hazards of soil erosion are virtually absent. The vegetation itself appears to be the main agent in promoting condensation.

Given these favourable environmental conditions, the question remains, how has the vegetation of the Jebels remained in an undamaged state? Elsewhere in the tropics, particularly in semi-arid and sub-humid regions, the presence of pastoralists and their livestock has caused or has accelerated ecological degradation and has been an important influence in the process of desert encroachment. Almost uniquely, the Jebali people, with their cattle, have occupied the Jebel Qara and Jebel Qamr regions for over 2,000 years without over-exploiting the grasslands and the woodlands. This situation is of the greatest interest, not only to Oman but also other countries situated in the arid and semi-arid zones which are experiencing desert encroachment. Two possibilities suggest themselves as reasons for the lack of over-exploitation of the vegetation.

a) The Jebali people could possibly have been aware of the dangers of damaging their habitat and they could have limited the numbers of their cattle voluntarily. If this were the case, they would be unique among pastoralists, and it is unlikely that voluntary restraint is even partially responsible for the limitation of cattle numbers.

b) One or more constraints, beyond the control of the Jebali people, could have been acting to limit both their own numbers and those of their livestock. Any one or more of the following constraints may have been crucial in limiting the human and livestock numbers.

- The population of Jebali people may have been limited by high mortality and/or low birthrate in the absence of modern medical facilities;
- the population may have been limited by circumstances connected with frequent local disturbances;
- the human population may have been limited by constraints on their main resource, cattle;
- the cattle population appears to be subject to unusual constraints. During the monsoon months of September and early October, great numbers of a biting fly (<u>Stomoxys</u> sp.) make it necessary for the Jebali people to keep their cattle in houses and caves during the daylight hours and to graze and water them at night. It seems probable that the number of cattle that can be kept in this way is severely limited, particularly since they are also restricted by relatively few sources of water, and by the grazing which is within one night's foraging range of the shelters and the water. It also seems possible that the absence of veterinary facilities for the cattle has played a part in limiting their numbers.

Whatever the limiting influences, the important fact remains that the cattle numbers do not exceed the long-term carrying capacity of the grasslands which remain in a highly productive state.

POSSIBLE THREATS TO THE ECOLOGICAL STABILITY OF THE REGION

The basic threat to the stability of the region is the possibility of damage to the grass and woodland vegetation through overgrazing and wood cutting. Removal of any of the present constraints on cattle numbers might lead to a considerable increase and to the risk of degrading changes in the grasslands. (Even a reduction in the height of the grass could reduce the amount of water condensed from the mists). Such an increase in numbers could result from (a) provision of additional water supplies, (b) a campaign to control the biting flies and (c) the introduction of veterinary treatment (to mention only three possible developments).

An increase in the number of people would create an increased demand for firewood and wood for building purposes.

The building of roads provides access for people from outside the Jebel Qara and opens the way for the collection of grass and wood in large quantities. This process, which has started with the opening of the new road, could lead to serious depletion of the woodlands and grasslands unless strictly controlled. The roads themselves replace valuable grasslands and careless road-making operations tend to destroy additional areas adjacent to the road.

The construction of residential areas and other building complexes tends to lead to ever-expanding development and to the proliferation of roads, tracks, water supplies, electrical installations, shops, offices, etc. Such development, if carried out at all, could threaten the survival of the plateau as an amenity for the country as a whole, and as a home for the Jebali people. The development of suitable rural aid centres is clearly desirable and should be done with due regard to the preservation of the Jebel's amenities.

At first sight the Jebel Qara appears almost ideally suited to the introduction of extensive agriculture and animal husbandry. However, the potential for such development which is compatible with the maintenance of the plateau as a water catchment area is probably limited. Well managed animal husbandry, which has a prime objective of conservation of the grasslands, could be a useful addition to the economy of the region. Extensive agriculture, with the prior necessity for ploughing, is likely to prove hazardous since it involves the certainty of soil loss by wind erosion and the reduction of water gathering capacity due to the removal of vegetation and exposure of the soil surface. Nevertheless, questions concerning the feasibility and advisability of animal husbandry and agriculture can be answered by experimentation on a small scale. Any attempt at extensive agricultural development without the benefit of pilot trials could be highly damaging.

The breed of small cattle kept by the Jebali people is of great practical and scientific interest. Its perpetuation as an undiluted breed should be one objective of the management of the region. The uncontrolled introduction of exotic breeding stock could quickly destroy the integrity of the Jebali cattle population. However, there could be little objection to limited experimental breeding programmes involving a part of the indigenous cattle population, provided care were taken to avoid indiscriminate cross-breeding in the population as a whole. The introduction of a well managed beef production scheme would almost certainly call for experimental breeding involving the local cattle and introduced stock.

A further threat to the Jebel Qara Region through development is the possibility of increased uncontrolled hunting resulting in the extermination of the wildlife species which have survived there to-date. The strict enforcement of wildlife conservation measures, at least in parts of the Jebel Qara and Jebel Qamr areas, could be achieved in conjunction with the maintenance of national parks and nature sanctuaries.

PROPOSALS FOR CONSERVATION AND MANAGEMENT

The management of the Jebel Qara and Jebel Qamr Regions should be based upon a fully integrated plan involving all aspects of the human and natural resources. Only with a reasonable fund of qualitative and quantitative information on the region can long-term management be planned. If the main objective of management is to be the maintenance of the Jebels as productive regions and water catchment areas, in the face of possible deterioration due to development activities, it is essential to obtain base-line information from which future ecological monitoring can proceed. Such information would be obtained through a thorough resource survey. The survey would document human population character-

istics (numbers, structure, distribution) in relation to resources and environmental factors; livestock and agriculture; other economic considerations; sociological attributes and constraints;
climate; hydrology; soils; geology; vegetation;
animal life. The resource survey could incorporate
or be co-ordinated with experiments and trials to
test the feasibilty of various regimes of grassland
management, agriculture and animal husbandry.

It would be expected that a survey would provide the knowledge upon which management recommendations could be based. It can be anticipated that
the recommendations might include proposals for the
zonation of the two Jebel areas for the following
land-use priorities:

a) preservation of the traditional Jebali
economy, in particular the maintenance of
the indigenous cattle breed;
b) forest reserves for maintenance of the
indigenous woodland and forest communities;
c) forest reserves for trial planting of both
indigenous and introduced species for the
provision of firewood and building timber;
d) intensive cattle husbandry area(s) for the
reinforcement of the existing beef production scheme;
e) national parks established for the main
purpose of conserving the indigenous plant
and animal life and to include complete
cross-sections of the eco-climatic zones
represented on the Jebels and in the adjacent lowland country. Such parks would provide the best opportunities for rehabili-
tating endangered wildlife species;
f) national parks primarily for the enjoyment
of the people of Oman and visitors from
abroad. Limited facilities for visitors
(lodges) might be constructed on the edge
of the parks; and
g) rural aid centres and other building complexes designed for the welfare of the
Jebali people, including water, medical,
veterinary, cultural and educational facilities.

The planning and management of the Jebel areas could
be accomplished effectively by a "Conservation and
Management Authority" composed of representatives
of all government ministries and departments concerned with the administration, economy and welfare

of the people, with livestock husbandry, range management, forestry, water management, and the conservation of natural flora and fauna. It could also include representatives from the Jebali people and from the livestock industry. The Authority would be responsible for the planning and implementation of a balanced and integrated management programme which would most appropriately lay stress upon the conservation of the natural resources of the Jebel areas. It would evaluate and, where appropriate, implement recommendations provided initially by the resource survey team and later by the ecological monitoring team which would succeed it.

It is anticipated that the resource survey team would work for at least three years to establish a basic description of the regions and would consist of perhaps five specialists whose interest would jointly cover the following aspects of the survey:

a) Sociology, demography and human resource ecology.
b) Grassland ecology and range management.
c) Forest and woodland ecology.
d) Livestock husbandry.
e) Soil survey; geology; geomorphology.
f) Climatology and hydrology.
g) Animal ecology and wildlife management.
h) Establishment of national parks and other protected areas.
i) Settlement and road planning and siting.

The ecological monitoring team to follow up the work of the survey team could consist of two widely based ecologists capable of maintaining a system of repeated quantitative measurement of such important statistics as human numbers and distribution; animal numbers, productivity and utilization; plant distribution and productivity in relation to climate and human and animal impact; climate and hydrology.

The survey could be planned and carried out effectively by a suitable commercial concern such as Huntings Technical Services. It is suggested that the opportunity should be taken to train several Omani field technologists at professional and technician levels so that they could become qualified field officers and possibly teachers. The survey and subsequent ecological monitoring programme would provide, through a counterpart scheme, an ideal training project.

In conclusion it should be mentioned that Oman is extremely fortunate in possessing the only surviving example of a virtually intact, near natural ecosystem in the whole Arabian Peninsula and Middle East. The ecosystem is the more remarkable since it incorporates a human population with its live-stock in apparent equilibrium with its environment. The value of this region to Oman in particular, and also to the world as a whole, cannot be measured in economic terms. It can only be described as a priceless heritage which must, at almost any cost, be preserved. It probably represents a former, more extensive Arabian upland flora and fauna. It would be to the great credit and fame of Oman if this rare and valuable example of nature should be conserved for posterity and it would indeed make Oman a leader and an example among the world's nations with regard to progressive conservation policies.

The significance of the Jebel Qara and Jebel Qamr Regions in the context of the conservation of the world's genetic resources is such that a very good case could be made for their inclusion in the Unesco Man and the Biosphere system of "Biosphere Reserves". Through this system these regions would be part of a network of scientifically monitored areas and their continued conservation and monitoring would receive international support.

Since this report was written, the Dhofar Province of the Sultanate of Oman, which includes the Jabal Qara, has been the subject of a reconnaissance land-use survey (Lawton, 1978) and an extensive fauna and flora survey (eds. Shaw Reade et al., 1980). In September 1983 a specialists' workshop on the ecology and development of the mountains and the marine environment of Dhofar will be convened at Salalah to consider the status of the region and to make recommendations for its sustainable development.

ANNOTATED BIBLIOGRAPHY

It appears that there was virtually no previous published knowledge on the Jebel Qara. Thomas (1932) mentioned "rolling yellow meadows, clumps of giant fig trees and wooded hillsides". With that exception, all the following references postdate this report.

Lawton, R.M. 1978. A reconnaissance survey of the Jebel Qara grazing land ecosystem, with particular reference to the impact of development.

Report to the Sultanate of Oman. Land Resources Development Centre (O.D.A.), London: 21 pp.
Lawton, R.M. 1980. The Forest Potential of the Sultanate of Oman. L.R.D.C. (O.D.A.), London: 39 pp.

Recommendations on forestry development include specific sites in the Jebel Qara Region.

Thomas, B. 1932. <u>Arabia Felix</u>. Jonathan Cape, London. 395 pp.

Shaw Reade, S.N.; Sale, J.B.; Gallagher, M.D.; and Daly, R.H. (Eds.) 1980. The scientific results of the Oman Flora and Fauna Survey 1977 (Dhofar). <u>J. Oman Stud</u>. Special Report No. 2.

This fine volume includes the contributions of twenty-two authors and a foreword by His Majesty Sultan Quaboos Bin Said. The subjects and authors are as follows:

Arnold, E.N. The Reptiles and Amphibians of Dhofar, Southern Arabia.
Branch, W.R. Chromosome Morphology of Some Reptiles from Oman and Adjacent Territories.
Buttiker, W. and Gallagher, M.D. First Records of Opthalmotropic Behaviour of Lepidoptera in Oman.
Gallagher, M.D. Introduction: The Environment of the Mountain Region of Dhofar.
Gallagher, M.D. and Rogers, T.D. On Some Birds of Dhofar and Other Parts of Oman.
Greathead, D.J. Beeflies (Bombyliidae, Diptera) from Oman.
Guichard, K.M. A Preliminary Account of the Sphecid Wasps of Oman (Humenoptera, Sphecidae).
Harrison, D.L. The Mammals Obtained in Dhofar by the 1977 Oman Flora and Fauna Survey.
Hoogstraal, H. Ticks (Ixodoidea) from Oman.
Mandaville Jr., J.P. Frankincense in Dhofar.
Mordan, P.B. Land Mollusca of Dhofar.
Popov, G.B. Acridoidea of Eastern Arabia.
Radcliffe-Smith, A. The Vegetation of Dhofar.
Rogers, T.D. Meteorological Records from the Mountain Region of Dhofar.
Sale, J.B. The Ecology of the Mountain Region of Dhofar.
Vachon, M. Scorpions du Dhofar.
Waterston, A.R. The Dragonflies (Odonata) of Dhofar.

Conservation of Jebel Qara Region

Wiltshire, E.P. The Larger Moths of Dhofar and Their
      Zoographic Composition.
Wright, C.A. and Brown, D.S.   Marine Mollusca of
      Dhofar.

Chapter Ten

SOCIAL RESTRAINTS ON RESOURCE UTILIZATION:
THE INDIAN EXPERIENCE

By

Madhav Gadgil
Centre of Ecological Sciences
  and Theoretical Studies
Bangalore, India

ABSTRACT

This paper reviews a variety of cultural practices
which helped the Indian society to maintain an ecologically steady state with the wild living resources from around 500 B.C. to 1860 A.D. The Indian
society is made up of a large number of endogamous
castes each with a restricted geographical range and
each with a hereditary profession. This hereditary
profession is so specialized that the different
castes, directly dependent on natural resources
utilize the different resources with little overlap
with other castes of the same region. Thus any
particular resource of a given region used to be
utilized over generations by a small homogeneous
breeding group which expected the same resource to
sustain its future generations as well. These conditions were particularly favourable for the evolution of cultural traits ensuring long-term sustainable utilization of natural resources. Such
practices included restraints on territory over
which a given human group may exploit the plants
and animals, the season in which the exploitation
is permitted, the method which may be used for
exploitation, the sex and stage in life history for
which exploitation is permitted, the method which
may be used for exploitation, the species or the
biological communities which may never be exploited
and the species in the exploitation of which a given
caste may be specialized. This equilibrium could
be maintained because the ruling classes only tapped
the agricultural surplus and a few select harvests
from the wild such as musk and sandalwood. After
the industrial revolution, however, many other raw
materials, including wood, acquired commercial
value, so that the forests, lakes, rivers and seas

which were earlier left to the local communities with the exception of hunting reserves of the princes now became a resource coveted by the ruling classes. Hence, the British Government wrested the control of these resources away from the Indian population as soon as they consolidated their hold on the country. The commercial interests which have been exploiting these resources since that time are only interested in immediate profit and have no stake in the long-term preservation of these resources. India's wild living resources have therefore been steadily depleted, and the old social restraints on preservation of these resources are breaking down. Apart from the depletion of natural resources, this pattern of development has contributed further to the impoverishment of the rural population which still largely depends on the wild living resources to meet many of its basic needs. It is now necessary to change this non-sustainable and inequitable pattern of development, restore to the local population a measure of control over their resources and reinforce the traditional practices of restraints on resource utilization. The Chipko movement in the Himalayas provides a ray of hope that we may indeed have begun to move in that direction.

INTRODUCTION

The continued existence of populations of all species of animals, including man, depends on the availability of a variety of resources. The population can crash and run the risk of extinction if the availability of any of the critical resources falls below a threshold value. But the availability of a resource will itself be affected by the animal population utilizing that resource. It may therefore happen that the utilization of a resource by an animal population may reduce it to levels at which that animal population can no longer sustain itself and may go extinct. In a book that has provoked much debate, Wynne-Edwards (1962) suggested that most animal species have evolved mechanisms of holding their populations at a level at which the resources are not reduced to such low levels, and Slobodkin (1968) further raised the question of whether animals behaved as "prudent predators" concentrating their hunting on prey of low reproductive value. The prevailing consensus, however, is that natural selection, acting as it does at the level of an individual, does not favour the evolution of such restraint on population growth or prudence in resource utilization except under very special circumstances (Williams, 1966; Dawkins, 1976). What happens, in fact, appears to be that animal populations tend to reduce the availability of various resources that they utilize to levels at which the population may occasionally go extinct, but more commonly exists in a balance such that it cannot increase any further (Lack, 1954; Hutchinson, 1978).

Human populations appear to behave in a basically similar fashion, increasing in size till the resources they depend on are depleted to a level at which the population cannot increase any further. This is however not the whole story, for with this symbolic language and cultural transmission of knowledge, man has acquired a vastly greater capacity of deliberately manipulating nature around him. This has enabled him to tremendously augment the resources which he can put to his own use, and it has also permitted the cultural evolution of socially exercised restraints on the utilization of resources (Harris, 1977). Man has in fact behaved from time to time as a truly prudent predator.

However, such prudence is far from a universal feature of human societies which have often totally wiped out the resources which sustained them, and in fact we seem today to be headed towards a global destruction of the resource base which sustains humanity (Martin and Wright, 1967; Brown, 1978; Ehrlich, 1980). An understanding of the conditions under which human societies did evolve effective methods of prudent utilization of the resources, and of the circumstances under which these practices broke down is therefore of vital importance in our endeavour to steer ourselves onto a course of sustainable utilization of the earth's resources (Gadgil, 1983). The present paper is an attempt to review this problem in the context of the Indian experience.

SOCIAL ORGANIZATION

The Indian society is made up of thousands of closed, self-governing communities or castes. Each of these castes is, or till recently used to be, characterized by the following four significant attributes:

Social Restraints on Resource Utilization

a)   Each caste is an endogamous group, i.e.
     all marriages are restricted within the
     caste. This is still by and large true,
     particularly in the rural areas.
b)   Each caste is distributed over a restricted
     geographical region. This is also still
     true by and large, except that few major
     urban-industrial centres have brought
     together a large number of people of all
     castes outside their traditional range of
     geographical distribution.
c)   Each caste is governed by a caste council
     which settles all disputes within the
     caste. This always was and continues to
     be more so with the lower, predominantly
     rural, castes. However the power of caste
     councils is being rapidly eroded.
d)   Each caste possesses a hereditary way of
     making a living. This again was and is
     much more true of the lower, predominantly
     rural, castes. These are the castes which
     depend most directly on the natural re-
     sources and traditionally each caste had a
     particular and often rather restricted way
     of utilizing the natural resources over
     its range of distribution. For example,
     in a region, one caste may catch freshwater
     fish, a second keep sheep, a third keep
     ducks, a fourth make salt from the sea
     water, a fifth maintain coconut orchards
     and so on. In addition, there would be
     castes of specialized artisans, enter-
     tainers, priests etc. Each small geographi-
     cal region is a mosaic of populations of a
     number of sedentary castes, of the order
     of ten to fifty, living together, yet
     independently, within that region. The
     same region would be visited by another
     ten to fifty nomadic or semi-nomadic castes
     of artisans and entertainers. These wander-
     ing castes would also have a very fixed
     geographic region over which they would
     move. All these castes had set up relation-
     ships of barter with each other.

This rural society was to a large extent self-
sustaining. It produced most of its own requirements within its own limits. Its interaction with
the urban society was restricted to surrendering a
fraction, sometimes moderate but sometimes exorbi-
tantly high, of the surplus of agricultural pro-

duction.

This social mosaic had developed over several centuries of interactions amongst a large number of tribal groups which had migrated into India at different times, the endogamous castes being largely derivatives of endogamous tribal groups (Karve, 1961). While the lower rural castes undoubtedly slowly changed their modes of subsistence over the centuries, each one came to occupy a rather well-defined and often quite narrow ecological niche in adjustment with the other castes sharing the locality with them. It is in this context that we must understand the cultural restraints on resource utilization that the Indian society has evolved.

CULTURAL PRACTICES

The Indian subcontinent abounds in a variety of traditions of restraints on the exploitation of wild plant and animal resources. These traditions relate to the territory over which a given human group may exploit the plants and animals, the season in which the exploitation is permitted, the sex and stage in life history for which exploitation is permitted, the method of exploitation and quantum which may be exploited, the species or the biological communities which may never be exploited by some or all castes, and the species in the exploitation of which a given caste may be specialized. We shall discuss below several specific examples of these various practices.

Territoriality

For most of evolutionary history human societies have been organized in hunting-gathering tribes each with its own exclusive territory (Lee and De Vore, 1968). This territoriality persisted in one form or the other with all Indian castes till recent times. Thus the beach-seine fishermen of Goa on the west coast report that seines from each fishing village would operate on the coast within a well-defined limit. Similarly, Nandivallas are a nomadic caste of entertainers of Western Maharashtra. They also engage in extensive hunting with the dogs for porcupines, monitor lizards, wild pigs, etc. Each group of the Nandivallas entertains and hunts within a well-defined territory (Mahlbotra 19). Similarly, pastorals like the Dhangar shepherds of Western Maharashtra wander extensively, grazing over an

area defined for and hereditarily controlled by
various groups of shepherds (Gadgil and Malhotra,
1983). This territoriality had two significant
consequences. Firstly, the pressure of exploitation
was evenly dispersed over the exploited plant and
animal populations. Secondly, each group had an
awareness that the resources of its hereditary territory had sustained it for generations, and were
to sustain its descendants, who would inherit the
territory and their mode of resource exploitation,
for generations to come. This facilitated the cultural evolution of a variety of other restraints on
the exploitation of living resources.

Closed Seasons
The Hindu month of Sravana (roughly August) which
coincides with the peak of the main rainy season
over most of India is a period during which many
castes abstain totally from consumption of fish,
poultry and meat and consequently suspend all hunting as well. The harvest of certain wild plants is
ritually restricted to certain days of the year
only. Thus in the Jakhol-Panchgai area of Uttarkashi
district of the Himalayas the tubers of a plant,
locally known as Nakhdun may be harvested only at
the time of a religious festival, as is also the
case with flowers of Brahmakamal a herb of alpine
meadows near the Nandadevi peak in Chamoli district
of Himalayas (Bahunga, 1980; Bhatt, 1981b).

Life History Stages
The famous Indian epic, Ramayana, begins with the
scene where the poet - a member of a hunting tribe
- is inspired to compose poetry for the first time
in his life on witnessing the killing of one of a
pair of copulating cranes by a hunter; such a killing being strictly against the prevailing ethic
(Shastri, 1959). In fact heronaries - breeding
colonies of storks, egrets, herons, ibises, cormor-
ants, pelicans, etc. - almost invariably receive
full protection from the village closest to the
heronary. For instance, in the Bangalore district
of south India is a village known as Kokre-Bellur
(literally village of the storks) where painted
storks and grey pelicans have bred on trees lining
the village streets since time immemorial. The
villagers not only chase away the hunters, they even
chase away photographers if they disturb nesting
birds. The villagers are often quite rationally

aware of the value of the bird guano, a fertilizer
for their fields.

In Bhandura district of Maharashtra the traditional fishing castes never disturb the spawning
aggregations of fresh water fishes in the hill
streams (Chitampalli, 1981), while the hunting
tribe of Phaseparadhis of Ahmednagar district of
Maharashtra whose main quarry is blackbuck report
that they traditionally let loose any calves and
pregnant does caught in their snares (Khomne,
Malhotra and Gadgil, in prep.)

Method of Exploitation

The freshwater fishes of the river Yamuna in its
upper reaches in the Himalayan district of Tehri-
Garhwal are exploited through netting as well as
poisoning. Traditionally, netting was permitted at
any time of the year, but poisoning was permitted
only at one time of the year, for a few days in
conjunction with a communal festival known as Maun
Mela. This festival is at a time when the river is
in spate and the effect of the poisoning is probably
quite restricted in time. The fish are poisoned and
consumed by all the meat-eating castes of the tract
as a communal endeavour (Bahuguna, 1980).

Many Indian villages maintained a village
forest on communal land. The village forests were
protected and carefully exploited by the village
community as a whole. There were often well specified limits on the quantum of exploitation for material such as fuel wood from these village forests.
Thus, only one member of each household gathers
fuelwood once a week from the village forest of
Gopeshwar in Chomoli district of Uttar Pradesh,
Himalayas. In consequence, this village forest is
still well preserved, although most of the neighbouring land has been completely deforested.

There occur, throughout India, patches of vegetation, or sacred groves which receive special
protection from the local community on grounds of
their association with some deity. As will be
explained below, most of these sacred groves were
traditionally totally free from any exploitation.
There are however groves known as Orans associated
with the goddess Jogmaya in the Aravalli hills of
western India where it was permitted to take away
wood for fuel so long as the collection did not
involve the use of any metal implements (Ishwar
Prakash, 1980).

Sacred Groves, Pools and Ponds

As Gause's (1934) classical experiments have shown, a very effective way of preventing the extinction of prey populations in a predator-prey system is to provide the prey with refugia or regions in which the prey is immune from predation. Such a traditional system of refugia in India was the network of sacred groves, ponds and pools in the courses of rivers and streams (Gadgil and Vartak, 1976-81). These were patches of land or water which were dedicated to some deity and were kept free of all exploitation, both of plants and animals. They ranged in extent from fifty hectares or more to a few hundred square metres. Where the network of sacred groves has remained intact till recent times, as in the South Kanara district of the west coast, one can see that they formed islands of climax vegetation at densities of 2 to 3 per sq km, ranging in size from a small clump to a hectare or more, and originally covering perhaps 5% of the land area (Karanth, 1981). This must have been a very effective way of preserving tropical biological diversity, for we are still discovering new species of plant, species which have disappeared from everywhere else, in these sacred groves, as for instance the recently discovered woody climber, Kunstleria keranlensis (Mohannan and Nair, 1981).

In Bangladesh every shrine has at least one pond attached to it, and the animals in such ponds are inviolate. Two such sacred ponds are of biological interest, for they harbour populations of endangered species; the Byazid Bostami has a turtle Trionyx nigricans, and Khan Jahan Ali has marsh crocodile. The former is of particular interest since it is the only known population of this turtle in the world. It is notable that the Muslim shrine of Byazid Bostami was apparently built around 800 A.D. at a spot which was earlier occupied by a Buddhist shrine. Thus the tradition of protection of the turtle and the sacred pond is likely to be an ancient tradition assimilated by Islam (Reza Khan, 1980).

Sacred Plants and Animals

In India a variety of plant and animal species have been considered sacred by one or more communities and therefore never destroyed (Presler, 1971). The most widely protected of such organisms is the peepal tree (Ficus religiosa), found depicted on a Mohanjodaro seal of around 2000 B.C. Other species of the genus _Ficus_ are also considered sacred, and were not felled traditionally by all Hindu castes. It is notable that _Ficus_ is now considered a genus of particular significance in the overall mainten- ance of tropical biological diversity - a keystone mutualist (Gilbert, 1980). In particular, its pres- ervation may have helped maintain high levels of populations of highly edible frugivorous birds, especially pigeons and doves.

Monkeys are a group of animals held as widely sacred as the _Ficus_ trees over most of India, except for Coorg, Kerala and the north-eastern tribal tract. They are never hunted even if they do con- siderable damage to the cultivated plants, but merely chased away. Unlike the _Ficus_ trees, it is difficult to see any rationale in their protection which may relate more plausibly to their close re- semblance to man.

Other plants and animals receive less universal protection, being sacred only in particular lo- cations or to particular castes. The peafowl, for example, is sacred to Lord Kartikeya and is never hunted, and is consequently abundant around Kartikeya temples in the southern state of Tamilnadu. It is more widely protected all over the western states of Gujarath and Rajasthan (per- sonal observations). The blue rock pigeon (_Columbia livia_) is considered sacred to the saint Hazrat Shah Jalal and is protected and encouraged to breed in artificial nest baskets in rural Bangladesh (Reza Khan, 1981). Even the rodents are protected and abound in the famous temple of Karnimata goddess in the state of Rajasthan (Ishwar Prakash, 1980).

Two notable animals which receive such local- ized protection in the vicinity of temples of cer- tain deities are the two most feared animals of India: the tiger and the cobra. Within a few kilo- metres of the temple of the tiger goddess Waghjai of Mahrashtra, for example, no tiger or panther is hunted. In turn, it is believed that the tiger or panther will never kill any man or domestic animal within that locality. In a similar fashion, no cobra is killed near certain temples and it is be- lieved that no snake-bite will ever be fatal in the same locality (personal observations). These taboos may help to remove the fear of these very dangerous animals, and may have survival value as, for example, if many deaths from snake-bite are due to fear of death rather than from the poison.

Many castes or clans within the castes have certain totemic plants or animals which they do not

destroy or let others destroy if they can help it.
Thus the Maratha clans or Mores and Ghorapades from
Maharashtra derive their clan names from their
totemic animals - peafowl and monitor lizard respectively, and will protect these animals, although
other clans of the same Maratha caste will hunt and
eat them (personal observations).

By far the most remarkable examples of protection of certain species is that of the Bishnoi sect
of western India (Ishwar Prakash and Ghosh, 1980;
Gadgil, 1980a). This Hindu sect, founded in 1485
A.D. enjoins its followers never to cut a green
tree, or kill any animal. They hold as specially
sacred the khejdi tree (Prosopis cinerarea), which
is by far the economically most valuable tree in the
desert tracts in which this sect originated. It is
recorded that in 1630 A.D., 363 Bishnois sacrificed
their lives to prevent the king of Jodhpur from
cutting down P. cinervea trees to furnish the fuel
for the lime-kilns to build a new palace. The
Bishnois also protect the wild animals including
blackbuck and chinkara. To this day, the tradition
is very much alive and the Bishnoi villages are a
refreshing scene of greenery and plentiful wildlife
in the Indian desert.

Niche Specialization

The various castes living within a small geographical region showed everywhere adjustments in their
utilization of natural resources, so that each caste
specialized in the use of some narrow range of resources and overlapped little with other castes of
the same region. The consequence was that a given
resource of a given locality sustained one relatively small homogeneous endogamous and self-
governing group over a long time span. These conditions must have facilitated the cultural evolution
of restraints on over-exploitation of living resources.

Two specific examples of such niche diversification may be cited here. The region of the crest-
line of the Western Ghats in Maharashtra around
18° N. lat. is inhabited by two major castes, Kunbis
and Gavlis. Of these the Kunbis practise paddy cultivation in the river valleys and shifting cultivation on the hill slopes. They indulge extensively
in hunting. They barter their cereal grains for
butter produced by the Gavlis. The Kunbis keep only
a few cattle for draft purposes. The Gavlis on the
other hand live on the upper hill terraces on which

they do a little shifting cultivation. Their major occupation is keeping buffaloes and cattle. They curdle the milk, consume the buttermilk at home and barter the butter for cereal grains from the Kunbis. The Gavlis get their protein supply from the buttermilk and do no hunting. Thus the cultivation of valleys and lower hill slopes is restricted to Kunbis and of hill terraces to Gavlis; maintenance of domesticated animals and exploitation of all fodder and grazing is restricted to Gavlis and hunting of wild animals to Kunbis (Gadgil and Malhotra, 1979).

Another interesting instance of niche diversification is provided by three nomadic hunting communities of semi-arid tracts of Western Maharashtra; Nandivallas, Phaseparadhis and Vaidus (Khomne, Malhotra and Gadgil, in prep.). The primary occupation of Nandivallas is entertainment and fortune telling, that of Vaidus dispensation of herbal medicines, while Phaseparadhis are specialist hunter-gatherers. The Nandivallas and Vaidus, unlike the settled castes, do a great deal of hunting in addition to their primary occupations. It turns out that the three castes use distinctly different hunting techniques and specialize on different prey species. Thus Nandivallas concentrate on hunting with dogs and go for wild pig, porcupine and monitor lizard. The Vaidus use baited traps for hunting smaller carnivores such as mongooses, civets, jackals and cats, while the Phaseparadhis specialize in snaring blackbuck and birds.

Protection by Rulers

The ruling classes of India collected agricultural surplus from the rural areas of their own territory as tax and from territories of other rulers as tribute or loot. Their demands on the wild plants and animals were minimal and largely restricted to items of special value such as cardamom, sandalwood, musk and ivory. An edict of the Maratha King Shivaji dated around 1660 A.D. forbids the cutting of fruit-bearing trees such as mango and jackfruit for use in building ships for his navy, on grounds that this would result in considerable suffering for the peasantry in his kingdom. Much more common were the attempts to protect special hunting preserves for the princes and forest habitat of elephants which were particularly valuable for the armies. Kautilya's Arthasastra, the fourth century manual of statecraft, prescribes the preservation of elephant forests near the borders of the kingdom, their strict supervision including periodic censuses of elephants based on their spoor, and death penalty for any poacher (Kaugle, 1969). The use of elephants for war declined only in the 18th century with the large scale introduction of gunpowder, while the practice of maintenance of hunting preserves for princes continued until the 1950s (Gee, 1964; Ishwar Prakash and Ghosh, 1980; Gadgil, 1980b).

HISTORICAL DEVELOPMENTS

The Indian subcontinent was probably colonized by hunter-gatherers as early as 50,000 B.C., and continued to support this mode of subsistence till the beginnings of agriculture in the river valleys of north-western India around 3000 B.C. The hunter-gatherers were presumably organized into tribes with their own territories and may have evolved cultural traditions of protecting resources within these territories. Restrictions on seasons of hunting and hunting of particular stages of life history are likely to have been the most primitive of such restraints. We know nothing of the impact of early agriculture and the Mohanjodaro-Harappa civilization on these practices. Our knowledge of history really begins with the invasion of primarily pastoral Aryans, equipped with horses and iron weapons, from central Asia around 1500 B.C. With their iron axes, the Aryans had the ability to clear thick forests and the next 1000 years record a long struggle between the pastoral-agricultural society of invaders and the native hunter-gatherers. At the end of this phase all arable land was taken over from hunter-gatherers, who were forced to accept a low status in the caste system, or to retreat to less productive terrain. The gradual spread of agriculture and pastoralism did continue till present times at a slow pace, although the settlement of the vast Indo-Gangetic plains was over by about 500 B.C. (Kosambi, 1965; Karve, 1967).

The caste society which crystallized out of this interaction in the first millenium of Christian era developed the whole system of sustainable use of living resources and remained ecologically in an approximately steady state till the consolidation of the British in the late 18th century. By this time Britain had largely exhausted its own forests and was hungry for forest raw materials, particularly teakwood for shipbuilding. They therefore strove to establish their hold on the natural resources of the country as quickly as possible, regarding the indigenous cultural traditions of restraint as mere obstacles in their way. This attitude is beautifully illustrated by Buchanan, reporting from the west coast of India in 1801: "The forests are the property of the gods of the villages in which they are situated, and the trees ought not to be cut without having obtained leave from the ... priest to the temple of the village god. The idol receives nothing for granting this permission; but the neglect of the ceremony of asking his leave brings vengeance on the guilty person. This seems, therefore, merely a contrivance to prevent the government from claiming the property" (Buchanan, 1802; reprinted 1956).

The village gods and the people had perforce to yield quickly to the will of the rulers who claimed a lion's share of the natural resources so carefully husbanded by the local village communities over the centuries. This takeover was followed initially by completely unregulated exploitation for the first hundred years of British rule till its final consolidation after the war of 1857. The 1850s saw the beginning of the laying down of the great network of railway lines through the length and breadth of the country to complete its conversion into a supplier of raw material and a market of finished goods for imperial Britain (Dutt, 1960). This generated an enormous demand for wood for railway sleepers. To meet this demand at as little cost as possible, the Government decided to legally take over a large fraction of communally owned forests without any compensation. This move was strongly resisted and there were agitations from 1860 to 1930 as the reservation of forests was continued in the more and more remote corners of the country. The agitations even led to shooting of people as at the Tiladi massacre of Tehri-Garhwal around 1930 (Bahuguna, 1980).

The burning of wood as fuel for trains quickly depleted the accessible forests, and the railways switched to using mineral coal. But other commercial uses for wood, such as for the paper and polyfibre industry were developed as time went by, and the growing urban and industrial sector also needed wood charcoal. The last century has therefore seen rapid depletion of India's forests through non-sustainable use for commercial purposes. The rivers, lakes and seas were also taken over by commercial interests and put one by one to non-sustainable exploitation.

When large tracts of forests, constituting more than one-fifth of India's land mass, were taken over by the Government for management, it had to lay down another set of regulations to ensure due restraint in the utilization of these resources. These regulations now had their rationale, not in tradition or religion, but in modern science, and this ushered in the era of modern scientific forestry in India (Sagreiya, 1967). As a renewable resource, the forest stock was supposed to be so manipulated as to result in maximum sustainable yield. A whole system of working plans and their execution was developed to implement this principle. There has, however, been a very wide gap between this theory and what has happened on ground. I would like to consider here just two case histories, that of bamboo resources of Karnataka and that of the Himalayan forests.

BAMBOO RESOURCES

The monsoon forests of India are very rich in bamboo stocks which have traditionally been the most important raw material for rural housing and various implements, and the basis of livelihood of a large community of basket weavers. The management of forests by the Governments has however entirely focussed on meeting commercial needs, totally ignoring the traditional needs of the rural population, or at best treating these requirements as privileges most grudgingly conceded and cancelled at the first opportunity. Since bamboo had no commercial value prior to its use by modern paper and pulp industry, it was considered as a weed and earlier forest working plans prescribed its eradication.

When bamboo became a commercial resource for the industry, working plans began to include prescriptions for its extraction based on the principle of sustainable yield. However, determination of such prescriptions needs a proper empirical data base which was totally inadequate. Therefore, the prescriptions that were made were essentially arbitrary and of doubtful value in ensuring the sustainability of the yield. Moreover, when commercial interests come into play, there is a drastic change in the whole attitude towards resource utilization. For now, those that utilize the resources have little stake in its continued existence, and unfortunately the paper industry is not genuinely concerned with the sustainable supply of bamboo resources for two reasons:

a) The profit margins are so large that the investment pays for itself very quickly, and the entrepreneur is not concerned if the paper mill has to be closed down and the capital invested elsewhere;

b) The entrepreneur can go on to the use of other resources such as softwoods and sugarcane bagasse. This pushes up the cost of paper production, but the market is a captive seller's market and the industry can jack up the paper price without suffering any loss of profit.

These vested interests are so strong that the attempts to ensure sustainable use of resources, themselves based on a totally inadequate empirical data base, are easily vitiated. As a result, the bamboo forests have been all but wiped out in recent decades in many of the Indian states (Gadgil and Prasad, 1978; Prasad and Gadgil, 1981; Gadgil, 1981).

HIMALAYAN FORESTS

The Uttarkhand region of northwestern Himalayas had retained a good tree cover until the early 1960s. This was because the road network in this hilly tract was very poor and there was little commercial exploitation of the forest. Beginning in the early 1960s, however, a good network of roads was developed and the forests were opened up for large-scale commercial exploitation. This commercial exploitation was based on working plans which had the objective of ensuring maximum sustainable yield. Unfortunately the working plans were again drawn up with an inadequate empirical data base and neglected several crucial factors. With an orientation towards supply of commercial timber, they left out of the reckoning the heavy demands on the forests by local population. They also ignored the vital role of tree cover in insuring the stability of soil in this geologically highly unstable zone. Furthermore, the vested interests often vitiated whatever discipline the working plans prescribed and prompted over-exploitation. The consequences were disastrous, landslides and floods resulting in loss of hundreds of human lives and damage to property worth millions of rupees (Bhatt, 1980).

RESPONSE OF THE PEOPLE

The situation in the Himalayas was of course qualitatively no different from what has been happening
for over a century, with the local inhabitants feel-
ing completely helpless to protect the living resources which still hold a key to their prosperity.
As Presler (1971) has described, the central Indian
tribes saw their traditional shifting cultivation
banned to them in the 1870s on grounds that it was
destructive of forests, only to witness forest con-
tractors move in and cut down thier sacred Saj
trees. In consequence, the local communities have
been losing or have already lost their own cultural
restraints on the utilization of living resources
and have become a party to their destruction.   In
fact the present pattern of land ownership is such
that a local villager or tribesman stands to gain
little for himself from a piece of tree covered
land, since these resources are managed exclusively
for the benefit of commercial interests.   On the
contrary, if he destroys that tree cover, he has
every chance of gaining control over that land for
cultivation. As a consequence, the local inhabitants
everywhere have been playing a role on a par with
the commercial interests in destroying the capital
of India's living resources (Gadgil and Malhotra,
1982b).
     While, however, the situation in the Himalayas
has been qualitatively the same, the magnitude of
suffering of the local population has been far
greater.   This is because the geologically young
Himalayas are very unstable, and the bare mountain-
sides are apt to come down in huge landslides.   The
disastrous landslides and floods of the recent years
have therefore brought a new level of consciousness
to the people of the Himalayas.   The result has been
a vigorous grassroots movement, known as the Chipko
movement, to save and to regenerate the forests of
Himalayas (Bhatt, 1980).
     It is this Chipko movement, and more particu-
larly the approach it has developed in the Chamoli
district, that is the one ray of hope that we may
yet turn back the mounting tide of destruction of
India's living resources.   The approach of this
movement may be summed up as follows:

     a) the most important role of forests for
         India is in meeting the minimum basic needs
         for fuel, fodder, fertilizer, fruit and
         fibre for the country's rural masses;

b) when the local inhabitants begin to derive genuine benefits from the tree cover they will once again have a stake in its preservation;

c) the tree cover can be preserved only under these conditions when those who benefit from it have a genuine concern for its sustainable utilization.

The Chipko movement has abundantly demonstrated its success, albeit on a restricted scale, in the catchment of Alakananda river and its tributaries. Here, they have succeeded not only in halting the pace of deforestation but also in inspiring the local inhabitants in taking up a vigorous programme of tree planting (Bhatt, 1981a).

ACKNOWLEDGEMENTS

A number of friends have helped me in putting together this material, and I am grateful to them all. In particular I wish to acknowledge my gratitude to: Sunderlal Bahuguna, Chandi Prasad Bhatt, Maruti Chitampalli, Ramachandra Guha, K. Sivaram Karanth, Sudhakar Khomne, Kailash Malhotra, V.M. Meher-Homji, Ishwar Prakash, M.A. Reza Khan, H.C. Sharatchandra, Indra Kumar Sharma, K. Usman and V.D. Vartak.

REFERENCES

Bahuguna, Sundarlal. 1980. Personal communication.
Bhatt, C.P. 1980. Ecosystem of Central Himalayas and the Chipko Movement. Dashuali Gram Swarajya Sangh, Gopeshwar, U.P., p. 40.
Bhatt, C.P. 1981a. Trees - a source of energy for rural development. Himalaya - Man and Nature 5 (4): pp. 7-13.
Bhatt, Chandi Prasad. 1981b. Personal communication.
Brown, L.R. 1978. The Twenty-ninth Day. World Watch Institute, Washington, p. 363.
Buchanan, F. 1956. Journey through the northern parts of Kanara. Karwar, Nagarika printers.
Chitampalli, M. 1981. Personal communication.
Dawkins, R. 1976. The Selfish Gene. Oxford University Press, Oxford, pp. 224.
Dutt, Romesh. 1960. The Economic History of India. New Delhi, Government of India Publications Division, Vol. I, pp. 312 and Vol. II, p. 476.

Ehrlich, P.R. 1980. The strategy of conservation in Soule, M. and Wilcox, B.A. (eds.) Conservation Biology, Sinauer, Sunderland.

Gadgil, M. 1980a. Guardians of green trees. Hindustan Times, New Delhi, 22 September 1980.

Gadgil, M. 1980b. Wild life resources of India: A review. Golden Jubilee Volume. National Academy of Sciences, Allahabad.

Gadgil, M. 1981. Indian Villagers Bamboozled by Paper Companies. IUCN Bulletin 12: 53-54.

Gadgil, M. 1983. Cultural evolution of ecological prudence, in T. Schultze-Westrum (ed) Eco-culture (in press).

Gadgil, M. and Malhotra, K.C. 1982a. Ecology of a pastoral caste: Gavli Dhangars of Peninsular India. Human Ecology 10: 107-143.

Gadgil, M. and Malhotra, K.C. 1982b. A People's view of Ecodevelopment. Environmental Services Group, New Delhi.

Gadgil, M. and Malhotra K.C. 1983. Adaptive significance of the Indian caste system: an ecological perspective. Ann. Human Biol. (in press).

Gadgil, M. and Prasad, S.N. 1978. Vanishing bamboo stocks. Commerce, 136: 1000-1004.

Gadgil, M. and Vartak, V.D. 1976. Sacred groves of the Western Ghats in India. Economic Botany. 30: 152-160.

Gadgil, M. and Vartak, V.D. 1981. Sacred groves of Maharashtra: an inventory in S.K. Jain (ed.) Glimpses of Indian Ethnobotany. Oxford University Press, Bombay.

Gause, G.D. 1934. The Struggle for Existence. Hafner, New York, p. 163.

Gee, E.P. 1964. Wild Life of India. Collins, London, p. 224.

Gilbert, L.E. 1980. Web organization and the conservation of Neotropical Diversity in Soule M.E. and Wilcox, B.A. (Ed.). Conservation Biology, Sinaner, Sunderland, Mass.

Harris, M. 1974. Cows, Pigs, Wars and Witches: The riddles of culture. New York: Random House. pp 276.

Harris, M. 1977. Cannibals and Kings. Collins, Glasgow, p. 255.

Hutchinson, G.E. 1978. An Introduction to Population Ecology. Yale University Press, New Haven, p. 260.

Ishwar Prakash. 1980. Personal communication.

Ishwar Prakash and Ghosh, P.K. 1980. Human-animal
    interactions in the Rahasthan desert. J. Bombay
    Nat. Hist. Soc. 75 (Suppl.) : 1259-1261
Karanth, K.S. 1981. Personal communication.
Karve, I. 1961. Hindu Society, an Interpretation,
    Decan College, Pune, p. 171.
Karve, I. 1967. Yugantha. Deshmukh. Pune, p. 287.
Kauglee, R.P. 1969. Arthasastra. An English trans-
    lation with critical notes. 3 parts. Univer-
    sity of Bombay, Bombay.
Khomne, S.B., Malhotra, K.C. and Gadgil, M. (in
    prep.) On the role of hunting in the nutrition
    and economy of certain nomadic populations of
    Maharashtra. Man in India (in press).
Kosambi, D.D. 1965. The Culture and Civilisation of
    Ancient India in Historical Outline. Routeledge
    and Kegan Paul. London. p. 243.
Lack, D. 1954. The Natural Regulation of Animal
    Populations. Clarendon, Oxford, p. 343.
Lee, R.B. and Devore, I. (Eds.) 1968. Man the
    Hunter. Aldine, Chicago.
Malhotra, K.C. 1974. Socio-biological investigations
    among the Nandivallas of Mashrashtra. Bulletin
    Urgent Anthr. Ethn. Sciences. (Austria) 16:
    63-102.
Martin, P.S. and Wright, H.E. (ed.) 1967. Pleisto-
    cene Extinctions: the Search for a Cause.
    Yale University Press, New Haven.
Mohanan, C.N. and Nair, N.C. 1981. Kunstleria
    Prain - a new genus record of India and a new
    species in the genus. Proc. Ind. Acad. Soc.,
    B 90: 207-210.
Prasad, S.N. and Gadgil, M. 1981. Conservation of
    bamboo resources of Karnataka. Karnataka State
    Council for Science and Technology, Bangalore,
    pp. 340.
Presler, H.H. 1971. Primitive Religion in India,
    Christ. Lit. Soc. Madras, pp. 349.
Rheza Khan, M.A. 1980. The holy turtle of
    Bangladesh. Hornbill 1980 (4): 7-11.
Rheza Khan, M.A. 1981. Personal communication.
Sagreiya, K.P. 1967. Forests and Forestry.
    National Book Trust, New Dehli, pp. 239.
Shastri, Hari Prasad. 1959. The Ramayana of Valmiki.
    3 Vols. Shanti Sadan, London.
Slobodkin, L.B. 1968. How to be a predator. Amer.
    Zool., 8:43-51.
Williams, G.C. 1966. Adaptation and Natural Selec-
    tion. Princeton Uni. Press, Princeton, pp. 307.

Social Restraints on Resource Utilization

Wynne-Edwards, V.C. 1962. <u>Animal Dispersion in Relation to Social Behaviour</u>. Oliver and Boyd. Edinburgh, p. 653.

Chapter Eleven

TRADITIONAL MARINE PRACTICES IN INDONESIA AND
THEIR BEARING ON CONSERVATION

By

Nicholas V.C. Polunin
Department of Biology
University of Papua New Guinea
Papua New Guinea

ABSTRACT

This paper discusses many of the ways that traditional Indonesian culture has helped to conserve
marine resources. Various marine areas are prohibited to people, are designated for particular
villages, families or individuals, or are concessioned out to individuals on an annual basis. Traditional limited-intrigue areas have been described
from many parts of Indonesia. Little is known of
their current status, though they may not have developed in several areas because of the instability
due to piracy and maritime seasonality. A number
of practices influence the allocation of particular
resources, and many controlled areas seem to have
resulted from conflict over specific resources. A
plea is made for additional information on traditional limited-intrigue areas, because these may
represent a valuable basis for managing coastal
resources, especially by enhancing local responsibility for shallow water habitats and exploited
marine populations on settled coasts.

INTRODUCTION

Marine reserves and other conservation measures in
the coastal zone are generally thought of as a
modern concept. This appraisal fails to recognize
that in some coastal societies controls on the use
of marine resources may have existed for centuries.
It is now appreciated that regulations and
attitudes of peoples in the island world of the
western Pacific have widely influenced patterns of
marine resource use there (Johannes, 1978), but what
of other well-populated archipelagos? In particular,

155

what of the island nations of southeast Asia, whence many inhabitants of the oceanic Pacific evidently came? There seems to be no work currently being carried out which might attempt to answer this broad question, but the available literature does contain many relevant anecdotes and I wish to bring together the Indonesian ones here. I will include a whole range of practices which, instigated for whatever reasons, tended to preclude some or all people from using particular marine organisms and areas. Much of this information seems to have been ignored or forgotten and I therefore hope that the present summary will return it to scrutiny. However, more important, at a time when plans for conserving critical marine species and habitats are being elaborated, is the realization that some traditional practices may have a part to play in modern developments. Hopefully this review will start to fill an important need identified recently by Unesco (1981), namely that of assessing the value of traditional arrangements for marine resource management in the light of today's pressures on the coastal zone.

While the present account attempts to be comprehensive in scope, other information may yet come to light, since I have based my review on readily available sources only. Additional literature, some of which may be relevant to the present topic, is harder to come by.

PERCEPTION OF THE SEA

The sea has traditionally been feared by many Indonesians. This attitude has probably come into being for a number of reasons. Dualistic perceptions are common in traditional Indonesian thought; amongst these, sea and coast are often seen as being in conflict with land and mountain. The sea is also a wild environment beyond the confines of human civilization. In addition, in a region where piracy has been rife for many centuries, the sea is to be feared as the direction from which raiders often came.

Symbolic antitheses are widespread in Indonesia (van der Kroef, 1954) and while dualistic perceptions of the sea have all but disappeared from the social organization of inland groups of people on large land-masses such as Kalimantan (the Indonesian portion of Borneo) and Sumatra, they remain an important element of traditional life on many smaller islands. On Solor and Flores, for example, such dualism evidently forms the basis of combats between fixed pairs of villages, each village representing one of the conflicting elements (Downs, 1955). Often hill-dwelling people were the symbolic inhabitants of the upperworld, while the coastal dwellers represented the underworld. This phenomenon has been most extensively referred to in the case of Bali, where Swellingrebel (referred to in van der Kroef, 1954) felt that the land/sea opposition dominated human existence. The mountains give forth water, a symbol of life, while the sea is downstream, a realm of calamity, sickness and death. The volcanic mountains are the home of the gods, and the sea is at the opposite pole - it is religiously dangerous, the home of evil spirits, and the repository of all worldly filth (Covarrubias, 1937; Hobart, 1978). Among many Indonesian societies, when disease strikes a community, it is symbolically discarded into the sea, or into waters which ultimately lead there (Frazer, 1922). In many areas, especially in the eastern part of the country, the soul is ritually put to sea in a boat. This is not for the soul to end up there, but rather so that it should cross the sea to reach its ancestral homeland; those who drown at sea, however, are left there (Frazer, 1922). On islands such as Lembata (Barnes, 1974), the Keis (Barraud, 1979), and on Pagai (Loeb, 1935), marine animals such as fishes, turtles and crocodiles are thought to be the forms ultimately assumed by many souls.

The Javanese have traditionally viewed the sea as a horrid wilderness beyond the control of human society (Lombard, 1980), and there are analogies with perception of the virgin forest, although on Java the latter habitat has now all but disappeared (Lombard, 1974). Both realms are regarded as sources of evil, and in both cases the people associated with them - particularly the maritime Bajau-Laut (Sopher, 1965) and the originally forest-dwelling Kalangs (Ketjen, 1877) - are, or were, held in some contempt. The Bajau-Laut in turn tend to be shy and wary of coming on land.

The threat of piracy, which was widespread into modern times, must have reinforced these attitudes in many places. The taking of slaves from Irian Jaya for pearl-diving in the Moluccas and other purposes made the local people aggressive to outsiders, so that even bold Buginese traders were afraid to go there (Anon., 1852). Piracy was an ever-present risk on the coast of many islands such as Sumba (Anon., 1855).

The consequences of these sources of instability are many. In areas such as Java, Bali, Timor (though not Roti; Bühler, 1937) and Sumba (Anon., 1918), people widely fear the sea. In Bali, few coastal dwellers are true Balinese (Earl, 1850). Little sea-fishing is carried out by local people on Seram (Ellen, 1978), on the south coast of Timor (Bruijnis, 1919), or in the Banggai Islands to the east of Sulawesi (Goedhart, 1908). This has commonly left the exploitation of profitable marine commodities such as trepang (sea-cucumber), turtle-shell, oyster-shell and shark-fin open to a minority of intrepid specialists. A dominant role in this business was long ago taken by the nomadic Orang Laut (western Indonesia) and Bajau-Laut (eastern Indonesia), who collected and otherwise hunted the valuable items, and the Buginese-Makassarese and a few other seafaring groups (Dick, 1975), who traded in them.

Traditional religious beliefs are widespread among those residents who do make use of the sea. Ceremonies are held to celebrate the beginning of a new seasons's estuarine fishing in eastern Sumatra (Gramberg, 1877) and coastal fishing in eastern Java (Mander, 1956), and to acknowledge a good catch in Irian Jaya (de Clercq, 1891). Magic is common in traditional marine exploitation, where care has to be taken to win the co-operation of the spirits whose domain is being infringed. Special words are used to avoid betraying the terrestrial origin of the fisherman (Schrieke, 1925), and to denote particularly sensitive species and places (Snouk Hurgronje, 1906; Endicott, 1970). People visiting Enu in the Aru Islands to collect turtle eggs observe special rituals (Compost, 1980). In the Mentawei Islands taboos surround turtle fishing (Loeb, 1935), while the skulls of dugongs and turtles are hung in sacred places to placate the spirits both there (Tilson, 1977) and in Irian Jaya (van der Sande, 1907). Magic is an important activity in the coastal fisheries of Aceh and Java (Snouck Hurgronje, 1906; Palm, 1962). The Pagai and Sipora islanders in the Mentaweis revere many types of spirits, one of which is regarded as protecting marine animals (Nooy-Palm, 1968). On Pagai, the crocodile is thought to be the servant of the "Mother of the Waters", and may be sent to punish those who disturb her domain, for example by throwing rubbish into the sea (Loeb, 1935). Vosmaer (1839) describes sacrifices made by the Bajau-Laut of southeastern Sulawesi to spirits of the sea and of certain coastal areas.

Coastal dwellers and fishermen are commonly looked down upon (Emmerson, 1980a), while marine specialists such as the Bajau-Laut are generally despised (Sopher, 1965). There are, however, notes of ambivalence in all these attitudes. Where the sea has been overcome, as it has been to a consider- able degree by the Buginese, it is possible to trace changes in perception from a position of fear to one of greater confidence in the face of the marine wilderness (Lombard, 1980). Even the Balinese can respect the sea as a dynamic system, transforming impure worldly waste into pure products such as clouds and fish (M. Hobart, pers. comm.). Such ambivalence of thought may be connected with the powerful Malay and Javanese god Batara Guru, who, through his exclusive possession of the water of life is able both to destroy life and also restore it; Batara Guru di Laut is the form of this deity who presides over the sea (Skeat, 1900). Like the forest to the Javanese (Lombard, 1974), the sea is viewed by many, such as the Toraja of Sulawesi, as a natural adversary which must be overcome if the child is to become man (Downs, 1955).

CONTROLLED AREAS

There are records from throughout Indonesia of various types of controlled area, and these fall into three categories. There are cases where entry or use was prohibited to everyone on a time-scale varying from weeks to generations. There are areas where the right to exploit marine resources is lim- ited to particular groups or individuals. There are also cases where exploitation is potentially open to anyone providing that a fee is paid.

In the Kei Islands, when a boat sets out on a long journey, the place previously occupied by it on the beach is regarded as sacred while the vessel is away at sea; infringement may lead to destruction of the boat (Frazer, 1922). More significant than this are the taboo areas established around the grounds habitually fished by a deceased man in the Sangihe Islands during his life; anyone caught using the area could be enslaved by the family of the deceased (Hickson, 1886). This prohibition presum- ably lasts or lasted, for several years. An area in which fishing has evidently been prohibited for centuries is that surrounding the sacred place of the sea goddess Loro Kudul at Parangtritis on the south coast of Java (Epton, 1974). Vosmaer (1839) described sacrifices made by the Bajau-Laut of southeastern Sulawesi to the spirits occupying particular islands, cliffs and points, and it seems likely that these places would not have been exploited.

Inter-village reserves, where only members of the community adjacent to the marine area could exploit resources, have been briefly mentioned for several parts of eastern Indonesia such as the Kei Islands (van Hoëvell, 1890b) and the north coast of Irian Jaya (van der Sande, 1907; Feuilleteau de Bruyn, 1920; Galis, 1955); they have been noted recently in the bay of Ambon in the Moluccas (C. Angell, pers. comm.). In the Kei instance, the seaward boundary apparently ended in about 20 m of water, while anyone was free to fish outside this area. There must have been some understanding, at least, over the use of tidal fish-weirs, which have been mentioned from several parts of the country such as Sapudi (Jochim, 1893) and the Leti Islands (van Hoëvell, 1890c), but no regulations have yet come to light. In the coastal swamps of eastern Sumatra, villages own particular stands of sago palm (Gramberg, 1881). At least on Tanimbar, the right to use certain reef areas is held by particular lineages; members of these groups are given access to such reserves on consulting a person called the "Lord of the Land", (LeBar, 1972). The role of the "Lord of the Land", or tuan tanah, is widely referred to in eastern Indonesia, but there has been little written about his potential function in the allocation of marine areas. In parts of the country such as Manggarai in Flores, the tuan tanah evidently monitors fishing areas (LeBar, 1972), and in the Arus the hunting of the dugong (Compost, 1980). An analogous framework for organizing the use of the coastal exploitation in western Indonesia is provided by the Sumatran marga, a traditional village commune system (Forbes, 1885; van Royen, 1927).

The fact that disputes over the use of marine areas arise is clear from a few accounts. Neighbouring villages on the north coast of Irian Jaya often fight over trade and fishing in their respective waters (van der Sande, 1907), a source of conflict which has been mentioned from further east by Malinowski (1918). Fights over access to reefs off Tanimbar, Aru and Salayar have been reported by Kolff (1840), van Hoëvell (1890c) and Kriebel (1919). Aru pearling-banks were a reason for conflict (Kist, 1938), no doubt in particular because they were off-shore and only intermittently occupied, and because the harvest began to decline in the last century (van Hoëvell, 1890a). Schot (1882) mentions disputes between groups of Orang Laut over fisning grounds on the eastern coast of Sumatra, which led to <u>adat</u> (traditional law) agreements over who should fish where. Snouck Hurgronje (1906) also speaks of conflict between boats fishing the same coastal area in Aceh. Evidently, as a result, the shore is partitioned between guilds of fishermen, each one with a designated individual to settle disputes. At least in Irian Jaya, right of access to certain marine areas can be held by the chief of the village (van der Sande, 1907), while off Salayar, reef and tidal-trap fishing areas are tenured and handed down from father to son (Kriebel, 1919).

The right to use many marine areas has traditionally been concessioned out to individuals or groups. One of the best described cases of this is the <u>marga</u> of Sumatra (van Royen, 1927). Here the right to fish and to cut nipah palm in estuarine areas is hired annually to the highest bidder. Turtle nesting beaches have traditionally been rented for the collection of eggs in many parts of western Indonesia (Somadikarta, 1962).

If there is little known about the nature and extent of these various protected-area practices, even less is known about their consequences. In the case of concessioned areas, it is not possible to establish whether resources have tended to be conserved or depleted. The fact that an individual often gained access to an area for only one year at a time might have led him to take more than he would otherwise have done. On the other hand, giving only one user access might have reduced the level of exploitation in the long term, below that which it would have been if everyone had been allowed in. On the rented turtle beaches egg-yields have, in several cases, declined significantly in recent years, although this could be as much due to the incidental taking of breeding turtles off-shore as to any short-comings of practice <u>in situ</u> (Polunin & Sumertha Nuitja, in press).

Several of the other controlled areas described above must have had the effect of reducing the pressure on resources, and promoting a certain efficiency in their long-term use, even though they may often have been established for reasons other than conservation. Such a beneficial effect may not have been the case where unique areas such as that at Parangtritis existed; it is not known in

this case whether any conserving effect was exceeded
by a more intensive exploitation in the area outside. It is more likely that some conservation of
resources accrued in the Sangihe Islands, where the
taboo areas respecting the deceased probably led to
a type of rotation on the fishing-grounds. Par-
titioning of the shore in Aceh may not have controlled the activities of those fishermen who were
in guilds, but presumably limited the total amount
of exploitation in the organized area. It is surely
the case that the other limited-entry areas, whether
established for villages, lineages or individuals,
enhance the conservation of resources. This is so
because not only is the number of people using each
discrete area limited, but it is also the domain of
resident fishermen, who would take greater care to
use it wisely than, say, a group of itinerant sea-
nomads.

PROTECTION AND ALLOCATION OF RESOURCES

Many conflicts over the use of particular areas such
as coastal reefs resulted from the high commercial
value of particular resources. Kolff (1840) and van
Hoëvell (1890c) have mentioned disputes between villages on Tanimbar over the harvesting of trepang,
while on islands off the north coast of Irian Jaya
inter-village reserves are established in particular
for trepang (Feuilleteau de Bruyn, 1920). Such
limited-entry areas have been discussed above.

Another evident source of conflict was that
within communities over the allocation of the catch,
because regulations for distributing it are widely
reported from Indonesia. For example, such rules
have been described for coastal fishing off Aceh
(Snouck Hurgronje, 1906), Java (ENI, 1921; Palm,
1962), and Irian Jaya (Feuilleteau de Bruyn, 1920),
for the catch of whales, turtles, rays and other
large animals off Lembata (Barnes, 1980), and for
the produce of stake-traps in southern Sulawesi
(Wiggers, 1893). While such rules refer primarily
to direct participants in the fishing activities,
it is clear in many cases that non-fishing individuals in the community can also benefit (Snouck
Hurgronje, 1906; Collier, Hadikoesworo & Malingreau,
1979; Emmerson, 1980b). Although catch-sharing
would not contribute directly to a conservation of
resources, it may reduce competitiveness within
communities and thus increase the efficiency with
which people use the resources available.

In many cases particular species are protected. This can usually be attributed to spiritual or religious reasons. In the southern Moluccas, crocodiles, turtles, eels and other species are prohibited to particular families because they are part of totemic systems and people believe that their ancestors take the form of these animals (Frazer, 1922). Crocodiles are forbidden species to the Tobelorese of Halmahera (Riedel, 1885), and to the Pagai Islanders, though not on neighbouring Siberut (Loeb, 1935). The Galelarese collect trepang, but these are apparently forbidden to the Tobelorese (Riedel, 1885). Crocodiles and snakes are traditionally taboo to many Malays while fishing (Endicott, 1970). Porpoises are not caught by Ambonese fishermen (Deane, 1979), whilst among plants the strand species Pisonia grandis is, or was, protected at Karang Bandong in southern Java, because of its association with the origin of kings (Teijsmann, 1855). In the case of such prohibited species, it is not possible to say whether any conserving effect resulted; information is needed on the numbers of people involved, the nature of exploited populations, and if, and how, attention is diverted to other species. Such details are not available.

Where Islam is important, it is forbidden to eat the meat, but not the eggs, of sea-turtles, though this has not prevented Mohammedans from catching turtles for others to eat, as described by Jochim (1893) for Sapudi Islanders bringing turtles to Hindu Bali. It has also not prevented partially-Moslem or animistic groups such as the Bajau-Laut (Vosmaer, 1839), Orang Laut (Pelras, 1972) or Siberut Islanders (Loeb, 1935) from eating turtle meat; the sea-nomads were in fact important in developing the trade based on these animals. In some cases, however, the Bajau-Laut evidently do not eat, or have stopped eating, turtle (Jochim, 1893; J.J. Fox, pers. comm.). An example where protection of a species has been instigated for functional reasons is that of sea-birds which nest colonially on certain rocks off northern Sulawesi (J.R. MacKinnon, pers. comm.); here the birds are valuable in helping to locate shoals of cakalang (tuna).

There are other practices which influence the way in which resources are used. One of these is the storing, or rearing, of all or part of the catch. An important example of this is the stunting of Milkfish-fry in tambak (brackish-water fish ponds) so that two harvests of adults can be obtained in spite of the seasonal scarcity of larvae (Schuster, 1952; Yamashita & Sutardjo, 1977). There are of course many facets to the impact of exploitation on stocks of this species, and almost nothing is known about any of them, but it is probable that the production of this marine species for human benefit has been increased greatly. Further, since larval mortality is likely to be high, a source of food is being made available which would otherwise have been lost to man, or even gone to waste. The keeping of edible sea-turtles in pens, as in southern Bali, might also be included here, but since turtle meat was traditionally dried and salted, it is not possible to argue in this case that storage has led to increased efficiency of use. Even in the past, when turtle-pens might not have been maintained, if more turtles were caught than were currently needed, these did not therefore go to waste. These turtles were not actually reared, but turtle-rearing from hatchlings or eggs has been carried out for some time, and a similar argument could be put forward for this activity as has been proposed for the milkfish above.

People using marine resources in Indonesia have been taxed quite heavily for a long time, either in kind or in money. This has, for example, been described for the Bajau-Laut of Sumbawa (Freys, 1859) and of east Kalimantan (von Dewall, 1855; Hageman, 1855), where they paid annual tribute in items such as _trepang_ and turtle-shell to the local rulers. Coastal fisheries and mangrove exploitation were also liable to tax, as on the east coast of Sumatra (Gramberg, 1877; Schot, 1883), at least in quite modern times. In the Bajau-laut case it is not possible to infer any effect on patterns of exploitation, but in the Sumatran case it is conceivable that some limitation was introduced, and that those who did enter the fishery tended to be specialists who could carry out the work more efficiently than less experienced individuals. At least in the case of the _trubuk_ fishery, however, the harvest had already fallen markedly in the 19th century (Gramberg, 1880).

Where species were not wholly protected, for whatever reason, there was undoubtedly often a certain awe connected with the exploitation of large species in particular. Galis (1955), for example, refers to turtle-demons in Irian Jaya, while Schot (1883) mentions the belief that dugongs are protected by spirits in Sumatra. Superstitions about crocodiles are widespread, as mentioned above and also by Skeat (1900). This returns us to the idea that the Indonesian sea and its inhabitants were fearful to many people. It seems likely that this attitude influenced the number and types of people who have used marine areas, and the pattern which marine exploitation as a whole has depicted in time.

AN OVERVIEW OF TRADITIONAL MARINE PRACTICES AND CONSERVATION

Practices which seem significantly to affect patterns of resource use and allocation are summarized in Table 11.1. Probably the most important types of practice are those which limit access to marine and coastal exploitation over extensive areas, such as the marga of Sumatra, tenured areas off Salayar, and inter-village reserves of the Moluccas and Irian Jaya. It is worth reiterating here that most of the available information on these come from old papers, many from the last century, so that their current status is for the most part unknown.

It is surprising that in a country where the sea has long been important as a source of food and trade commodities (Polunin, in press a), there are so few data on activities such as fishing and on any ways in which they might be controlled. This lack of evidence may mean that such regulations do not exist, or perhaps that there has been little study of them. Against the former point, there is the indication that regulations do occur, and at that quite widely, in the country, as suggested by Table 11.1. On the latter view, it is clear that there has been surprisingly little work on maritime southeast Asia (Emmerson, 1980a). While I tend to support the latter view-point, I do think that traditional measures for controlling the use of resources may not be as extensive as they might be predicted to be on simple theoretical grounds. Significant causes of this may be both the result of traditional fear of the sea together with the expansion in the trade in marine products in the last two or three centuries, and also of the influence of seasonality in coastal districts.

Some original attitudes to the sea have been described above. At least partly because of this timidity, the opportunity for exploiting valuable marine species was widely left open to a few specialists. These people, in particular the sea-nomads and traders such as the Buginese-Makassarese, were themselves in many cases pirates, who protected

Table 11.1 - Important Types of
and Allocation of Marine

Type of Practice		Area
1. Restricted species	i	Sumatra, Java, Kalimantan (Mohammedans)
	ii	N. Sulawesi
	iii	S. Maluku
	iv	Halmahera (Tobelorese)
2. Storing/rearing	i	Java, Sulawesi
3. Sharing of catch	i	Sumatra (Acehnese)
	ii	Java
	iii	Lembata
	iv	Irian Jaya
4. Concessioned areas	i	Sumatra, Java, Kalimantan
	ii	Sumatra
	iii	Sumatra
5. Tenured areas	i	Sumatra (Battam Orang Laut)
	ii	Sumatra (Acehnese)
	iii	Sumatra
	iv	Salayar (S. Sulawesi)
	v	Tanimbar
	vi	Kei
	vii	Irian Jaya (Geelvink)
	viii	Irian Jaya (Humboldt)

their livelihood through piracy and came to pervade
the country. While making marine exploitation an
unstable profession for others, many of them were
by nature wandering opportunists who, if resources
ran low in one area, could presumably move on to
another locality. Under such conditions, they would
have been unlikely to regulate their use of marine
areas, because these were extensive and under-
exploited. The domination of the archipelago by
these maritime people is, however, a comparatively
recent event, so that many practices which formerly

Traditional Practice Influencing the Use Resources and Habitats in Indonesia

Resource or Habitat	Sources (examples)
Turtle meat	Polunin & Sumertha Nuitja (in press)
Sea-birds	J.R.MacKinnon (pers.comm.)
Various species, depending on family	Frazer, 1922
Crocodiles	Riedel, 1885
Milkfish fry	Schuster, 1952
Fish	Snouck, Hurgronje, 1906
Fish	Palm, 1962
Whales, turtles, rays	Barnes, 1980
Fish	Feuilleteau de Bruyn, 1920
Turtle-nesting beaches	Somadikarta, 1962
Nipah and mangrove use (marga)	van Royen, 1927
Estuarine fishing	van Royen, 1927
Coastal fishing	Schot, 1883
Coastal fishing (guilds)	Snouck Hurgronje, 1906
Sago stands	Gramberg, 1881
Reefs, coastal fishing	Kriebel, 1919
Reefs (Trepang)	LeBar, 1972
Reefs	van Hoëvell, 1890b
Reefs	van der Sande, 1907
Reefs	Galis, 1955

existed may have been lost in the scramble for valuable commodities. Some concern for the way in which marine resources are used should rather be sought amongst societies which have a more stable history. A case can be made for explaining the presence, or perhaps survival, of marine practices such as inter-village reserves in eastern Indonesia in this way, because the influence of people such as Bajau-Laut in this region came late and remains sparse (Sopher, 1965; Fox, 1977). A comparable case could be made for the marga of eastern Sumatra, a part of the country which it is true has had a turbulent history, but where extensive coastal swamp-forests must have afforded some protection from the outside world.

A second major reason for which resource regulations may not be more extensive than it is possible to predict, is the fact that in most parts of the country the weather varies seasonally, so that fishing is not feasible throughout the year. Fishermen can, and usually do, turn to other methods of sustenance during the rough season, and there is even prehistoric evidence that coastal sites were only seasonally occupied (cf. Brandt, 1976). Under these conditions coastal people could hardly be expected to attach the importance to marine resources that they do in areas where they are more exclusively dependent on them (cf. Johannes, 1978). If certain traditional measures have disappeared in some areas, this would not seem to have been due to commercialization per se, because trade in marine species has also been carried out for a long time in areas where limited-entry practices are still extant today (e.g. for Irian Jaya see Anon., 1852 and de Clercq & Schmeltz, 1893; for the Keis see Bosscher, 1855 and van Hoëvell, 1890b; for eastern Sumatra see Schot, 1883 and Croockewit, 1853). In any case, as noted above and observed by Kriebel (1919) off Salayar, the more productive an area is, the more likely is its use to be regulated.

It is not known exactly how measures such as limited-entry areas came into existence. I have inferred above that at least in some cases these arrangements resulted from conflicts within and between communities of coastal people. It is possible that such conflicts were accentuated by the depletion of marine stocks in particular localities, and that the controlled areas were thus established because the limits of natural resources were recognized. A proper answer to the question may come partially from detailed studies on areas where these practices are still maintained. In any case, it is possible that the analogous measures observed on western Pacific islands (Johannes, 1978) do have their origin in Indonesian, and other southeast Asian, practices.

It is probable that for the time-being traditional regulations limiting access to coastal areas have at least as much a role to play in development as the often unenforced measures attempted by a central government acting at a distance of hundreds or thousands of kilometres. This will be discussed below, after first assessing the character of modern marine environmental problems.

MODERN MARINE ENVIRONMENTAL PROBLEMS IN PERSPECTIVE

Marine exploitation has been carried on for at least a few millenia (van Heine-Geldern, 1945; Gorman, 1971), and international trade in Indonesian sea-produce has existed for many centuries (Rockhill, 1914-15). The last decades have, however, seen an escalation of human impingement on the sea (Polunin, in press a). This has been intimately involved with rapid population growth and in some cases through precipitate introduction of new technology and ideas.

In the 19th century the first measures began to be taken to curb some of the problems which were arising. The realization that Java could be supplied with increasingly valuable protein by fisheries (van Soest, 1861) led to the removal or reduction of taxation on fishing activities in the 1860s. In the 1850s regulations had already been imposed on the oyster fishery in the southern Moluccas, and with the entry of steam-powered vessels, stake-trap fisheries needed to be confined in busy sea-lanes (ENI, 1921). From the 1890s, a series of legal measures was brought in to attempt to regulate other fishing activities (mesh-size of nets, use of poisons) more widely in the country. In a few cases, such as the estuarine trubuk fishery of eastern Sumatra (Gramberg, 1880) and the oyster-shell yield of the Aru banks (van Hoëvell, 1880a), production was already declining. Demand had evidently exceeded local supply of milkfish fry for fish-ponds, because these had long been brought from outside Java, and of turtle meat, because this was being imported to Bali (e.g Jochim, 1893).

The growing need actively to develop coastal fisheries around Java, in particular, followed from investigations such as that of the 1904-05 Welfare Commission (Verloop, 1906). Exploratory trawling was soon carried out in the Java sea (van Roosendaal and van Kampen, 1907). In the 1920s motorized fishing on a large scale began with the commercial Japanese muro-ami fisheries of the western Java Sea, but attempts at the mechanization of local fisheries only started in the 1930s with the payang fishery of Java (Furnivall, 1937). Nevertheless, at the end of the colonial period Java remained a major importer of fish, though surrounded by productive sea (Bottemanne, 1959). In the last 30 years Indonesian fisheries have developed considerably: the country is no longer a net importer of fish, and marine produce is now a valuable source export commodity (Anon., 1979). Traditional small-scale operators, however, still constitute some 98% of Indonesia's fishing population (Sidarto and Atmowasono, 1977); their activities are sail-powered and comparatively inefficient (Kartono, 1958). Although fish production has increased, the catch per fisherman has decreased since the 1950s (Krisnandhi, 1969), and the waters of the northern coast of Java and much of the eastern coast of Sumatra are considered to be seriously over-fished (Sujastani, 1980), although they support the vast majority of fishermen. The fact is that some 69% of Indonesia's population is concentrated in only 7% of its land area, around Java and Bali (Anon, 1978). This has led to incipient pollution and extensive coastal habitat modification, as well as tne over-exploitation of stocks. Concern about pollution has been brought to a head by the deteriorating condition of Jakarta Bay waters and fears of high oil-hydrocarbon concentrations, habitat modification by the silting-up of deltas, the replacement of mangroves by fish-ponds, salt-production areas and settlements, and over-fishing due to the conflict between traditional and mechanized fishing. For some time the government has endeavoured to alleviate population pressure in Java and Bali by encouraging people to "transmigrate" to sparsely inhabited parts of the country. Among these poorly-populated areas are coastal swamp habitats, and although projects for developing such environments have been started in a number of areas, there is doubt as to whether these will succeed (Hanson & Koesoebiono, 1979; Burbridge, Dixon & Soewardi, 1981). In the meantime extensive deltaic areas are being transformed.

Although many major environmental problems are centred on Java and Bali, there are also many areas of growing concern outside these islands. An important one of these is the conflict between development and protection of mangrove forests, the former alternative for wood and organics, fish-ponds, salt-production and other uses, the latter for shore-protection and as a basis for certain fisheries. Coral reefs are being widely affected by mining and fishing with explosives, although they are important in traditional fisheries (Unar, 1979) and potentially also in large-scale ones (Cusing,

1971). As rain forest inland is felled, increasing siltation, salt-intrusion and other effects on the coast can be expected (Brubridge & Koesoebiono, in press). It is to the coastal zone that most concern is directed.

TRADITIONAL MARINE CONTROLLED AREAS IN THE MODERN CONTEXT

Many of the problems which have been briefly summarized above reflect a poor state of knowledge about the ecology and use of coastal areas. Lack of action, however, often also reflects a lack of responsibility. Ineffectiveness in enforcing regulations usually results from an incomplete commitment to the established objective, and this is commonly because legal controls applied by government are little respected by local people. How can a fuller commitment be achieved?

A major role can clearly be played in coastal zone development by protected areas, particularly where these are seen as covering a whole range of states of control, from "Resource Reserves" to "National Parks" (Polunin, in press b). I have shown above that various types of controlled area have long existed in Indonesia; the idea of restricting access to particular zones is not a new one. These traditional areas of limited entry have also demonstrated that widespread local responsibility for the use of marine resources has long existed. Measures such as the marga of Sumatra, tenured reefs of Salayar, or inter-village reserves of Irian Jaya and the Moluccas may once have existed in Java, but there is apparently no record of them now. It cannot be claimed therefore that such practices could alleviate the critical problems of coastal fishing in that area. This is not the case for the outer, less populated, parts of the country, for many of which there is evidence that traditional limited-entry areas exist, or existed until quite recently. If these systems of coastal tenure and concession still exist, why worry about them? An answer is that in at least two cases, quite widely separated in the country, traditional systems are threatened with replacement apparently without anyone being aware of their existence. One of these cases is afforded by the Sumatran marga, which are evidently being supplanted in transmigration areas (Hanson & Koesoebiono, 1979). The other example is Ambon in the Moluccas, where attempts by the central government to establish a marine nature reserve at Pombo Island have met with little success; the reef has, for example, been heavily damaged by explosives (Sumadhiharga, 1977). A recent survey proposed that accessible parts of Ambon Bay are appropriate as nature reserves (J.W. McManus, pers. comm.) although inter-village reserves are already present here. In parts of the country for which they have been reported, however, nothing is known of the current status of these controlled areas.

The inclusion of traditional protected areas in conservation work may not be consistent with a purist view that in reserves nature should ideally be left entirely to its own devices. Inclusion of these measures, however, is increasingly acceptable to those who seek a more functional approach to marine protected areas, and view strict nature reserves as one extreme in a spectrum of degrees of control by which coastal waters can be zoned in critical areas. Traditional controlled areas may have certain disadvantages; for example, they may not be able to assimilate the effects of rapid population growth, particularly that resulting from immigration. They do, however, provide a basis for local responsibility in resource management, and a greater effort should be made to incorporate them in regional planning procedures. They could represent a valuable device for reducing habitat destruction and regulating fisheries on settled coasts. To this end it is clearly essential to know more about their distribution, structure and varied functions in the country. If this information is not soon made available, then a valuable forum for coastal-zone planning may be lost before it has been properly considered.

ACKNOWLEDGEMENTS

This work was carried out under contract to the International Union for Conservation of Nature and Natural Resources (IUCN), Gland, Switzerland, in co-operation with the United Nations Environment Programme (UNEP). I am grateful to Jeffrey McNeely for making it possible for me to write on the topic. I thank Tristam Rily-Smith, Simon Strickland, J.J. Fox, R.E. Johannes and K.E. Ruddle for reviewing the draft manuscript.

REFERENCES

Anon. 1852. Ceram Laut Isles. J. Indian Archipelago and Far East. 6: 689-691.

Anon. 1855. Beschrijving van het eiland Soemba of Sandelhout. Tijdschr. Ned.-Indie 17(1-6): 277-312.

Anon. 1918. A manual of Netherlands India (Dutch East Indies). London: Naval Staff Intelligence Department. 548 pp.

Anon. 1978. Statistik Indonesia. 1977. Jakarta: Biro Pusat Statistik. lxxii + 1202 pp.

Anon. 1979. Fisheries Statistics of Indonesia 1977. Jakarta: Direktorat Jenderal Perikanan. xxxviii + 83 pp.

Barnes, R.H. 1974. Kédang. Oxford: Clarendon Press. xiv + 350 pp.

Barnes, R.H. 1980. Cetaceans and cetacean hunting, Lamalera, Indonesia. Gland, Switzerland: World Wildlife Fund. 82 pp. (mimeo).

Barraud, C. 1979. Tanebar-Evav, Une Société de Maisons Tournées Vers le Large. Cambridge: Cambridge University. xii + 283 pp.

Bosscher, C. 1855. Bijdrage tot de kennis van de Keijeilanden. Tijdschr. indische taal - Land en Volkenk 4: 423-458.

Bottemanne, C.J. 1959. Principles of Fisheries Development. Amsterdam: North-Holland. lX + 651 pp.

Brandt, R.W. 1976. The Hoabinian of Sumatra: some remarks. Mod. Quatern. Res. S.E.Asia 2: 49-52.

Bruijnis, J.K. 1919. Twee landschappen op Timor. Tijdschr. K. ned. aardrijksk. Genoot. 36: 169-198.

Bühler, A. 1937. Bericht über die im Jahre 1935 auf Timor, Rote und Flores angelegten ethnographischen Sammlungen. Verh. naturf. Ges. Basel 48: 13-37.

Burbridge, P., Dixon, J.A. & Soewardi, B. 1981. Forestry and agriculture: Options for resource allocation in choosing lands for transmigration development. Appl. Geog. 1: 237-258.

Burbridge, P. & Koesoebiono (in press). Coastal zone management in southeast Asia. In: Chia Lin Sien & C. MacAndrews (eds.), Frontiers for Development: the Southeast Asian Seas. Singapore: McGraw-Hill.

Collier, W.L., H. Hadikoesworo and M. Malingreau. 1979. Economic development and shared poverty among Javanese sea fishermen. pp. 218-236. In: A.R. Librero & W.L. Collier (eds.), Economics of Agriculture, Sea-fishing and Coastal Resource Use in Asia. Manila: Philippines Council for Agriculture and Resource Research.

Compost, A. 1980. Pilot Survey of Exploitation of Dugong and Sea Turtle in the Aru Islands. Bogor: Yayasan Indonesia Hijau. 63 pp. (mimeo).

Covarrubias, M. 1937. Island of Bali. London: Cassell. xv + 417 pp.

Croockewit, J.H. 1853. Aanteenkeningen omtrent de bevolking en den handel van het eiland Billiton. Tijdschr. indische Taal-Land-en Volkenk. 1: 77-88.

Cushing, D.H. 1971. Survey of Resources in the Indian Ocean and Indonesian Area. Rome: FAO Indian Ocean Fishery Commission. viii + 123 pp. (1OFO/DEV/71/2).

Deane, S. 1979. Ambon. London: Murray. 222 pp.

de Clercq, F.S.A. 1891. Rapport over drie reizentinaar het Nederlandsche gedeelte van Nieuw-Guinea. Tijdschr. indische Taal-land-en Volkenk. 34:117-169.

de Clercq, F.S.A. and Schmeltz, J.D.E. 1893. Ethnographische beschrijving van de West-en-Noordkust van Nederlandsch Nieuw-Guinea. Leiden: Trap. xv + 300 pp.

Dick, H.W. 1975. Prahu shipping in eastern Indonesia Part 1. Bull. Indonesian Econ. Stud. 11(2): 69-107.

Downs, R.E. 1955. Head-hunting in Indonesia. Bijdr. Taal Landen Volkenk-Ned.-Indie 111: 40-70, 280-285.

Earl, G.W. 1850. The trading ports of the Indian Archipelago. J. Indian Archipelago and Far East 4: 238-251, 380-399, 483-495, 530-551.

Ellen, R.F. 1978. Nuaulu Settlement and Ecology. Verh. K. Inst. Taal-Land-en Volkenk. 83, xi + 265 pp.

Emmerson, D.K. 1980a. The case for maritime perspective in southeast Asia. J. Southeast Asian Stud. 11: 139-145.

Emmerson, D.K. 1980b. Rethinking artisanal fisheries development: western concepts, Asian experiences. World bank Staff Working Pap. 423, x + 97 pp.

Endicott, K.M. 1970. An Analysis of Malay Magic. Oxford: Clarendon. viii + 188 pp.

ENI. 1921. Enclyclopaedie van Nederlandsch-Indië. Volume 4. ("Visscherij"). The Hague: Martinus Nijhoff. 922 pp.

Epton, N. 1974. Magic and Mystics of Java. London: Octagon. 212 pp.

Feuilleteau de Bruyn, W.K.H. 1920. Schouten-en Padaido-Eilanden. Herz. door A. Meyroos. Meded.
Bureau Bestuurszaken, Encyclop. Bureau 21, x + 193 pp.

Forbes, H.O. 1885. A Naturalist's Wanderings in the Eastern Archipelago. London: Sampson Low, Marston, Searle and Rovington. xix + 536 pp.

Fox, J.J. 1977. Notes on the southern voyages and settlements of the Sama-Bajau. Bijdr. Taal-Land-en Volkenk. 133:459-465.

Frazer, J.G. 1922. The Golden Bough. London: Macmillan xiv + 756 pp.

Freys, J.P. 1859. Schetsvan den handelvan Sumbawa. Tijdschr. Ned.-Indie 21(2): 268-285.

Furnivall, J.S. 1936. Studies in the social and economic developments of Netherlands East Indies. IVd. Fisheries in Netherlands India. Rangoon: Burma Book Club. 9 pp.

Galis, K.W. 1955. Papua's van de Humboldt-Baai. The Hague: Voorhoeve. 293 pp.

Goedhart, O.H. 1908. Drie Landschappen in Celebes (Bangai, Boengkoe en Mori). Tijdschr. indische Taal-land-en Volkenk. 50: 442-548.

Gorman, C. 1971. The Hoabinhian and after: subsistence patterns in southeast Asia during the late Pleistocene and early Recent periods. Wld. Archeol. 2: 300-320.

Gramberg, J.S.G. 1877. De troeboekvisscherij. Tijdschr. indische Taal-Land-en Volkenk. 24: 298-317.

Gramberg, J.S.G. 1880. De visscherij en bezwering van troeboeko Indische Gids 2(2): 331-346.

Gramberg, J.S.G. 1881. De Oostkust van Sumatra. Indische Gids 3(1): 356-372, 586-593, 788-795, 1036-1046.

Hageman, J. 1855. Aanteekeningen omtrent een gedeelte der Oostkust van Borneo. Tijdschr. indische Taal-Land-en Volkenk. 4: 71-106.

Hanson, A.J. & Koesoebiono. 1979. Settling coastal swamplands in Sumatra. pp. 121-175. In: C. MacAndrews & Chia Lin Sieh (eds.), Developing Economics and the Environment. Singapore: McGraw-Hill.

Hardenberg, J.D.F. 1931. The fish fauna of the Rokan mouth. Treubia 13: 81-168.

Hickson, S.J. 1886. Notes on the Sengirese. J. anthrop. Inst. 16: 136-142.

Hobart, M. 1978. The path of the soul: the legitimacy of nature in Balinese conceptions. pp. 5-28. In: G.B. Milner (ed.), Natural Symbols in Southeast Asia. London: School of Oriental and African Studies.

Jochim, E.F. 1893. Beschrijving van den Sapoedi Archipel. Tijdschr. indische Taal-land-en Volkenk. 36: 343-393.

Johannes, R.E. 1978. Traditional marine conservation methods in Oceania and their demise. Ann. Rev. Ecol. Syst. 9: 349-364.

Kartono, R.A. 1958. Comparison of fishing efficiency between A. longline and "rawai" (Prawe) B. trawl and "dogol" C. various types of 'pajang'. Proc. Indo-Pacific. Fish. Coun. 7(2-3): p. 83.

Ketjen, E. 1877. De Kalangers. Tijdschr. indische Taal-Land-en Volkenk. 24: 421-436.

Kist, F.J. 1938. The geo-political and strategic importance of the waterways in the Netherlands Indies. Bull. Colon. Inst. Amst. 1: 252-262.

Kolff, D.H. 1840. Voyage of the Dutch brig of war Dourga. London: James Madden. xxiv + 365 pp.

Kriebel, D.J.C. 1919. Grond en waterscrechten in de onderafdeeling Saleijer. Koloniaal Tijdschr. 8: 1086-1109.

Krisnandhi, S. 1969. The economic development of Indonesia's sea fishing industry. Bull. Indonesian Econ. Stud. 5(1): 49-72.

Le Bar, F.M. (ed.) 1972. Ethnic groups of Insular Southeast Asia. Volume 1. Indonesia. New Haven: Human Relations Area Files. viii + 236 pp.

Loeb, E.M. 1935. Sumatra, its History and People. Wiener Beitrage zur Kulturgeschichte und Linguistik 3, ix+350 pp.

Lombard, D. 1974. La vision de la forêt à Java. Etudes Rurales 53-56: 473-485.

Lombard, D. 1980. Le thème de la mer dans les littératures et les mentalités de l'archipel insulindien. Archipel 20: 317-328.

Malinowski, B. 1918. Fishing in the Trobriand Islands. Man 18: 87-92.

Moss, R. 1925. The Life after Death in Oceania and the Malay Archipelago. Oxford: Oxford University. xii + 247 pp.

Nooy-Palm, H. 1968. The culture of the Pagai-Islands and Sipora, Mentawci. Tropical Man 1: 152-241.

Palm, C. 1972. Notes sur quelques populations aqua-
tiques de l'archipel nusantarien. Archipel 3:
133-168.

Polunin, N.V.C. (in press a). Marine resoûrces of
Indonesia. Oceanogr. Mar. Biol. Ann. Rev.

Polunin, N.V.C. (in press b). Marine "genetic resources" and the potential role of protected
areas in conserving them. Environ. Conserv.

Polunin, N.V.C. and Sumerta Nuitja, N. (in press).
Sea turtle populations of Indonesia and
Thailand. In: K. Bjorndal (ed.), Biology and
Conservation of Sea Turtles. Washington, D.C.:
Smithsonian Institution.

Riedel, J.G.F. 1885. Galela und Tobeloresen. Z.
Ethnol. 17: 58-89.

Rockhill, W.W. 1914-1915. Notes on the relations and
trade of China with the Eastern Archipelago
and the coasts of the Indian Ocean during the
fourteenth century. Parts I and II. To'ung
Pao 15: 419-447. 16: 16-159, 236-271,
604-626.

Schot, J.G. 1883. De Battam-Archipel. Indische Gids
4(2): 25-54, 161-188, 476-479, 617-625.
4(1): 205-211, 462-479.

Schrieke, B. 1925. De zee in ethnographie en volks-
kunde. pp. 283-286. In: D.A. Rinkes, N. van
Zalinge & J.W. de Roever (eds.), Het Indische
Boek der Zee. weltevreden: Volkslectuur.

Schuster, W.H. 1952. Fish culture in brackish water
ponds of Java. Spec. Publ. Indo-Pacif. Fish.
Coun. 1, 143 pp.

Sidarto, A. and Atmowasono, H. 1977. Policies and
programmes of artisanal fisheries development
in Indonesia. pp. 157-162 In: B. Lockwood &
K. Ruddle (eds.), Small Scale Fisheries Development. Honolulu: East-West Center.

Skeat, W.W. 1900. Malay Magic. London: MacMillan xiv
+ 685 pp.

Snouck Hurgronje, C. 1906. The Achehnese (translated
by A.W.S. O'Sullivan): Volume 1. Leiden:
Brill. xxi + 439 pp.

Somadikarta, S. 1962. Penyu Laut di Indonesia. Buku
Laporan Kongres Ilmu Pengetahuan Nasional Kedua
5 (C-Biologi): 573-585.

Sopher, D.E. 1965. The sea nomads. Mem. natnm. Mus.
Singapore 5, x + 422 pp.

Sujastani, J. 1980. A review of the current state of
the Indonesian marine fishery resource exploitation. Manila: South China Sea Fisheries
Development and Coordinating Programme 28 pp.
(mimeo).

Sumadhiharga, O.K. 1977. A preliminary study on the ecology of the coral reef of Pombo Island. Mar. Res. Indonesia 17: 29-49.

Teijsmann, J.E. 1855. Iets over de Widjojo Koesoemo (Pisonia sylvestris Teijsm. Binnd.). Natuurk. Tijdschr. Ned.-Indië 9: 349-356.

Tilson, R.L. 1977. Social organization of Simonkobu monkeys (Nasalis concolor) in Siberut Island, Indonesia. J. Mammal. 58: 202-212.

Unar, M. 1979. Perairan karang sebagai taman laut dan aspek sumber perikanannya bagi tujuan pengusahaanya. Bio Indonesia 6: 53-61.

Unesco. 1981. Marine and coastal processes in the Pacific: aspects of coastal zone management. Unesco Rept. mar. Sci. 6, 20 pp.

van der Kroef, J.M. 1954. Dualism and symbolic anti-thesis in Indonesian Society. Am. Anth. 56: 847-862.

van der Sande, G.A.J. 1907. Ethnography and anthropology. Nova Guinea 3, 390 pp.

van Heine-Geldern, R. 1945. Prehistoric research in the Netherlands Indies. pp. 129-167. In: P. Honig & F. Verdoorn (eds.), Science and Scientists in the Netherlands Indies. New York: Board for the Netherlands Indies, Surinam and Curacao.

van Hoëvell, G.W.W.C. 1890a. De Aroe-eilanden, geographische, ethnographisch en commerciëel. Tijdschr. indische Taal-Land-en Volkenk. 33: 57-101.

van Hoëvell, G.W.W.C. 1890b. de Kei-eilanden. Tijdschr. indische Taal-Land-en Volkenk. 33: 102-159.

van Hoëvell, G.W.W.C. 1890c. Tanimbar en Timorlaoet-eilanden. Tijdschr. indische Taal-land-en Volkenk. 33: 160-186.

van Roosendaal, A.M. and van Kampen, P.N. 1907. Verslag van der verrichtingen van het onderzoekingsvaartuig "Gier" gedurene de tijdvak 2 September 1907 (datum van indienststelling) tot 1908. Meded. Visscherij Sta. Batavia 4: 1-36.

van Royen, J.W. 1927. De Palembangsche marga en haar grond en watersrechten. Thesis, Rijksvmversiteit, Leiden.

van Soest, G.H. 1861. De visscherijen in Indie. Tijdschr. Ned.-Indië 23(2): 9-23.

Verloop, G.N. 1906. Beschouwingen over de voorstellen der Welvaart-commisie in zake visscherij. Tijdschr. Nijv. Landb. Ned.-Indië 73: 213-239, 337-349.

von Dewall, H. 1855. Aanteekeningen omtrent de nord-
    oostkust van Borneo. Tijdschr. indische Taat
    Land-en Volkenk. 4: 423-458.
Vosmaer, J.N. 1839. Korte beschrijving van het zuid-
    oostelijk schiereiland van Celebes Verh.
    batav. Genoot. Kunst. Wet. 17: 61-184.
Wiggers, H.D. 1893. Schets van het Regentschap
    kadjan, onderafdeeling Kadjan, afdeeling
    Oosterdistricten, Gouvernement Celebes en
    onderhoorigheden. Tijdschr. indische Taal-
    Land-en Volkenk. 36: 247-278.
Yamashita, M. and Sutardjo. 1977. Engineering
    aspects of brackish water pond culture in
    Indonesia. pp. 261-280. In: Joint
    SCSP/SEAFDEC Workshop on Aquaculture Engineer-
    ing, Volume 2. Manila: South China Sea
    Fisheries Development and Coordinating Pro-
    gramme. (SCS/GEN/77/15).

This paper was prepared for IUCN's Commission on
National Parks and Protected Areas in co-operation
with the United Nations Environment Programme.

Chapter Twelve

CUSTOMARY LAND TENURE AND CONSERVATION
IN PAPUA NEW GUINEA

By

Peter Eaton
University of Papua New Guinea
Papua New Guinea

ABSTRACT

Many problems have been encountered in acquiring
and leasing customary land for national parks. A
major alternative is to permit customary groups to
retain their ownership rights, and involving them
in park development. Wildlife management areas
already provide a precedent where some customary
rights are maintained but there is agreement on
rules of hunting and exploitation.

INTRODUCTION

At the Conference on the Human Environment in the
South Pacific held at Rarotonga this year, one of
the areas for conservation recommended as being of
particular regional importance was defined as follows:

> The study of traditional land and marine
> tenure systems and their reconciliation
> with environmental management, especially
> in relation to conservation and the desig-
> nation and management of reserves.

In this paper I shall attempt to examine this relationship of customary land tenure to conservation
in one of the countries of the region.

In Papua New Guinea traditional societies have
their own forms of resource management and conservation, but these have not always proved adequate
to cope with changes resulting from population increase and new forms of economic activity. In many
areas unique natural environments are threatened and
there is a need to set aside land for conservation

purposes. However, these purposes may be imperfectly understood and often unappreciated by local land-owners who are frequently among the poorest and most neglected members of the population. Conservation areas often have to compete with other forms of land utilization which appear to offer more immediate profits. Furthermore, the system of land tenure often makes it difficult to acquire land for national parks and even when they have been established, the former landowners may feel that they retain customary rights such as access, hunting, burning the vegetation and clearing the land for cultivation. These problems may be partly a result of misunderstanding or ignorance of the aims of national parks; they are also associated with a concept of land tenure in which land inherited from ancestors cannot be permanently transferred outside the tribal group.

CUSTOMARY LAND TENURE IN PAPUA NEW GUINEA

In Papua New Guinea this type of customary land tenure is prevailing over 97% of the country. Absolute ownership of the land is vested in the kinship group or clan which retains control over its allocation, use of transfer. Certain rights are usually exercised concerning sweet potato, taro, yams and cassava. Sago is a staple food in some areas and a variety of fruits and vegetables are also produced. Pigs are the main domestic animals kept; they feature largely in ceremonies and gift exchanges, their possession conferring social prestige on the owner; they do not provide a regular supply of meat. In some areas hunting may make up for deficiencies in diet; it may also be plumage and other ornaments for decoration and ceremonial purposes. Wildlife hunted includes wallabies, crocodiles, bandicoots, echidna, pigeons, birds of paradise and cassowaries. In coastal areas dugongs and turtles are caught; fishing is important on the coral reefs and in the estuaries.

In many ways the customary land tenure system encouraged the conservation and management of wildlife resources. It excluded hunters and collectors who did not come from the land-owning group. Rights to bird of paradise display trees, megapode breeding grounds and caves where bats lived were all jealously guarded. There were also controls within the groups; if a particular bird or animal seemed to be becoming scarcer then village leaders might decree a ban on hunting it for a period of maybe six months or a year. Other moratoria on hunting might be associated with a taboo on a piece of land following the death of a relative.

Traditional religious and magic beliefs control the hunting or eating of many forms of wildlife. Some groups may have a particular association with a species of animal or bird which prevents them from killing it, perhaps because it acts as the totem for their moiety or because of a belief that they were once descended from it. There is often a prohibition against the hunting of wild dogs; sometimes because they are regarded as guardians of a community, in other cases because it is feared that if you kill one they will steal a child in return. It is also believed that certain insectivorous birds, such as wagtails should not be killed in gardens because they are really ghosts; this protects them and also helps to keep down insect pests.

There may also be temporary bans on hunting and eating wildlife at particular times of the year. These are often associated with agricultural activities. In parts of the Highlands, cassowaries may not be hunted during the taro planting season and in some coastal areas turtles are not hunted during the yam harvest.

In the territories of most Papua New Guinea villagers there are sacred areas where access is restricted; here vegetation and wildlife should not be disturbed. Some of these places are cemeteries, others are associated with initiation rites. There are also places which belong to the spirits, ples masalai, and are therefore protected.

Traditional beliefs and techniques have helped to protect the environment in the past and in many areas are still operative. They have not, however, proved comprehensive or strong enough to withstand many of the present-day pressures associated with population increase and mobility, the growth of the case economy and the adoption of new techniques of hunting using the shotgun and nylon nets. Many types of wildlife are becoming scarce and their continued existence threatened. In addition, large areas of forests have been destroyed by the activities of shifting cultivators, logging companies and commercial agricultural projects. Traditional controls are no longer sufficient to deal with these threats; new approaches have proved necessary.

Customary Land Tenure in Papua New Guinea

CONSERVATION MEASURES

The main piece of specialist legislation protecting
wildlife has been the Fauna (Protection and Control)
Act. This provides for the declaration of protected
fauna which can only be hunted by the indigenous
inhabitants and then only by traditional methods and
for traditional purposes. The Act also provides for
the establishment of sanctuaries, protected areas
and wildlife management areas.
    In wildlife management areas, the land remains
in the possession of the customary landowners who
form their own management committee which makes
rules to control the hunting of wildlife within the
designated boundaries of the area. Altogether
thirteen management areas have been declared and
many more have been proposed but not yet gazetted.
The first management area to be established was at
Tonda in Western Province. This is an area rich in
wildlife where the local people have made rules
restricting hunting by outsiders. Any visitors must
buy a licence or pay fees if they wish to hunt deer,
shoot duck or go fishing.
    Other wildlife management areas are at Pokili
and Garu in West New Britain. Here the main aim is
to protect the breeding grounds of the megapodes
who lay their eggs in the warm sands near volcanic
springs. These eggs have traditionally been a source
of food and income for the local people; they became
worried about over-collection, hunting of the birds
and the destruction of their habitat by tree-
felling. The rules of these areas now forbid shot
guns, dogs and logging in the breeding areas; the
number of eggs collected is controlled and outsiders
are not allowed to take any.
    Some wildlife management areas are designed to
protect marine resources. One at Maza in the Western
Province is concerned with the control of dugong
hunting; another on Long Island aims to protect
turtles from over-exploitation.
    The great advantage of wildlife management
areas is that local people are involved in their
initiation and management; they are not imposed by
the government from outside. There are no problems
of transfer of land, all rights are retained by the
customary owners. The procedures involved are sufficiently flexible to allow each area to be treated
as a separate case and for rules to be drawn up
according to the particular local problems. Their
main limitation would seem to be that although they
may be very effective in restricting the activities

184

of outsiders, they do not always provide rigid
enough controls over hunting by members of the group
themselves.

In addition to the Fauna (Protection and Control) Act, other environmental legislation includes
three acts passed by Parliament in 1978. The Environmental Planning Act requires developers to
submit a plan outlining the environmental impact of
any project they propose to put into effect. The
Environmental Contaminants Act was intended to prevent and control different forms of pollution. Unfortunately neither of these acts has been fully
implemented although development plans for large-
scale projects now usually have an environmental
content. These may include the setting aside of
certain areas as reserves for the protection of a
particular species.

One example of these reserves is to be found
in the Kumusi timber project in the Northern Province. Here three parts of the timber rights purchase
area have been set aside to preserve the habitat of
the Queen Alexandra Birdwing, the world's largest
butterfly. A fortunate factor in this case is that
the vine which is the butterfly's only source of
food grows best in secondary forest which is not the
most productive area for logging. A problem with
this and other protected areas in timber projects
is that the owners of the reserves will have to
forgo the royalties which are paid to their neighbours. The question arises here, as in other types
of conservation areas, as to whether customary landowners should receive any compensation in return for
forgoing the financial benefits that might accrue
to them from the development of their resources.

The third piece of legislation, the Environmental Planning Areas Act, was passed in 1978. This
provided for conservation of sites and areas having
"particular biological, topographical, geographical,
scientific or social importance". Under the Act
land would not change ownership but it would be
administered by a management committee on which the
customary landowners would be represented. Any
development which would alter the existing use of
land in a conservation area is forbidden unless it
has the approval of the Minister for Environment and
Conservation. No conservation areas have yet been
declared, mainly it seems because of shortage of
staff to carry out the initial work of investigation
and establishment of the areas. There also still
seems to be some confusion over the function and
status of these areas in relation to the existing

national park system.

NATIONAL PARKS

The first areas to be renewed for national parks in Papua New Guinea were the McAdam Park in 1962 and Variarata in 1963. Both were placed under the supervision of the National Parks Board when it was established in 1967. Since then several smaller parks have been declared under different classifications. Two small islands off East New Britain coast, nanuk and Talele, have been designated as a provincial park and a nature reserve respectively. A two hectare area at Cape Wom, which was the site of the Japanese surrender in the country at the end of the Second World War, has been declared an international memorial park. Another historical site associated with the war has been gazetted at Namenatabu near Port Moresby. Other types of park are the Kokoda Trail Walking Track and the Baiyer River Sanctuary; the latter is important for its collection of birds of paradise and other indigenous fauna.

The first full national parks, Variarata and McAdam, were established on what was considered to be government land, but this has not always presented land disputes which have affected their development. McAdam provides a good example of the problems that may arise due to conflicting land rights. This park occupies an area of 2,080 ha on the western side of the Bulolo River Valley. It is of particular interest because of its natural vegetation of hoop and klinki pine. In the past its steep and precipitous topography had been a deterrent to both shifting cultivation and to commercial logging operations. The land was in fact originally part of an area acquired by the colonial government as being "waste and vacant". After self-government it was decided that compensation would be paid to local people who had claims to historical ownership of the land. The prospect of a cash settlement stimulated three groups to assert rival claims to the land on the grounds that their ancestors had fought, hunted and made gardens in the area. Attempts at arbitration failed and eventually the case went before a local land court where, after much deliberation, it was decided that any payments should be divided between the three groups.

Other problems in McAdam were caused by mining activities. Gold is mined in a series of small-scale operations from the alluvial sands and gravel along the valley of the Bulolo River. This has caused some confusion concerning park boundaries. At one time the boundary ran along the river and included some of the areas leased for mining, but it has now been amended to exclude them. Problems have still arisen when miners have illegally squatted on park land and cleared forest to make gardens. A threat from mining interests on a rather larger scale occurred when the large Australian corporation, Broken Hill Proprietory, applied for a prospecting licence in an area which included the park, but this application was withdrawn after opposition from the National Parks Board.

In Variarata National Park, extension of the park area has been prevented by the local Koiari people who have disputed the government's title to land adjacent to the park. There have also been problems of burning the forest in the park area.

Most of the new areas proposed for national parks are on land at present held under customary systems of tenure. This involves either outright purchase by the government or some type of lease from the customary landowners. The initial procedures involved are similar in that they both require investigation, negotiation, survey and evaluation of the land. Nevertheless, leasing does have a number of very distinct advantages. The local landowning group will not feel they are losing their land permanently. They should maintain an interest in park area and its development; in some cases, such as Mount Gahavisuka in the Eastern Highlands, they have expressed an interest in taking over the management when the lease comes to an end. Financially, it means that the initial costs to the government are reduced, while the customary landowners are guaranteed a regular income from the rent. Under the lease arrangements the customary owners may also be allowed to retain certain traditional rights. Examples of these that have been discussed in relation to proposed parks include crocodile hunting in Lake Dakataua, fern collecting on Mount Wilhelm and fishing on Horseshoe Reef. The problem that would seem to arise here is to determine to what extent the maintenance of these traditional rights is compatible with the conservation aims of the park. Should they be extended to include rights to clear and burn areas of bush? Generally, it has been felt that the low population densities in the areas affected should allow multiple land use without conflict between declaration of the park should prevent major damage to its resources which might occur through mining, timber projects, industry or commercial agricultural development.

At present, the effectiveness of lease arrangements cannot be fully evaluated. Negotiations to establish a provincial park at Mount Gahavisuka in the Eastern Highlands seem to have been successful. In the case of Mount Wilhel, the highest mountain in Papua New Guinea, the negotiations to lease the area have been abandoned and instead the National Parks Board decided on outright purchase. Frequently, lease arrangements have met with delays and obstacles, as in the following case study of a proposed national park at Lake Dakataua.

LAKE DAKATAUA

Lake Dakataua is located in the northern part of the Willaumez Peninsula in West New Britain. It is a caldera lake in an area of volcanic activity; natural features include hot springs, mud flows and dormant volcanoes. The main natural vegetation is lowland rain forest and there is a variety of wildlife which includes crocodiles in the lake.

The area around the lake is sparsely populated. The main village is called Bulu Miri and it has about 150 inhabitants. The people live mainly by subsistence agriculture, hunting and fishing; shell collecting is also a source of income.

In nearby areas of West New Britain there had been considerable economic development associated with the timber industry and oil palm growing. It was feared that the unique natural environment of the area around the lake might be destroyed unless measures were taken to protect it.

Original suggestions for a park included both Lake Dakataua and Mount Bola to the south, but the latter was excluded because timber rights had already been purchased for part of the area. Investigations began in 1974 when a meeting was held between National Parks officers and the customary landowners at Bulu Muri village. Leaders of three clans and nine sub-clans were present and they agreed to lease land to the Government for a park.

In 1975, a submission was made to the Cabinet by Mr Stephen Tago, who was then Minister for the Environment and Conservation. It proposed a park of approximately 10,350 ha which would include the lake and the land around it. Other government departments were consulted and raised few objections;

there were not thought to be any valuable minerals or other resources in the area.

At this stage, when it seemed likely that the park would be established, a group of local landowners started to protest against it. They seem to have been led by a local government councillor who had been absent from the meeting when the park was first discussed. It was decided that the Minister himself should visit the area. He held another meeting at the village, attended by about a hundred people, and left satisfied that all had agreed to the park. There did, however, still seem to have been some doubts among the landowners. Among the questions they asked were:

a) Would they or the government get the entrance fees from the visitors to the park?
b) How long would their land be alienated for?
c) Would the National Parks Board build a road to the park from the nearest town, Talasea?
d) Would their traditional rights to hunting be allowed?

Only a week after the meeting, a group of 11 men visited the office of the Provincial Commissioner and expressed their concern about their lack of knowledge and understanding in relation to the proposed park development. The National Parks Board was again asked to send an officer to hold another meeting with the people. The Board was not able to send anybody at that time because of shortages of staff and travel funds, and since then there has been little progress in establishing the park.

The Lake Dakataua case does illustrate some of the difficulties in negotiations with customary landowners. There is the need for general agreement with the group to the transfer of land. There are problems caused if landowners are absent during the early investigations and meetings. There are obstacles caused by dissension within the group and political aspirations among its members. There is also the difficulty that the landowners may have in understanding the implications of park development and natural resource conservation. The landowner may perceive the establishment of a park as a means by which he can get greater benefit from the resources of the area. In addition to the rent or purchase price, there may be income from tourists or from employment in the park. There may also be the opportunity to obtain roads and other forms of service. However, if other types of development,

such as a timber project, seem to offer greater
monetary rewards and services, then it is inevitable
that many rural people from poor and disadvantaged
areas will prefer this type of development. The
need to protect wildlife is understood, but the
establishment of a conservation area is often seen
as something which protects the animals and birds
from the depredations of outsiders and not something
which affects their own hunting rights.

The education and extension role of National
Parks officers is obviously important in helping to
explain the objectives and implications of park
development. There is a need for full discussion
during investigations and to follow these up when
problems arise. Lack of staff and finance have too
often been restraints in preventing park investigation and establishment.

CONCLUSIONS

The problems and delays that have occurred in attempts to acquire or lease customary land, make it
worthwhile examining alternative methods by which
parks may be developed. There have, for example,
been cases where local groups have expressed an
interest in making gifts of parts of the land to be
developed as parks. This has occurred at Mount
Brown and Mount Miria in Central Province, although
the inaccessibility of these mountains has to date
prevented any further development.

Outright gifts will probably be rare, but
another possibility is that customary groups should
retain their ownership rights but allow the park
authority to develop footpaths and other facilities.
The landowners could be involved in park development, which would provide some employment and
income. The scenery, natural vegetation and wildlife could be preserved by means of agreements and
by-laws restricting other forms of land use. Wildlife management areas already provide a precedent
for this in Papua New Guinea; the customary landowners maintain their rights but agree on rules to
hunting and other forms of wildlife exploitation.

In many countries national parks have been developed on privately owned land, there is no reason
why they should not be established on customary
owned land. There would be a need for full agreement and understanding between the park authorities
and landowners on the rights involved. These might
well allow the customary owners to retain their

cultivation, hunting and food collection rights, while the park authorities are given the right to develop footpaths and other facilities, with visitors having rights of access to the park. If a zoning system of land use was also a feature of park management, there could be provisions for a wilderness reserve area in which there would be no disturbance of the natural environment.

Parks on customary land could be started at relatively low costs to the Government and with the minimum disturbance of the traditional economy and systems of tenure. At the same time it would be development compatible with the fourth national goal as expressed in the Constitution: "... for Papua New Guinea's natural resources and environment to be conserved and used for the collective benefit of us all, and be replenished for future generations".

Chapter Thirteen

TRADITIONAL MARINE RESOURCE MANAGEMENT
IN THE PACIFIC

By

Gary A. Klee
Associate Professor of Environmental Studies
San Jose State University
San Jose, CA 95192, USA

ABSTRACT

Many South Pacific islanders possessed and continue
to possess a wealth of environmental knowledge, including traditional systems of resource management.
Traditional conservation practices of many South
Pacific cultures were once highly effective, and,
if supported or adapted to modern conditions, could
continue to be so. What follows is a brief overview
of various cultural practices that have traditionally affected marine resource management in the
Pacific.

INTRODUCTION

The types and importance of marine conservation in
Oceania dwarfs all other forms of traditional conservation practices - as one might expect of peoples
who live along the margins of the sea. In most areas
of the Pacific, fishing, the gathering of shellfish,
the hunting of different kinds of sea mammals, and
the capture of turtles constituted an important
source of protein which supplements a diet of terrestrial plants and animals. These aquatic resources
were safeguarded by a variety of means: (1) a high
degree of environmental awareness, (2) skilled conservation officers and master fishermen, (3) a
complex system of marine tenure, (4) a variety of
magico-religious taboos, enforced by (5) strict
fines and punishment, and (6) a variety of methods
to conserve sea foods[1].

Environmental knowledge was central to most forms
of traditional conservation practices in Oceania.
The native islanders by necessity lived close to

nature and had the ability to read the diurnal, monthly, and seasonal cycles of their environment. To the Polynesian, Micronesian, and Melanesian, the heavens and the phases of nature served as a clock and calendar to be read and sometimes acted upon. The position of the sun, the rising and setting of the stars, the waxing and waning of the noon, the ebb and flow of the tide, the changing wind directions, the height of the breakers on the reef, the natural smell within the village, the seasonal variances of terrestrial flora and fauna, and the aquatic cycles, all served as a system of time reckoning, and, consequently played a major role in the understanding of life histories, mating seasons, habitat requirements, and other basic knowledge of the plants and animals within their environment.

With this high degree of environmental awareness, many island cultures were able to regulate their harvest and use of wild plants and animals on a sustained yield basis. Daily activities were geared to the cycles of nature. Fishing, being the most cyclical of human activities, was carried out according to the reading of the heavens as well as the phases of nature. The moon, tides, stars, and fish migrations had a direct bearing on the movement and activities of island fishermen. Since the reef, lagoon, and sea were primarily the domain and habitat of the men, it was natural that the men led a life that was closest to the cycles of nature.

Although the women would occasionally comb the tidal flats for shellfish, sea urchins, sea cucumbers and some varieties of small fish, their activities were primarily concentrated on the land in the cultivation of taro, an activity that varies little with the seasons.

Master fishermen who acted as fisheries' ecologists and conservation officers were predominant in Polynesia, Micronesia, and Melanesia[2]. In the Lau Islands, for example, R. Allen records the following interesting passage[3]:

> Each of the Lau Islands also enjoyed the service of a _ndau ni nggoli_, a master fisherman and authority on the island's fish lore and fishing techniques. The master fisherman's job was to act as a fisheries' ecologist, studying the habits of all the edible marine species, the state of the fishing grounds, the incidence of toxic plants that might render fish poisonous, and all other matters

affecting fisheries. No large, organized fishing parties were formed without his permission, and he led all communal turtle hunts. The master fisherman thus protected the island's marine resources from over-exploitation, and by taking advantage of his knowledge of the optimum conditions for fishing, ensured an optimum take.

Marine tenure systems that placed restrictions on geographic area, season, specific species, and food type helped regulate the harvesting of aquatic resources.

Fishing rights to specific areas surrounding an island were often controlled by local chiefs or simply claimed as their own personal property[4]. In the former case, islanders would have to ask permission of the chief to fish in the lagoon, on the reef, and out at sea. In the latter case, villagers were completely restricted from the chief's choice fishing spots. In both cases, some form of regulation was involved.

The opening and closing of fishing seasons was also a tool in managing marine exploitation. Sometimes the restriction was for economic reasons to allow a depleted supply to recover or to conserve the supply for some festival in the near future[5]. At other times, it was applied as a mark of respect in the death of the ruler or some other ethnical or religious purpose[6]. Closed seasons were also applied to reserve particular aquatic life for the ruler or chiefs[7].

Specific species regulation was also incorporated into traditional tenure schemes of marine management. During their spawning season, specific fish such as albacore, bonito, and rock cod were protected in the Society Islands[8]. P.H. Buck records the regulation of more exotic aquatic life, such as the octopus, in the Mangareva Islands. In order to keep this "royal fish" in abundant supply, the Mangareva islanders would erect a tree branch as a sign to warn others that particular islet on the outer reef was restricted territory for octopus fishing. After a closed period of time, a master fisherman would then gather some octopuses and present them to the king. The restriction was then withdrawn[9].

Food avoidances also played a role in maintaining aquatic resources. Some species could only be eaten by chiefs, or chiefs and priests[10]. In other cases, certain animals were restricted to

members of particular tribes, each tribe having a
few such restricted species[11]. Food avoidances
according to one's sex or class were also prevalent
in the Pacific. In the Marquesas Islands, for
example, yam, coconut, breadfruit, and most kinds
of fish were free to everyone; but bananas, pigs,
and such marine life as turtle, cuttle-fish, bonito
and albacore were off limits to women and lower
class men[12].

Most marine tenure systems were integrally
dependent upon the political authority of village
elders and were buttressed by a set of ethical rules
proclaimed by the religious leaders within the community. Areal, seasonal, specific species, and food
restrictions placed on aquatic resources were reinforced by a complex set of magico-religious
taboos. Taboos could be issued in the form of
chieftain decrees, clan taboos, or private ownership
taboos[13].

In the latter case, those villagers who privately owned sections of a reef would periodically
institute taboos on fishing to allow the fish to
multiply[14]. Master fishermen often ruled the
sea by tabooing fishing at certain times; these traditional "fisheries ecologists" had power beyond
that of mere advising[15].

In addition to the taboos dealing with areal,
seasonal, specific species, and aquatic food resource, taboos were also placed on the reef, lagoon,
or sea for a variety of other reasons. Taboos were
decreed to regulate the numbers of fishermen on the
reef at any one particular time. For example, the
fishermen of Ngake Village in Pukapuka would an-
nounce that they might fish in the lagoon for one
night. For that period the lagoon was taboo (off
limits) to all other villages except Ngake; other
villages got their turn to harvest the reef on subsequent nights[16]. Taboos were issued placing
regulations on the first fishing expeditions of the
season[17]. On the death of a king or clan member, the sea was declared taboo and fishing was
prohibited[18]. Taboos even existed that barred
women from participating in particular types of
fishing[19].

To illustrate the close relationship between
tenure system (in this example, reef rights in the
Marshall Islands) and the workings of magico-
religious belief systems, the following select pass-
ages are provided from J.E. Tobin's field work in
Micronesia[20]:

Throughout the Marshalls the reefs were claimed by the _iroij_ (king or paramount chief) as _emo_ (forbidden, taboo) or personal property if the fishing was good around them... After this taboo was instituted, no one else was permitted to fish that particular reef... Other people were afraid to disobey the taboo until it was lifted by government edict... Small islands were also occasionally tabooed, e.g. Kaben, a small island with a few trees on it on Wotto Atoll, was taken by the _iroij_ for his personal use because of the abundance of coconut crabs on it. _Emo_ (forbidden) fishing sites were in existence on every atoll.

These magico-religious taboos that governed Pacific island tenure systems were enforced by strict fines and punishment. Offenders could sometimes expect severe if not fatal punishment for what seems a trifling matter. In Pukapuka, E. Beaglehole recorded that trespassers in a fishing reserve which belonged to another village might be punished by fines in nuts levied by the guards of the village whose reef was violated[21]. If one trespassed on tabooed fishing reserves in the Marshall Islands, one could expect the penalty of death or expulsion from the island[22]. Severe punishments of taboo violations were recorded in Hawaii and Mangareva, as well as many other islands throughout the Pacific region[23]. These penalties for breaking taboos held the people in strict obedience.

The conservation of sea foods was the final major means by which Pacific islanders conserved their aquatic resources. Traps and fish ponds were used to capture, raise, and maintain fish or turtle crop until needed or until they reached the desired size. Taro fields were also used to provide an area in which shrimp and small fish were maintained[24].

Food preservation methods were widespread and helped stretch the available supply of aquatic resources. Basically, three methods were used: sun drying, smoking, salting, or combinations of salting, soaking in brine, and sun drying[25].

INADVERTENT V. RECOGNIZED CONSERVATION PRACTICES

A good number of the above-mentioned techniques were employed consciously and explicitly for conservation

purposes. However, a number of practices were frequently bound up in religious and social rituals
and customs, and, consequently, were not actually
recognized for their conservation qualities. Other
practices were only sometimes carried out for their
conserving qualities.

Marine resources were conserved by using such
clearly recognized practices as using an overseer
of fisheries resources, restricting the harvesting
of specific species, restricting the numbers of
fishermen on a reef at any one time, conserving sea
foods through traps and fish ponds, preserving sea
foods by sun drying, smoking, salting, and using a
system of taboos for restricting purposes, and using
a system of fines and punishment for offenders.

Clearly inadvertent practices that conserved
aquatic resources were those such as restricting the
eating of certain foods to certain social classes,
sexes, or clans, prohibiting fishing on the death
of an important individual, and prohibiting women
from particular types of fishing.

Certain practices such as allocating fishing
rights to specific areas, and the opening and closing of fishing seasons were sometimes but not always
initiated for the purpose of conserving resources.
In the first case, fishing rights to specific areas
were often claimed by local chiefs for strictly
selfish reasons. On the other hand, master fishermen sometimes controlled fishing rights in an area
for the express purpose of regulating the exploitation of aquatic resources. In the second case,
the opening and closing of fishing seasons was sometimes done for the express purpose of allowing a
depleted supply to recover; other times, this
measure was merely instituted as a religious sign
of respect for a dead ruler.

DEGREE OF EFFECTIVENESS

Examination of past forms of traditional marine resource management in Oceania would seem to indicate
that most of the region's peoples were effective
conservationists. Several authors have specifically
cited the effectiveness of traditional marine conservation techniques[26]. Robert Johannes, a marine
biologist, states the problem most clearly:

> "But did these practices really work?" it
> might be asked. Certainly not all of them
> worked, any more than all western conser-

vation measures work. But I am confident
that some did work. The inhabitants of
Oceania have had centuries to test these
measures by trial and error. Even in
Hawaii, where the fishermen, by virtue of
their more intense contact with the West,
have probably lost more of their traditional marine lore than elsewhere in
Oceania, their knowledge of marine ecology
clearly surpasses that of the marine biologist in some ways. I went as a consult-
ant to a fishermen's meeting in Hawaii a
few months ago and came away having
learned more from them than they learned
from me27/.

REVIVING, REINFORCING, AND/OR MODIFYING
TRADITIONAL CONSERVATION PRACTICES

It is possible to hypothesize about the lapsed or
dying-out attitudes and practices that might be
revived, reinforced, and/or modified. Such marine
conservation practices as fishing seasons, specific
species regulation, traps and fish ponds, and
methods of food preservation could probably be
revived and/or reinforced within an area without
too much difficulty or modification.

However, re-establishing the degree of environmental awareness, the concept of "master fisherman",
fishing rights to specific geographic areas, magico-
religious taboos, and related fines and punishment
would often require a high degree of modification
to fit present-day conditions. For example, the
"conservation ethic" behind an indigenous religion
might be revived and reinforced without doing the
same for the magical aspects (i.e. many Christians
support the Ten Commandments without actually be-
lieving or supporting the origin of these ideas).
The severity of fines and punishment might also be
modified a bit to meet universally excepted humani-
tarian standards.

Food avoidance based on class or sexual differences probably could not (and should not) be
revived or reinforced: the notion of equality, as
well as ethnic pride, is sweeping throughout the
islands. However, if food avoidances according to
class or sex lines remains to some degree in a particular culture, the practice should not be discouraged for it does play a role in conserving resources.

CONCLUSION

These older, long-standing systems of conservation and resource management have much to teach the modern-day resource manager. First and foremost, the modern-day resource manager can heighten his own awareness of the local environment by mentally combining two culturally different temporal frameworks. By fusing his own system of time-reckoning (the Swiss watch and the Gregorian calendar) with that of the indigenous culture's system (the movement of the sun, moon, stars, tides, and so on), the modern-day resource manager can see the heavens and the phases of nature in new perspective.

To be more specific, the western marine biologist can learn a variety of types of information, such as the lunar periodicity of the spawning of fish; the location and traditional regulation of marine preserves; the fishing grounds used by a particular village; the effect of rainfall, winds, currents, and temperature on fishing conditions and the habits of certain fish; the times, places, and seasons of optimum fishing; the peculiarities of different islands and different parts of the coasts of larger islands on fish habits and migration; the incidence of toxic plants that might render fish poisonous; the traditional regulations regarding fishing rights, closed seasons, and specific species; the optimum days for particular fishing techniques; the construction and proper use of traps and ponds for fish conservation; the various methods of fish preservation; the traditional conservation ethic; and related fines and punishment. According to E.S.C. Handy and others, "the experienced native fisherman is possessed of a store of precise knowledge that may be truly characterized as natural science"[28].

Traditional conservation methods should be respected, emulated, and possibly preserved, not thoughtlessly replaced; little time remains to identify, record, and possibly preserve some of these traditional systems of conservation management.

REFERENCES

1. P.H. Buck. Ethnology on Mangareva (Honolulu. B. P. Bishop Museum Press, 1938), p.289; K.P. Emory. Kapingamauangi; Social and Religious Life of a Polynesian Atoll (Honolulu: B.P. Bishop

Museum Press, 1965), p. 345; and B. Malinowski, Soil-Tilling and Africultural Rites in the Trobriand Islands (Bloomington: India University Press, 1965), p. 51.

2. E.S.C. Handy. Houses, Boats, and Fishing in the Society Islands (Honolulu. B.P. Bishop Museum Press, 1932), p. 74; W.H. Alkire, "Lamotrek Atoll and Inter-Island Socio-economic Ties" in Illinois Studies in Anthropology (Urbana: University of Illinois Press, 1965), p. 69; and R. Allen, "Eco-development and Traditional Natural Resource Management in the South Pacific", paper presented at the Second Regional Symposium of Conservation of Nature, Apia, Western Samoa, 14-17 June 1976, p. 10 (mimeographed).

3. Allen, op. cit. footnote 2.

4. P.B. Sauder. "Guam: Land Tenure in a Fortress", in Land Tenure in the Pacific, ed. Ron Crocombe (Melbourne: Oxford University Press, 1971), p. 192; Handy, op. cit., footnote 2; and J.E. Tobin, "Land Tenure in the Marshall Islands", Atoll Research Bulletin (Washington, D.C.: Smithsonian Press, 1952), p. 11.

5. K.B. Cumberland and J.S. Whitelaw, New Zealand (Chicago: Aldine Publishing Company, 1970), p. 22: N. Meller and H. Horwitz, "Hawaii: Themes in Land Monopoly", in Land Tenure in the Pacific, ed. Ron Crocombe (Melbourne: Oxford University Press, 1971), p. 27; and M. Ticomb, Native Use of Fish in Hawaii (Honolulu: University of Hawaii Press, 1972), p. 13.

6. R.W. Williamson. The Social and Political Systems of Central Polynesia, (Cambridge University Press, 1924), p. 250.

7. Buck, op. cit., footnote 1, p. 161.

8. Handy, op. cit. footnote 2.

9. Buck, op. cit., footnote 1 p. 302

10. Meller and Horwitz, op. cit., footnote 5, p. 27; Williamson, op. cit., footnote 6, p.146; and E.S.C. Handy, Polynesian Religion (Honolulu: B.P. Bishop Museum Press, 1927, p. 129.

11. Handy, op. cit., footnote 2, p. 129.

12. Williamson, op. cit., footnote 6, p. 147; and M. Titcomb, op. cit., footnote 5 p. 11.

13. Alkire, op. cit., footnote 2; Handy, op. cit., footnote 2; and R.P. Owen, "The Status of Conservation in the Trust Territory of the Pacific Islands", Micronesia, Vol. 5. (1969), p. 303.

14. J.L. Fischer. The Eastern Carolines (Connecticut: Pacific Science Board in Association with the Human Relations Area Files, 1957), p. 139.

15. M. Mead. "The Samoans", in <u>Cooperation and Competition Among Primitive Peoples</u>, ed. M. Mead (Boston: Beacon Press, 1961), p. 291.

16. E. Beaglehole and P. Beaglehole. <u>Ethnology of Pukapuka</u> (Honolulu: B.P. Bishop Museum Press, 1938), p. 32.

17. Williamson, op. cit., footnote 6.

18. Buck, op. cit., footnote 1 p. 494; and Alkire, op., footnote 2.

19. Williamson, op. cit., footnote 6. 295.

20. Tobin, op. cit., footnote 4.

21. E. Beaglehole and P. Beaglehole. op. cit., footnote 16, p.33.

22. Tobin, op. cit., footnote 4.

23. Titcomb, op. cit., footnote 5, p. 13; and Buck, op. cit., footnote 1, p.494.

24. F.M. Reinman. "Fishing: An Aspect of Oceanic Economy", Fieldiana: Anthropology, Vol. 56. (1967), p. 192.

25. Reinman, op. cit., footnote 24, pp. 192-193.

26. Allen, op. cit., footnote 2; Reinman, op. cit., footnote 24, pp. 192-193; and Owen, op. cit., footnote 13.

27. R.E. Johannes. "Exploitation and Degradation of Shallow Marine Food Resources in Oceania", in <u>The Impact of Urban Centers in the Pacific</u>, eds. R.W. Force and Brenda Bishop (Honolulu: Pacific Science Association, 1975), p. 60.

28. Handy, op. cit., footnote 2, p. 76.

Section Four

CONSERVATION AND ENVIRONMENTAL PLANNING
BY THE PEOPLE

INTRODUCTION

Thus far we have pointed to management systems that
work through and with the local people, and we have
emphasized the value of the traditional knowledge
base. At some point in the argument and the historical process, management ceases to be top-down
and the tasks of conservation are taken over by the
people. At this point, conservation reflects a
popular ideology and ethic. In many ways this is
the ideal goal seldom realized and we have very few
accounts of such success stories, nor do we know
what kinds of social contexts and dynamics favour
this process. Some experiences of conservation by
the people are presented here and a future task
should certainly be to encourage research and action
in this area.

Chapter Fourteen

PEOPLE, TREES AND ANTELOPES IN THE INDIAN DESERT

By

K.S. Sankhala
21 Duleshwar Garden
Jaipur 302 001, India
     and
Peter Jackson
CH-1171 Bougy, Switzerland

ABSTRACT

Wildlife has been decimated in the past half century
in most of India, and only recently have official
conservation programmes been successful in holding
the line. Even so, the plains that once swarmed with
antelope and gazelle are now barren - except in some
extensive tracts of the desert state of Rajasthan
and neighbouring areas where herds roam freely in
the fields and among the livestock of the Bishnoi
community. Four hundred years ago a young man of the
area perceived that protection of nature and wildlife was necessary for human welfare. His 29 principles of life, from which his followers took their
name of Bishnois or "Twentyniners", included a conservation ethic which has survived the centuries and
is as much a reality today as always.

When you travel west from Delhi the soil quickly
becomes sandier and the vegetation sparser. Patches
of sand become more frequent and larger, and there
are fewer trees. You are entering the Thar desert
and you could travel in these arid lands right
through Iran to the Middle East, where they join the
deserts of Arabia and continue across North Africa
to the shores of the Atlantic.
     The Thar was not always like this, for great
fossil tree trunks embedded in the soil show that
moister conditions existed tens of millions of years
ago. Even 100 years ago, when arid conditions
already held sway, trees, bushes and grasses adapted
to the climate spread across the landscape, providing food, shade and shelter for vast herds of blackbuck (the Indian antelope, <u>Antilope</u> <u>cervicapra</u>) and
gazelles (Chinkara or Indian gazelle, <u>Gazella</u>

gazella), for wolves, foxes, hares, eagles, buz-
zards, falcons, bustards, sandgrouse and a host of
other animals. The human population consisted of
Bhils, hunter-gatherers whose origin is lost in the
mists of time, and the Aryan Hindus, who arrived
some 3,000 years ago with their herds of cattle,
sheep and goats, and pushed the Bhils into less
favourable areas.

The grazing and browsing herds increased in
numbers and ravaged the vegetation, eating the
leaves and grasses, seeds and seedlings, while large
trees fell to the axe. The advance of the desert
accelerated; the capacity of the land to withstand
the periodical droughts diminished; and long migrations became necessary to find fodder in hard
times. In the past century the wildlife has been
hunted nearly to extinction, particularly since the
Second World War, when firearms proliferated and
the go-anywhere jeep opened up vast areas which
were formerly difficult of access and had served as
refuges for the wild animals.

The traveller reflecting on this sad story as
he passes through the barren land will suddenly be
brought up short by what seems a vision. A herd of
blackbuck grazes peacefully near the roadside;
chinkara nibble at bushes; a covey of partridges
scurries across the road; and he realizes that real
trees cover the landscape, which is dotted with
villages and farms. In a devastated world it seems
unbelievable. But it is real. This is the land of
the Bishnois, a Hindu sect for whom protection of
trees and wild animals is a religious duty.

Such a vision confronted me when I drove into
the Thar desert with Kailash Sankhala, Rajasthan's
Chief Wildlife Warden. I was eager to photograph
the blackbuck and chinkara in these idyllic surroundings, but as we manoeuvred into position a
woman emerged from a nearby house and shepherded
the animals away from us. We were surrounded by
men and boys, who demanded to know who we were, and
why we were "harrying" the herds. Fortunately, we
were able to explain that we were wildlife conservationists, and expressed our pleasure at seeing
how well wild animals and trees were cared for in
that area. I say "fortunate" because the Bishnois
have been known to assault, and even kill poachers.
With our credentials established we were hospitably
received and invited to join in refreshments.

And there I learned more of the remarkable
Bishnois. In the late 15th century a young man
named Jambeshwar, who was the son of the headman of

the village of Pipasar, grew up fascinated by the nature around him. When herding the family cattle he lay in the shade of the trees and watched with wonder the graceful antics of the blackbuck and chinkara. Already much destruction of the vegetation had taken place, and, when droughts came, food for man and livestock became scarce. As conditions worsened during one prolonged drought he realized that humans had themselves contributed to their plight by cutting trees and allowing their cattle, sheep and goats to overwhelm the vegetation. The wild animals he loved were hunted down for food. But still people and livestock starved.

Jamboji, as the young man was familiarly known, had a vision in which he saw man bringing disaster on himself by destroying nature. It led him to renounce his inheritance and undertake a mission to teach people to care for their health and environment. Jamboji enunciated 29 principles for living, and his followers became known as Bishnois or "Twentyniners".

The 29 principles set out forms of worship, including prayer, fasting and sacrifice of grain and ghee (clarified butter) to fire, the symbol of God. They prescribe hygiene through daily bathing, purification of water, and non-acceptance of food from unpurified people. Menstruating women must not do household work. A Bishnoi should refrain from eating meat, from taking drugs of all kinds, and renounce anger, desire and illicit sex.

Among the principles are three which demonstrate Jamboji's extraordinary environmental perception - Bishnois are enjoined to love all forms of life, to protect beneficial animals, and not to cut living trees.

Jamboji's preaching had immediate impact and his following grew quickly. Today there are tens of thousands of practising Bishnois. The men dress in white and sport large turbans to protect their heads from the hot sun. Women favour red and make a colourful sight as they gather at the village wells or work in the fields.

Bishnois today may not live up to all Jamboji's precepts - for instance, they are not above enjoying a dab of opium on their tongues when taking tea - but their environment shows that they have certainly protected animals and trees for centuries, while destruction continued all around.

The handsome Bishnoi women once demonstrated their convictions in a truly remarkable way. In 1730 the Maharajah Ajit Singh decided to build a

People and Wildlife in Indian Desert

new palace of the local red sandstone on the tower-
ing rocks of Jodhpur. Lime was needed for construction, and therefore wood to fuel the kilns. There
were few trees around, however, except in the
Bishnoi village of Khejadali, about 30 km from
Jodhpur, and the Maharaja's men headed there.

When they announced that they had come to cut
trees the Bishnois forbade them because they were
protected by their religion. Back in Jodhpur, the
Maharaja's minister, the Dewan, was enraged and
ordered the work to proceed. A confrontation
between the Maharajah's men and the Bishnois ensued,
and when the axemen moved in on the trees, one of
the Bishnoi women, Amrita Devi, rushed forward with
three of her daughters and hugged the trees to protect them. The axemen were disconcerted, but the
angry Dewan ordered them to go ahead and cut down
the trees - and the women with them. They did so
and the women's blood flowed. Far from being in-
timidated, more Bishnoi women rushed forward to hug
trees and were cut down in their turn. Legend has
it that 363 Bishnois sacrificed their lives for
their trees.

The Bishnois' mass sacrifice may sound incred-
ible, but it comes from an area where such actions
were not uncommon. There are several instances
when Rajput warriors, when all was lost, sallied
forth in saffron wedding robes to die in battle
against Muslim invaders, while their women threw
themselves on huge funeral pyres.

(Incidentally, the reverberations of the
Bishnois' action have echoed into the present day,
for their actions inspired the Chipko (hugging)
movement to save trees and prevent erosion in the
Himalayas, which has been one of the dramatic
people's movements for conservation in India.)

Maharajah Ajit Singh was horrified when he
heard what had happened and rode out to Khejadali
to apologize to the Bishnois. His promise to respect
their religious beliefs was inscribed on copper
plate and decreed punishment for those who cut trees
or killed animals. Bishnois were authorized to
challenge hunters, including members of the Royal
Family, and could even be excused killing them.
They exercise that right to tackle suspected
poachers even today - some Army officers have been
prosecuted, a team from All India Radio was attacked
after one of them fired a shot in Bishnoi territory,
and some poachers have actually been lynched.

Today a small white-washed shrine at Khejadali
stands at the site of the episode. Inside, an oil

lamp burns before a garlanded portrait of a white-bearded Jamboji, and nearby stands a gnarled survivor of the trees which were cut down. Every year during the September full moon there is a five-day fair where tens of thousands of Bishnois gather to commemorate their community's great sacrifice. A roped-off patch of earth marks the spot where the victims of the massacre were buried, and water is poured on it from pitchers as a tribute. It is noteworthy that, unlike most other Hindus, Bishnois do not cremate their dead, because that would require cutting down trees for the funeral pyre.

Undoubtedly the greatest tribute to the Bishnois is the flourishing land in which they live in the midst of the Thar desert in Rajasthan and extending into neighbouring Haryana and Madhya Pradesh states. Groves of khejdi trees (Prosopis cinerea) dot the landscape. To Bishnois this is "Kalpa vraksha" - the tree that fulfils all wishes - providing shade, fodder for livestock, and pods which make a delicious curry. Of all trees it is the most sacred to Bishnois.

In the fields bounded by thorny khejdi branches are the cattle which are the mainstay of the Bishnois, and among them roam blackbuck and chinkara. As evening comes a desert fox may be seen chasing a black-naped hare. Jackals howl in chorus, to the satisfaction of the Bishnois, who believe that when that eerie sound is no longer to be heard, a village is doomed. One might even see a wolf, that most persecuted and rare of animals.

The Moghul Emperor, Akbar the Great, recorded his amazement at the wealth of wildlife in Bishnoi areas in the 16th century. It is even more remarkable today, when the blackbuck, which swarmed over much of the Indian plains only half a century ago, has been virtually wiped out elsewhere and survives only in a handful of small reserves. In just one part of Jodhpur district there are 10,000 blackbuck and 8,000 chinkara, while similar concentrations can be seen in many other areas, roaming freely in the fields as the Bishnois go about their daily routine.

The Bishnois are by no means a primitive community. Tractors are to be seen everywhere and motorcycles are a common means of transport on the dusty roads. Bishnois are prominent in business, the civil service and politics - Bishnois have been Chief Ministers of Rajasthan and of Haryana. They have formed an All India Bishnoi Jeev Raksha (Life Protection) Committee, for which they elected

Kailash Sankhala as Chairman, on the grounds that he has been one of Rajasthan's great protectors of nature throughout his career in the Forest Service, even if not actually a Bishnoi. The Committee has awarded prizes for outstanding wildlife conservation work, the recipients having included the Field Director of the Ranthambhor Tiger Reserve, Fateh Singh Rathore, and the Chief Wildlife Warden of Kashmir, Mir Inayatullah.

Religious faith has faded in many parts of the world, even to some extent in parts of India, where generally it remains strong. But there is no sign of weakening among the Bishnois, a community which realizes that the natural world and its wildlife are an essential requirement for human welfare.

Chapter Fifteen

INTERACTIONS BETWEEN PEOPLE AND FORESTS IN EAST KALIMANTAN

By

A.P. Vayda, Carol J. Pierce Colfer
and Mohamad Brotokusumo (*)

ABSTRACT

The paper points to many myths in understanding how local people react to changing circumstances. Too often a pessimistic model has been used and we have not recognized the creativity that is inherent often in people's relationship with both the environment and the outside. A situational model may be most useful both to explain and guide future policy. The paper documents situations in interactions between people and tropical forests in East Kalimantan and stresses the role of human flexibility, creativity and responsiveness.

INTRODUCTION

East Kalimantan is a large, economically booming Indonesian province on the island of Borneo. It covers a total land area of 21,144,000 ha or about 11% of the total land area of Indonesia. Natural forest accounts for 17,292,000 ha of East Kalimantan's land. Tropical rain forests are among the last remaining reserves of economically valuable land in the world[1]/, and East Kalimantan has, predictably, become a prime target for development.
The potential timber volume of East Kalimantan's production forest is about 530 million cubic metres of commercially exportable timber and about 270 million cubic metres of non-exportable timber[2]/. Stimulated by such factors as the greatly

---

(*) A version of this paper appeared in "Impact of Science on Society", Vol. 30, No. 3, 1980.

increased Japanese demand for tropical hardwoods
and the passage of Indonesian laws conducive to
foreign investment in the forestry sector3/, 4/,
logging in East Kalimantan developed quickly after
1967. Of the almost 13 million ha of production
forest allocated for mechanical logging, about 2
million have already been logged, and there are now
some 100 timber concessionaires operating in East
Kalimantan.

This rapid development in logging has led to
extensive ecological and social disruptions, including some associated with movements of people at-
tracted by the economic boom. Sixty-two per cent
of the increase from a population of 725,000 in East
Kalimantan in 1971 to 960,000 in 1976 resulted from
immigration from other provinces; many more migrants, especially farmers from the island of
Sulawesi (Celebes), have come since the new road
between East Kalimantan's two largest cities,
Samarinda and Balikpapan, was opened to the public
in 19765/. Because of the rapidity with which
social and ecological changes are occurring in East
Kalimantan, it has become urgent to make forest management in the province more effective and to combine it with development that benefits the people
who live in or by the forest and use it.

Policy-makers attempting to achieve these objectives have been handicapped by the lack of information on existing uses of forests by people in East
Kalimantan. Such information is especially needed
to enhance the social and ecological soundness of
policies with respect to the following:

- Containing, eliminating, or improving shifting cultivation, depending on the various
  forms it takes and consequences it has.
- Resettlement of forest-using people in East
  Kalimantan.
- The use of existing local-level knowledge and
  existing practice in agriculture, forest-
  product collection, and trade as foundations
  for integrated agroforestry (or forest-
  farming) development.
- The nature and extent of participation by
  people in their development and in the management of resources on which they depend.

Recognizing this need for information, Indonesian
and American social and biological scientists
jointly began a project of research in September
1979 entitled "Interactions between People and For-

ests in East Kalimantan". Broadly, this research, which is part of Indonesia's Man and Biosphere Programme[6]/, is intended to show: (a) the range of people's forest-related knowledge; (b) their repertoire of forest-related activities; (c) the variety of situations in which decisions to engage in those activities or to change them are made; and (d) the environmental and socio-economic effects that these activities have.

FOCI OF THE RESEARCH

Three main locations were chosen for the research because of the opportunities they afford for studying significant variations in shifting cultivation and other forest-related activities, and in the conditions under which they are practised. One location, the Apo Kayan, is a lofty interior plateau isolated from commercial centres and timber concessions in the lowlands by extensive and impassable river rapids. It is the home of nearly ten thousand Dayak people living in long-house communities, possessing a wealth of forest-related knowledge, and practising an apparently stable, long-fallow, forest-maintaining form of shifting cultivation.

A second location is the Telen River lowland area where settlements of Dayak migrants from the interior plateau were established prior to the timber boom and where the subsequent granting of timber concessions has led to further changes in the physical and socio-economic conditions to which th Dayak migrants are adapting. The third location is the vicinity of East Kalimantan's booming capital city of Samarinda. Lands along the new roads constructed by the Government and by timber companies have become readily accessible for the first time here, and the agriculture, practised in logged-over forests in the vicinity of Samarinda by newly arrived inter-island migrants as well as by long-established residents of East Kalimantan, includes the dry-field farming which, because of long cropping periods and/or short fallows, is apparently the most damaging to the tropical forest environment. In addition to the investigations specific to each of these locations, research is also proceeding in all of them (and along the trade routes connecting them) on the collection and trading of rattan, incense wood, and other so-called minor forest products. Explication of the rationale of this project calls for a discussion of the relationship between

our research and certain issues in development
theory and anthropology. It is appropriate to
review here three general models or views that have
been dominant at various times concerning the economic behaviour of such rural and tribal people who
are among the important subjects of research in the
project.

The first two of these models were formulated
and gained adherents largely in the absence of substantial information about the diversity, variability and situational specificity of the economic
behaviour in question, i.e. in the absence of the
kind of information being collected in this research
project. All three models or views may be said to
vary with respect to two important issues. These
are the rationality or irrationality of people's
behaviour, and their capacity for or resistance to
change. Important policy and research implications
of the models are discussed below.

A common but possibly now waning view portrays
rural and tribal people as unquestioning tradition-
alists, lacking in initiative and decision-making
capabilities, kept from modern technology either by
superstition and ignorance or by cultural barriers,
docile prisoners of age-old customs and magical or
mystical ideas that make them use their land irrationally and inefficiently[7]. In recent years
much evidence has accumulated to cast doubt on this
view[8], but many policy-makers, developers, and
researchers still subscribe to it[9].

A frequent concomitant of this view is an acceptance of a unilineal view of human history and
development. From this perspective, hinterland
people gaining their subsistence by hunting and
gathering are, for example, at an earlier, less
advanced stage of evolutionary development. The
policy implication of the view is that wholesale
change of the beliefs and behaviour is required, to
draw people from their backwardness and (further up
the evolutionary ladder) towards that highest stage
represented by modern metropolitan society.

Though few anthropologists explicitly subscribe
to this view, the traditional anthropological con-
ceptualization of culture as an integrated whole -
a persisting system in a specific community or some
comparable unit - as well as the evolutionary theories that have waxed and waned in the field over
the years, have served to reinforce this first model
of human beliefs and behaviour. The focus of much
of applied anthropology on the identification of
cultural barriers to change, proceeding from the

assumption that "the major problems in technological development are embedded in the society and culture of the community itself"[10], has meshed nicely with prevalent notions about rural traditionalism and resistance to change.

We find this view to be of little value for realizing our project's goal of obtaining policy-relevant information on interactions between people and forests in East Kalimantan. Traditionalism is hardly what is demonstrated by some of the activities and processes in which we are most interested in this project - for example, the spontaneous migration of thousands of Bugis farmers from the island of Sulawesi in order to convert East Kalimantan forest land into plantations of pepper, a crop the people had not grown in their homeland; the movement of Dayak from the interior plateau to lowland areas where they have eagerly taken to using chain-saws and "perahu" (canoes) with outboard motors in their activities as shifting cultivators; and the greatly increased allocation of time and effort to the collection of incense wood by Dayak from Apo Kayan when the price traders were paying for that commodity rose.

EVOLUTIONARY INTEGRATION OF CULTURES

These examples are also indicative of difficulties with (a) assigning the way of life of a people to a particular evolutionary level, and (b) construing this way of life as necessarily a functionally interconnected whole that maintains its integrity by resisting change. According to commonly accepted evolutionary schemes, shifting cultivation belongs to a "primitive" level[11] whereas use of chain-saws and outboard motors and participation in a cash economy would be considered indicators of a more "advanced" level. Yet the same people engage in various combinations of these so-called primitive and advanced activities. In the Samarinda area, there are even shifting cultivators - recent migrants from the island of Buton (Butung) - who commute to their fields in shared taxis from their urban residences. Such examples, illustrative of the behaviour we are trying to understand in the project, must be interpreted by means of concepts and approaches other than those used to show the integration of cultures at particular evolutionary levels.

In a somewhat different view that has gained

currency in economic and development circles in recent years, present-day rural land use is seen as efficient and rational but stagnant because trial-and-error development over many generations has made it impossible for the small farmers to effect further significant improvements in the allocation of traditionally available means and resources. In the words of one economist subscribing to this view, traditional farmers are "caught in a technical and economic equilibrium trap"[12]. The development policy associated with this view concentrates on making new means available to the traditional farmers, in the form of modern agro-chemical inputs. In this view, then, the people have no irrational resistance to change, but the means for change must be provided from the outside.

The implications in anthropological research, in this view, are minimal or non-existent. The economist Schultz says, for instance, that "since differences in profitability are a strong explanatory variable, it is not necessary to appeal to differences in personality, education, and social environment"[13]. The main research task, in this view, would then be economic investigations of "differences in profitability" rather than anthropological studies encompassing the social contexts or situations in which economic behaviour operates. Whereas the first model discussed above exaggerates the differences between modernized and traditional people, this second model attributes undue universality to the ends that people seek and the means that are suitable for attaining them.

PERTINENCE OF ECONOMIC MOTIVATION

So far, most of the people we have been studying have been found to be responsive to economic opportunity. Being responsive does not mean, however, that they are ready to consider all possible alternative uses of their labour, land, or capital, and then to choose from them those likely to be most profitable. If there is an opportunity to gain profit in a particular way, the people frequently respond to that without necessarily considering whether or not there might be other ways even more profitable.

Thus, some, like most of the Bugis migrants, see the new roads through the forests in the Samarinda vicinity as presenting opportunities for pepper farming. The path towards profit seen by others, including poorer members of the Banjar and Kutai ethnic groups, lies in combining shifting cultivation with the removal of wood from the forests in the form of beams, planks, and shingles for sale. Yet others, including urban as well as rural residents in East Kalimantan, concentrate on having logged-over forest cleared so that they can establish their claims to land either simply to be sold for profit in the future or else to be worked by wage labourers or share-croppers.

The motivations of the farmers vary as much as their means. Some are the poor, subsistence-orientated, land-hungry farmers who have been characterized in other parts of the world as "shifting cultivators by necessity"[14]; others, including many of the migrants from Sulawesi, seek to gain enough wealth to be able to advance themselves socially by such means as making the pilgrimage to Mecca; and others have turned to farming as a supplementary occupation because their incomes from urban wage-earning are inadequate for maintaining middle-class creature-comforts. Miracle's comment on the view put forward by Schultz is apt: "We can ill afford to use an economic shorthand which implies that the critical characteristics of all small-scale farmers are the same."[15]

The third and most current view - and the one most congruent with our research perspective - focuses on continuing responsiveness to changing circumstances. Associated with this view is attention to the following kinds of phenomena, among others.

Firstly, the continuing exercise of decision-making capabilities by rural people[16]. Some observers have concluded that a lack of obvious long-term planning by people in some rural areas implies an absence of decision-making capabilities. But the people we are observing in this project repeatedly demonstrate their willingness to use their minds actively rather than slavishly following a plan. Indeed, one can argue that in the absence of a firm, comprehensive plan, more, not less, decision-making is required.

For example, in Long Segar, a Dayak settlement on the Telen River, where a variety of options exist for productive activity, each individual makes daily decisions about how to allocate his or her time, taking into consideration such factors as current household and agricultural labour needs, exchange obligations within the village, cash requirements, and personal preference, as well as a number of more external factors such as the market price of various products, the weather, the current labour needs of the nearby plantation and timber company, and so on. Compare this with the decision-making demands awaiting a factory worker in an industrialized nation as a new day dawns.

The absence of rigid planning among the Kenyah people among whom our research is being conducted seems to be accompanied by a recognition of the advantages to be gained by decision-making in the course of action[17]. Thus an Apo Kayan man, when asked by a project investigator what he would do for the day, laughed and said, "I don't know now... I have many plans." When another man was asked how long his trading trip to Malaysia would take, the answer was maybe a month, maybe two or three, depending on what happened along the way[18].

Secondly, the rationality of the rejection of some externally advocated innovations[19]. The Banjar farmers who left the government-subsidized Keluang Pantai resettlement area in East Kalimantan's Pasir district did so not because they were irrationally rejecting progress or change but because they knew they could not obtain good harvests from fields in imperata grasslands. Similarly, in Dayak communities along the Telen River, the efforts of government extension workers to persuade the people to switch from shifting cultivation of dry rice to permanent wet-rice cultivation have consistently failed because the Dayak farmers know the lands proposed for such conversion are not fertile and well enough watered to sustain wet-rice cultivation without expensive additional effort. Their knowledge of the long fallows required for stable, shifting cultivation to maintain the forests, has also made them resist official efforts to persuade them to confine their farming to smaller areas than previously used. Indeed, both here and in other areas of East Kalimantan, where soils, topography and water supply are appropriate (as, for example, in the Krayan area in the north-west of the province), the Dayak readily engage in wet-rice cultivation.

ADJUSTMENTS AND VARIATIONS

Thirdly, continuing capability for "situational adjustment"[20]. By this we refer to people's modification of existing routines or habits and manipulation of existing norms so that the actions they take to gain their ends can be appropriate to their immediate situations. Thus a Bugis norm is that labour exchanges for important tasks should be restricted to kinsmen because non-kin, not being <u>sejiwa</u> (literally, "one spirit"), cannot be trusted. In frontier areas where kinsmen are few and labour is needed for such tasks as land clearance, Bugis migrants have been able to find help in accord with their norms by construing all people with a common village of origin in Sulawesi to be kin.

We may also consider the situations resulting from the granting of timber concessions on land used by shifting cultivators. Privation because of being denied access to land formerly used by people may be an expected result and has indeed been reported from another province of Indonesian Borneo[21]. It must be noted, however, that Indonesia's land laws include numerous conflicting stipulations (e.g. that local people are entitled to use land in their customary manner; that people residing in timber concessions are restricted to certain areas; that all land within 2 km of a river is available for use by local inhabitants). We are finding that some East Kalimantan shifting cultivators take advantage of the fuzziness of the laws by continuing to cut forest within the timber concessions. (We are also funding, incidentally, situational adjustment by timber-company personnel, some of whom have success-fully argued that the activities of shifting culti-vators have interfered with their production and that the government should therefore allow them to log more tracts in a given year than originally specified in their agreements.)

Fourthly, a great range of variation in the conditions under which the indicated capabilities and rationality are exercised[22]. If we look, for instance, at two Apo Kayan communities, Sungai Barang and Long Ampung, we can observe that the former is surrounded by a great deal of forest, whereas the latter is not. The people of Sungai Barang, then, have relatively easy access to the forest for hunting and for making their rice fields, and can readily obtain wood for building, firewood, and other uses. The differences between the two communities in forest accessibility are reflected in major differences in daily activities. Sungai Barang, unlike Long Ampung, is also near heath (<u>kerangas</u>) forest from which the best incense wood can be obtained. Such differences - and many more might be mentioned - are enough to make the exercise of rationality and decision-making capabilities in the two different communities produce very different results.

Fifthly, practical knowledge that people have gained, through experience, about the varying conditions under which they must make decisions and act[23]. A wide variety of information has already been brought to light in the course of this project, through the use of the people as consultants. In Long Segar, the people looked on with amusement as agricultural extension workers planted their experimental wet-rice fields in swampy, alluvial soil that the local inhabitants knew to be unsuitable. Similarly, the Sungai Barang people know about the unsuitability of heath-forest soils for their farms[24].

ECOLOGICAL AND SOCIO-ECONOMIC CONSIDERATIONS

The policy implications of this view are considerably different from those of the other two views discussed. Combining recognition of the great diversity of existing ecological and socio-economic circumstances with the view that behaviour and beliefs are mutable (in response to changing external conditions) suggests that development-related human diversity is even greater than heretofore recognized. The development of effective strategies for change will require greater attention to this variability; different situations will require different approaches. Moreover, current land-use strategies and the knowledge of people of their environment can be tapped in the effort to develop locally appropriate change. This view suggests also that diverse paths to improved living conditions exist, and that development efforts should focus on utilizing existing local-level knowledge, strategies and creativity to solve particular development problems, rather than attempting to remake the people in a uniform and more advanced stage of development. As suggested in a recent article on upland "problem soils" in Indonesia, the local people might well be regarded as qualified consultants on how development in their areas can proceed[25].

Besides having the policy implications noted above, this third model, with its focus on human adaptability, responsiveness, and initiative, has far-reaching implications for research in social science. The following five shifts or changes are particularly fundamental.

First, much research and analysis have been directed towards determining the goals of a society as a whole and ways in which it maintains itself. We are focusing instead on the ways particular individuals, acting together or separately and using whatever technological organizational, and cultural means are available to them, respond to changing circumstances.

Secondly, a traditional concern in social science has been with the norms or rules people follow in their daily lives. In our research, we are investigating those areas of social life that are characterized by inconsistency, conflict, and ambiguity; we are interested in seeing how people utilize such determinacy to achieve certain immediate ends.

Thirdly, there has been a tendency to single out problems (e.g. over-population or protein deficiency) and ascribe them to people on a global scale or to broad categories of people, like "peasants" or "Amazon Indians". Our research includes a recognition of the need to determine empirically which of many possible problems have urgency for particular people at particular times.

Fourthly, an orthodox disciplinary objective has been explaining culture or regularities of social process. We are replacing this with an attempt to understand, explain and predict specific human actions that have specific, practical significance.

Fifthly, the literature in social science is replete with statements which imply a basic dichotomy between rural and tribal peoples on the one hand, and modern urbanites on the other. But the third view, set forth in this section, implies no such dichotomy. Indeed, as we turn to the analysis of situations in the next section, the artificiality of such distinctions becomes clearer.

Recognizing the responsiveness of people to changing circumstances, and wanting to provide useful information that is congruent with the policy implications outlined above, we have opted for a research strategy that focuses on situations rather than communities. We remain firmly within the anthropological tradition in our commitment to the holistic premise that problems can only be understood if they are considered part of a complex of interacting causes and effects. But we do not assume that the boundaries of that complex necessarily correspond to the boundaries of a community or its culture. The approach that we have developed includes identifying particular behaviours that affect or can affect the forest and then attempting to understand those behaviours by analysing the situations in which they occur. Starting with a particular human behaviour, we trace the complex of relevant influences and impacts outward, obtaining, in the end, an understanding of the important factors that must be attended to by the relevant actors. Such use of situational analysis to elucidate behaviour corresponds to the methods and goals of the situational analyses advocated by some philosophers[26].

Consider, for example, certain activities observed by one of us among the Dayak of Telen River communities: cutting wood form the forest and making from it balok (beams, usually 10 x 10 cm) for sale. We discuss below some important factors that we have already discovered to be operating in the situations in which people decide to make balok. Selling balok represents a comparatively profitable utilization of time. In one day of hard work, using a chain-saw, two persons can expect to cut one cubic metre of balok, grossing approximately Rp. 20,000. This represents a much greater return than the available wage labour in the area which pays from Rp. 800 to 1,500 per day. Some of the people have established direct trading connections with Samarinda where they are paid Rp. 40,000 per cubic metre for balok, thereby increasing their profit.

The work setting is compatible with Dayak preferences. Specifically the cutter can work at his own rate, at times that are convenient to him (cf. the earlier discussion, page 184, of Dayak flexibility). Furthermore, the cutter can continue to live at home, in contrast to what is required by the other main sources of wage labour - the Georgia Pacific logging camp and the oil palm plantation - both of which are too far from the village for practical commuting and too close to fit into the traditional category of an income-seeking adventure.

Lastly, the legal status of these activities must be explained. Cutting and selling ironwood from within a concession is legal if a tax is paid to the government at the sub-district, or kecamatan, level. Cutting other kinds of wood within a concession is legal only if a royalty (currently Rp. 5,500 per cubic metre) is also paid to the concession owner. These payments are rarely made because: (a) there are very few official personnel to enforce the regulations; (b) when balok-cutting comes to the attention of timber company personnel, the only actions taken by the latter are to confiscate the balok and to give some compensation to the cutters;

and (c) there is informal agreement in the area that most _balok_-cutting is done to feed or house one's family and is therefore an honest and proper activity, even if inconsistent with the rules mentioned.

TRACING THE THREADS OF INFLUENCE

Decisions about what specific factors to investigate and how far to pursue them are taken on the basis of empirically-assessed impacts on the forests, the people and important development questions in the region. Following this strategy we judge the ideas, goals and operating strategies of the personnel at Georgia Pacific, for instance, to represent more productive topics for investigation than do the details of the form of religion (Christianity) practised within the confines of any particular community of shifting cultivators. We are not allowing the scope of inquiry to be limited by the geographical boundaries of conventional spatial units such as villages. Indeed, our research on the trade in incense wood is taking us from the Dayak collectors in the heath forests of Sungai Barang to Chinese traders in the river ports of East Kalimantan and ultimately to the buyers and warehouses of Hong Kong[27].

The situational approach also provides a convenient framework for organizing our research in the Samarinda vicinity. Since the situation (rather than a "community"), defines the appropriate sphere of investigation, we are free - and indeed required - to pursue leads and trace threads of influence in many directions. The problem of defining the target population that has plagued researchers wanting to do holistic research in urban setting is obviated by this approach. One of our fundamental concerns is with human activities that change the forest. Therefore the behaviour and beliefs of government officials and other professionals who clear logged-over forest near Samarinda with the intention of either having land for speculating purposes or establishing absentee-owned commercial plantations are as important to understand, from our perspective, as are the behaviour and beliefs of the poor Butonese who make farms on the hilltops near Samarinda and have migrated there because of poverty and land shortage in their home island.

Just as we are rejecting rigid spatial frameworks for inquiry, so too are we rejecting rigid temporal ones. Historical research is providing us with important insights regarding some of the actions and situations we are analysing. An example is the movements of land-clearing Bugis pepper farmers in East Kalimantan. As a result of documentary research and the collection of case histories, we can see these movements not as discrete, individual migrations but rather as part of an ongoing and well-organized long-term colonization process with the potential for moving Bugis to almost all accessible areas of East Kalimantan where pepper can be profitably grown[28/].

Many developers have recognized the importance of understanding relevant human behaviour from a holistic perspective; but anthropological contributions have frequently been criticized as lacking in focus. Policy-makers and planners do not want to read through pages of ethnographic description of cultural features that are only marginally relevant to development concerns. This situational approach provides a good framework for providing data that are germane, focused, and holistic.

In conclusion, we have planned a research project based on recognition of human flexibility, creativity, and responsiveness to changing conditions. We are documenting interactions of people in East Kalimantan with the tropical forest there and are making these interactions intelligible by showing the situations in which they occur. The research is resulting in information that will be useful to development planners and forest managers.

Our findings to date tend to indicate the heuristic value of this dynamic view of behaviour and suggest that this kind of situational analysis is an efficient and productive way to gather policy-relevant information. Furthermore, this approach, in our view, represents a more realistic appraisal of human interaction with the biosphere than do the other views discussed. This human responsiveness to changing conditions is the characteristic that accounts for both creativity in problem-solving and the opportunism that is instrumental in creating problems.

THE INADEQUACY OF EDUCATION

In our investigations we are finding that people typically act in what they consider to be their best interests; and, indeed, much of the people's forest-destroying or land-degrading action is profitable to them. An important, but often ignored, implication of this not too surprising finding is that education and propaganda will be insufficient to change what people do. Some concrete and profitable alternatives will have to be created if we want to protect the forests and other features of our biosphere.

To date, in development planning circles, the destructive aspect of human behaviour has been duly recognized. Yet the creativity that we are finding to be the other side of that coin has been vastly underestimated and correspondingly under-utilized. We are convinced that the decision-making capabilities, the capacity for situational adjustment and the rationality of people that we are finding in this project, combined with the knowledge these people have of their diverse environments, represent an important, neglected resource that, if used, could substantially improve the results obtained in development projects and resource management.

REFERENCES

1. D. Poore, Ecological Guidelines for Development in Tropical Forest Areas of South East Asia (IUCN Occasional Paper No. 10, 1974).
2. Laporan Universitas Mulawarman, Pengaruh Ekspor Kayu dan Kesempatan Kerja, 1976.
3. C. Manning, "The Timber Boom, with Special Reference to East Kalimantan", Bulletin of Indonesian Economic Studies, Vol. 7, No. 3, 1971.
4. A. Sumitro, Foreign Investment in the Forest-based Sector of Indonesia: Increasing Its Contribution to Indonesian Development, Yogyakarta, Fakultas Kehutanan, Universitas Gadjah Mada, 1975.
5. K. Fischer; Y. Rasyid, Population and Social Structure, TAD Report No. 8 (East Kalimantan Transmigration Development Project), Hamburg, Institute for International Economics, 1977.
6. K. Kartawinata; A. Vayda; R. Sambas Wirakusumah, "East Kalimantan and the Man and Biosphere Programme", Berita Ilmu Pengetahuan dan Teknologi, Vol. 21, No. 2, 1977 (reprinted in Borneo Research Bulletin, April 1978).
7. C. Hutton; R. Cohen, "African Peasants and Resistance to Change: A Reconsideration of Sociological Approaches", in I. Oxaal, T. Barnett and D. Booth (eds.), Beyond the Sociology of Development: Economy and Society in Latin America and Africa, London, Routledge & Kegan Paul, 1975. See their discussion of "obstacle man".

8. G. Helleiner, "Smallholder Decision
Making: Tropical African Evidence", in L. Reynolds
(ed.), Agriculture in Development Theory, New Haven,
Conn., Yale University Press. See, for example, his
review of the tropical African evidence.
9. R. Seavoy, "Social Restraints on Food
Production in Indonesian Subsistence Culture",
Journal of Southeast Asian Studies, Vol. 8, No. 1,
1977, p. 15-30; and Indonesian Resettlement Team,
Resettlement in Indonesia. ASEAN Workshop on Land
Rehabilitation and Resettlement, Samarinda -
Surakarta, 28 February - 8 March 1979. See above
for examples relating to Indonesia.
10. G. Foster, Applied Anthropology, p. 94,
Boston, Little, Brown & Co., 1969.
11. See the references in T. Grandstaff, "The
Development of Swidden Agriculture (Shifting Cultivation)", Development and Change, Vol. 9, 1978.
12. R. Stevens, Tradition and Dynamics in
Small-farm Agriculture: Economic Studies in Asia,
Africa, and Latin America, Ames, Iowa State University Press, 1977.
13. T. Schultz, Transforming Traditional Agriculture, New Haven, Conn., Yale University Press,
1964.
14. R. Watters, Shifting Cultivation in Latin
America, Rome, FAO Forestry Development Paper No.
17, 1971.
15. M. Miracle, "The Smallholder in Agricultural Policy and Planning: Ghana and the Ivory
Coast, 1960 to 1966", Journal of Developing Areas,
Vol. 4, 1970.
16. A. Hoben, "Decision-making for Development: An Anthropological Perspective". Unpublished
prospectus, 1979; M. Miracle, Agriculture in the
Congo Basin, Madison, Wis., University of Wisconsin
Press, 1967.
17. Cf. S. Ortiz, "Uncertainties in Peasant
Farming: A Colombian Case", London, Athlone Press,
1973. (London School of Economics Monographs on
Social Anthropology, No. 46).
18. T. Jessup, Intra-project correspondence,
28 December 1979.
19. G. Castillo, "A Critical View of a Sub-
culture of Peasantry", in C. Wharton (ed.), Subsistence Agriculture and Economic Development, Chicago,
Ill., Aldine Publishing Company, 1969; see reference
No. 7; and see Helleiner's (reference No. 8) concept
of "the wise rejector".
20. Cf. S. Moore, "Epilogue: Uncertainties
in Situations, Indeterminacies in Culture", in S.

Moore and B. Myerhoff (eds.), Symbol and Politics in Communal Ideology: Cases and Questions, Ithaca, N.Y., Cornell University Press, 1975.

21. G. Adicondro, "The Jungles are Awakening", Impact, September 1979; J. Weinstock, Land Tenure Practices of the Swidden Cultivators of Borneo, thesis, Cornell University, Ithaca, N.Y., 1979.

22. R. Eckaus, Appropriate Technologies for Developing Countries (Chapter 6), Washington, D.C., National Academy of Sciences (see reference No. 16); P. Hill, Studies in Rural Capitalism in West Africa, Cambridge, Cambridge University Press, 1970.

23. D. Barker; J. Oguntoyinbo; P. Richards, The Utility of the Nigerian Peasant Farmer's Knowledge in the Monitoring of Agricultural Resources. Report No. 4, London, Monitoring and Assessment Research Centre (MARC), Chelsea College, University of London, 1977; R. Chambers, Managing Rural Development: Ideas and Experience from East Africa, Uppsala, Scandinavian Institute of African Studies (Africana Publishing Co.), 1974; A. Vayda, "Human Ecology and Economic Development in Kalimantan and Sumatra", Borneo Research Bulletin, Vol. II, No. 1, 1979.

24. Cf. P. Richards, "Soil Conditions in Some Bornean Lowland Plant Communities", in Symposium on Ecological Resources in Humid Tropics Vegetation, Kuching, Sarawak, 1965.

25. P. Driessen; P. Burman; Permadhy, "The Influence of Shifting Cultivation on a 'Podyolic' Soil from Central Kalimantan", in Peat and Podyolic Soils and their Potentials for Agriculture in Indonesia, Bogor, Soil Research Institute. (Bulletin No. 3, 1976).

26. K. Popper, Objective Knowledge: An Evolutionary Approach, Oxford, Clarendon Press, 1972; I. Jarvie, The Revolution in Anthropology, London, Routledge & Kegan Paul, 1964.

27. N. Peluso, Intra-project correspondence, 27 January 1980.

28. Cf. A. Vayda, "Buginese Colonization of Sumatra's Coastal Swamplands and its Significance for Development Planning", Proceedings of the Programmatic Workshop on Coastal Resources Management, held in Jakarta, September 1979, Tokyo, United Nations University (in press).

Chapter Sixteen

SHONA PEOPLE, TOTEMS AND WILDLIFE

By

Chris Tobayiwa
131 St. Patrick's Road
Hatfield, Zimbabwe
    and
Peter Jackson
CH-1171 Bougy, Switzerland

ABSTRACT

The Shona people of Zimbabwe have a totem system
based on wildlife, which regulates much of their
social life, including marriage and succession to
chieftainships, and provides collective inspiration.
Each person has a totem animal, or part of an animal, whose name is received through the father.
Poems in praise of totem animals, which have evolved
with the system, show close observation and attachment to nature. Conservation can be served by encouraging this interest and a major effort is being
made on the outskirts of Harare, where a natural
park stocked with wildlife is being developed with
educational and recreational facilities.

When I lived with my grandmother, back home in the
back of beyond, sadza, our staple maize dish, was
best with delicacies like locusts, certain types of
beetles, caterpillars and mice. Whenever I brought
these home, she thanked me profusely and told me
what a fine child I was. One day I brought home a
hare. My grandmother ululated, clapped and
declared:

> Thank you so, oh Moyo -
> The Heart, the Heart of Hearts.
> Your ancestry is so beautiful, wise,
> With cattle pens always so full
> Of fat hornless cows,
> Providing milk to fill every bowl,
> Manure to fill all the furrows,
> Skin to tan and meat to eat to the full.
> Your ancestry radiates royalty;
> Is benevolent even to laity,

> Officiates all chieftainships in the land,
> And oversees all Zimbabwe and beyond.
> Thank you again, my Moyo,
> Yesterday, today and in the days to come.

Her recital touched my heart then, as it still does and always will, for she was telling me that the Heart (Moyo) was my totem. However, as I grew older, I realized that I was not alone in having a grandmother, mother or aunt telling me that I had a totem - all the boys in the neighbourhood were learning that they too had totems. I was not the only prince in the land. Time nurtured my pride, transforming it into a formidable sense of my own identity, my history derived from, and transmitted through the totem system in our Shona society.

The understanding of the totem system - known to us as Mutopo - is one of the bases for understanding Shona society. I do not speak of it as an expert, but rather as someone who grew up taking it for granted, like creation, until someone said he was interested.

Our oral history offers us no tangible facts to explain the system scientifically - but the totem system is a living reality that has survived the weather of development, changing only subtly, and always to facilitate social customs like marriage patterns, chieftainship succession, collective inspiration, and the inter-clan feuds and fights of the past. Common knowledge suggests links between some dynasties within Shona society. It seems probable that at some distant time it became impossible to determine chieftainship and marriage patterns within one community. Feuds may have developed too frequently and some sage could have chosen a method of distinguishing people. What choice could be better than the different animals that populated the surrounding forests?

Another theory says that the Mutasa people came from Mozambique, from a place that had many zebra (Tembo). When they met other migrating peoples they were asked:

> "Where do you come from?"
> "From the place of many Tembo."
> "Oh, Mbizi?"
> "Yes."
> "Fine, you of Mbizi Tembo."

Such exchanges established an identity within different communities.

230

As time passed, too many people claimed to be Mbizi-Tembo, and it became necessary to subdivide. Feuds developed and breakaway groups changed their totem to "Shumba-Tembo", "Shumba-Mhazi" and others. Similar patterns are to be found in other dynasties, lordships or clans within the Shona community. Some people say precise rituals were performed before one could adopt an animal as one's totem.

The exact origin of the system is obviously beyond my reach and one can really only quote generally-accepted explanations. Many people are happy to accept that we have always had a totem system. Some elders suggest that, long ago, each family had a medicine chest with recipes that included viscera of a particular animal, which became the family totem.

The totem system is paternal in that every child is born into the totem of the father - an animal, or a part of one, chosen somehow in the dark corridors of history, and perpetuated and passed on through our ancestors as a patent for a people with one origin.

A lot of taboo is interwoven into the totem system. It is taboo to marry within one's own totem; taboo to eat certain parts of certain animals; taboo to touch one's totem - some fear a spell which leaves them unprotected from misfortune e.g. that teeth will fall out if one eats one's totem animal. No devout Chuma person will touch a tortoise - their name means "beads", which is a synonym for tortoise.

In practice, the system serves to identify people and create social order. The system was dynamic and continued to serve as the guiding yardstick in society. The three factors that often caused changes in the totem system were the accidental, or, in some rare cases, intentional marriage of closely-related people; scrambles for succession to chieftainships; and, in former times, inter-clan feuds and fights.

The descendants of any one totem are entitled to the chieftainship of their totem group, tribe, clan or community at some stage in their history. As people increased in numbers, the line of succession became complex and naturally contestants for a chieftainship often fought and separated, subdividing themselves in the process.

People were sometimes banished from their community for wrong-doing. In their flight they often subtly changed identity and established a new line of succession as they started a new life.

The reverence afforded to one's "Mutupo" animal takes many forms. Fundamentally, a special effort was made to highlight those qualities of the totem animal in which it excels. A summary of that deep observation of the animal has been passed on in the form of inspiring praise poems that have, in fact, expanded further to include the history of a people. These evocative and accurate observations of animals could only come from living in harmony with nature.

Animals that show no elegance, gaiety, dignity, strength, nor dominance in some positive way were not chosen as totems. There is no hyaena totem, for the animal is associated with witches, and is one of several animals regarded as lacking in fine qualities. And I have not heard of a "Mr Zongororo" - millipede.

Tembo-Mbizi, the zebra, is admired for its beauty, colour, and its graceful, ballet-like movements; Shato, the python, for its wonderful colour and strength - it is the only snake totem. Chuma, the tortoise, lives a long time and is clever, honest and self-reliant. Soko the monkey, although small, is loved by the Mbire people as an expression of strength in numbers and they always refer to its hair as beautiful. People of the Dziva totem, which means a big pool of water, respect the power of thunder and the Sabi river, and they do not eat a certain type of fish - but they do drink water. The mighty lion, represented by Shumba and various synonyms, is obvious. Shiri Hungwe Matapatira, the great fish eagle, has a very impressive flight and is a lord of the skies. Nzou, the elephant, is admired for its size, strength and wonderful tusks, which give rise to derivative totem names, such as Ndoro, meaning a symbol of authority often worn round the neck and made of ivory, and Nyandoro, bearer of the symbol of authority.

Many Shonas have double-barrelled names, such as Shumba-Tembo or Moyo Ndizvo, which represent the inclusion of an honorific, or stress or characterize the owner's identity.

In a way, the system has meant that nobody is ever a stranger for long. People can always unearth a relationship somewhere in history. However, problems can arise, particularly involving marriage. Trying to identify relations from strangers is like a walk in a maze. Imagine being at the centre of a spider's web of relationships. The correct place to marry is at the periphery. As soon as the marriage occurs, the centre shifts radically. A marriage within the same totem requires such arduous rituals that it is scarcely worthwhile trying, but exceptions did - and do - occur.

A complete stranger, who is not Shona and does not have a totem, cannot easily mix in the Shona community. One white missionary found it essential to adopt a totem. He chose Shumba (Lion) and thus he became part of the community with which he worked and lived.

Have you ever thought of being born a member of a wildlife society? It makes sense in a Shona community. In a totem system like ours, nature is a part of one's being. The need to have virgin forests full of wildlife is not debatable. A totem system without animals is nonsense. A Mr Shumba who may never see a lion is a living contradiction. A Shona people without a totem system would be a people without a culture.

In youth, I sat by the woodfire in wooden huts at night, listening joyfully, and sometimes in fear, to our folklore and fairy tales, mostly about the life of the wilderness.

Many times we went hunting in forests nearby. We were taught the joys and the dangers of doing right and wrong to the wilderness - a treasury of what one needed, and not more - as if the forests could be angered.

"If you find rotten fruits, do not curse the tree, lest you fail to find your way home", they told us.

"If you see any creature too small or too ugly, do not gasp or laugh, its creator might be offended."

We learned what wild fruits to eat, when and where. We killed animals and birds for meat.

In earlier times our forefathers also got leather and feathers from which they made blankets and ornaments, medicine chests and musical instruments - a notable one is the kudu horn. It seemed a beautiful time and place to be born, and many of our names come from the wilderness. Often we watched our elders sit on wooden stools in the shade, making wooden handles for tools. They shared beer brewed on wood fires and sang about themselves and about the animals in neighbouring forests.

Of course, our environment was not the perennial paradise I have made it seem to be. Many nights were sleepless, and many days were restless. Baboons and monkeys were gluttons for our mealies. Elephants sometimes made highways through our fields. Snakes often played havoc in our chicken runs. Scorpions, wasps and the deadly malarial

mosquitoes were rampant. The way through the forests was, to say the least, unpleasant. Coming from
an area so remote, developed regions inevitably
seem like heaven on earth. The 20th century, as it
has been thrust upon us, must be sweet like stolen
waters.

Some Shona names and expressions emanate from
a close relationship with nature, just as in the
totem system:

- Mutyambizi means "one who fears the zebra".
- Mutambanengwe means "one who plays with the
  leopard".
- Shumbayarara means "the lion has slept".

These are literal translations. In each case the
name often has an historical significance for the
family.

The following expressions both mean "dawn",
but the translations are interesting as they show
contact with nature:

- Mashambanzou means "when the elephant
  washes".
- Rufuramhembwe means "when the duiker feeds".

The detail is as fascinating as it is endless.

I believe our purpose is to generate enthusiasm
for conservation. I believe we are searching for
meaningful tools. I believe we are aware that the
sheer necessity to exploit our natural resources in
order to live is the biggest obstacle to conservation. I also believe that those who live near
virgin forests, who are in a way the trustees of
our wildlife heritage, are also often so poor that
they need to harvest the forests the most. I also
believe that those who derive ornaments and pleasure
from plundering the wilderness to wear animal skin
coats or decorate their homes are a force to reckon
with in the long run. This does not rule out controlled exploitation of wildlife resources for human
benefit.

I believe we are aware that nature appreciation
is not governed by a universal attitude. People
interact with animals in different ways and for
different reasons. The balance of nature as a
scientific concept does not appeal to the man whose
fields are devastated by kudus, monkeys and baboons.

It is enough here to say that the totem system
in Shona society was developed through observation
and profound appreciation of nature. Times have

changed and collective benefit from the wilderness has to be reciprocated by collective responsibility for what we each take from it. An effort must be made to induce a collective understanding that the wilderness cannot provide us with its resources forever unless we care for it.

Education thus becomes an essential element in conservation. To be effective, it is necessary to be sensitive to, and make use of, existing experiences and outlooks. Conservation themes must go further, to include rebuilding of what we have already lost.

In Zimbabwe we have a project designed to capitalize on the deep cultural involvement of the Shona people with wildlife and nature. This is the Mukuvisi Woodland, only five km from the centre of the capital, Harare. An area of 274 ha of wooded savannah with a river flowing through it, which was once scheduled for housing development, has been leased for $2 a year to a non-profit conservation association by the municipality, and is being stocked with indigenous animals, most of them already family totems of many people living nearby. It offers a unique opportunity to educate some 100,000 school children every year and an innumerable number of adults. This will generate a positive interest in the animals, and is, therefore, an opportunity to encourage further interest in wildlife and conservation as a whole. The project includes a lecture hall, and interpretative exhibitions and nature trails.

The Mukuvisi project, which has been approved by IUCN/WWF, needs every support so that it can do a good job right from the start. Getting it right first time is the stated policy. Success could encourage similar projects elsewhere in the world. The project is well under way; and conservationists should make every effort to nurse it from its childhood to the massive educational giant it is intended to be.

Shona People, Totems and Wildlife

Some Common Family Names
Frequently Found Among Shona People

Chuma - Tortoise
Dziva/Hove - Fish
Gumbo - Leg
Hungwe - Great Fish Eagle
Makoni - Buffalo
Matemai and Shava - species of antelope
Mhazi - Lion
Moyo - Heart
Mutasa - Zebra
Ngara - Sheep
Nyandoro - Elephant
Shumba - Lion

Section Five

WHERE WE ARE GOING

INTRODUCTION

Even though we only have a small proportion of the
research, data and models on which to build a
culturally-oriented conservation, it is still important to evaluate this material as a stepping
stone to planning more appropriate activities. We
have therefore collected together a number of different disciplinary and sectoral perspectives united
by a common focus on culture, conservation and development and based in part on a commentary of contributions to this volume. But our aim is not a
restricted contemporary debate and these final
papers speculate on the future in a way that should
stimulate controversy.

Conservation, and especially conservation from
below, is interdisciplinary and intersectoral by
nature and definition. One can enter the garden by
any gate and all disciplinary perspectives will be
necessary in the team that will tackle future problems.

Of course there are important disciplines,
notably economics. Many argue that economic criteria dominate in any discussion of the environment. Conservation may be regarded by some national
governments as a luxury with few cash benefits and
many costs. But another economic argument is being
developed: the ultimate value is perhaps not what
people are thought to need in terms of goods and
services but what they want, what they value and
cherish culturally and what they can manage themselves. Conservation may have a central part in
this populistic and neo-utilitarian theme in economic development.

One further point: although we have tried in
this volume to think in a national context, in terms

of concrete cases, we must never forget the socio-economic superstructure and the "one world" environment we all inhabit. International activities then are not just a question of tidying up conflicts on the boundaries or the commonlands, they are very often the key to what happens internally in any nation. So international, intersectoral, environmental planning, is of the greatest importance, even if it is often planning without teeth, without the sanctions that make rules stick.

The importance of the total socio-economic structure means the creation of new disciplines which can handle the linkages between the natural and social processes. Of course there are different approaches to this. Our intention is not to come to a judgement on any one appropriate approach - we merely introduce some of the elements for the debate. The rethinking that is going on about culture and conservation needs flowers from many different fields.

Chapter Seventeen

CULTURE AND CONSERVATION:
SOME THOUGHTS FOR THE FUTURE

By

C. de Klemm
21, Rue de Dantzig
75015 Paris, France

ABSTRACT

The purpose of this paper is, in a very preliminary
way, to attempt a review of the different types of
traditional cultures as they relate to the natural
environment and of the factors that may have contributed to their survival or disappearance. The
documents on which this review is based are essentially those that were submitted to the Bali Congress and to the IUCN Commission on Environmental
Planning on the theme of culture and conservation.
In addition, it would seem that if traditional cultures are to be preserved, some of the means that
could assist in achieving this result should be
explored. Two of these possible means; the legal
recognition of customary rights and the revival of
territorialism are therefore examined in some
detail. These are, to a certain extent at least,
legal concepts. It may be symptomatic of the importance of inter-disciplinary work that most of the
documents reviewed have ignored them completely.

INTRODUCTION

In our modern world traditional cultures are disappearing at an increasing rate. Although considerable
research work has been undertaken by anthropologists, a lot of important information has already
been lost as old people die and their knowledge is
not transmitted to younger generations and remains
unrecorded. Moreover, anthropologists have tended
to concentrate on subjects such as languages, religion, social structures, arts and crafts and to
neglect ecological relations between man and his
environment. This may be due to the fact that ecol-

ogy is still a relatively new science, the importance of which was, sometimes, not sufficiently recognized. Yet, ecology is the key to a better understanding of the place that man occupied in nature
and of the religious and customary rules that he
developed to assist him in his survival. With the
disappearance of many traditional customs and the
death of those, such as fishmasters or masters of
the land, who enforced them, a lot of extremely
valuable information will be lost for ever.

The subject has, however, now received increased attention on the part of conservationists.
As early as 1963, the Ninth Technical Meeting of
IUCN, held in conjunction with the Union's Eighth
General Assembly in Nairobi, dealt extensively with
the Ecology of Man in the Tropical Environment which
was its main subject. Several papers presented at
that meeting specifically discussed the role and
impact of pre-industrial man. More recently, the
World Conservation Strategy emphasized the importance of traditional knowledge to assist in conservation-based rural development and the 15th IUCN
General Assembly meeting in Christchurch, New
Zealand, in October 1981, adopted a resolution (Resolution 15/19) on the role of traditional lifestyles
and local populations in conservation and development. There are several reasons why traditional
cultures are important for conservation:

a) "rural communities often have profound and
detailed knowledge of the ecosystems and
species with which they are in contact and
effective ways of ensuring they are used
sustainably" (World Conservation Strategy,
ch. 14, para. 10). In particular, traditional societies have been using for
centuries a large number of wild plant
species for food or medicine; it would be
a tragedy if that knowledge was irretriev-
ably lost;

b) many traditional methods of living resource
management are worth rescrutiny or reviving
either in their original or in modified
forms (World Conservation Strategy, ch. 14,
para. 11). These methods are often based
on religious customary rules which may
prove useful to conservation today as they
allow for non-destructive or sustainable
ways of exploitation of the natural environment;

c) last but not least, all cultures form a part of the cultural heritage of mankind and should therefore, as much as possible, be kept alive for their intrinsic value independently from the economic or conservation benefits which may be derived from them.

For these reasons and as a result of the Christchurch resolution, the subject of "culture and conservation" has now become an important element of the IUCN programme and several papers dealing with the relationship between protected areas and indigenous peoples were presented at the Third World National Parks Congress in Bali in October 1982. Other papers were presented to the IUCN Commission on Environmental Planning under the general heading of "culture and conservation" (IUCN/CEP Work in Progress No. 13) as a background document to support further research into the lifestyles, conservation and development practices of traditional communities and to define further action.

TRADITIONAL CULTURES AND THE NATURAL ENVIRONMENT

There are considerable variations in the methods used by human societies to utilize the natural resources of their environment. Their methods may, however, be regrouped under two major headings: direct predation and farming, including stock-raising, although the two may of course be combined.

Man as a Predator

Hunters and gatherers. Ethnical groups for which hunting, fishing and gathering are the only means of subsistence usually live in remote areas generally unsuitable for agriculture. Examples are the Eskimos or Inuit in Arctic tundras, the Bushmen in the Kalahari Desert and the Aborigines of the arid regions of Australia. Other groups in the same category inhabit dense tropical rain forests as, for instance, African Pygmies and the Negritos of southeast Asia.

All these peoples occupy vast areas and their population density is very low. Hunters are nomadic and their movements are governed by the local abundance of game. Societies are divided into individual groups or clans, each one living on its own territory, from which all others are excluded. Their behaviour is strongly territorial.

Many of those cultures have disappeared after coming into contact with outsiders. Physical extermination, the transmission of diseases against which their members were not naturally immune, genetic swamping and habitat destruction were probably the major causes of their fall. Among surviving groups many are in a precarious situation.

Farmers-hunters. Predation is however a characteristic of all cultures and of all times. It is a means to supplement food obtained by farming, especially protein rich food such as meat or fish. It can also be a commercial or a recreational activity. As a means of subsistence it continues to play a very important role in many developing areas of the world[1]/.

Predation was, however, generally severely regulated in traditional societies. Each ethnic group had its own territory where members of the group were not allowed to hunt except by permission of the chief. Examples of such customs are mentioned, for instance, in the report of the Third International Conference for the Protection of the Fauna and Flora of Africa (Bukavu, 1953). In many areas of the former Belgian Congo, now Zaire, hunting was restricted to the tribal territory. It was a collective endeavour undertaken for the benefit of the community as a whole. Game meat was equally apportioned between all members of the group. Hunting for personal gain was not allowed, chiefs often had the power to establish game reserves where all hunting was forbidden. Offenders incurred strict penalties.

Similar customs are found in many parts of the world. Examples are the collectively-owned lands of Papua New Guinea, from which hunters and collectors who do not belong to the landowning group are excluded[2]/. The allocation of megapode nests in certain Pacific islands to family groups or the practice to allow only one village at a time to harvest a coral reef in Pukapuka in the south Pacific[3]/ are other examples.

Other conservation practices include religious taboos against the taking of certain species and the establishment of protected areas such as sacred groves and ponds[4]/. Most of these customs on religious traditions are now, however, rapidly disappearing as a result of the opening of tribal ter-

ritories to outsiders, the introduction of modern
equipment, weapons and gear and the centralizing
emanating from governments in the name of national
unity. As early as 1953, the report of the Bukavu
Conference was already noting the fact that wild
animal populations were rapidly decreasing in many
areas as a result of the disruption of customary
practices and the development of commercial hunting.

Farmers and Pastoralists

Shifting cultivators. Many traditional societies
have practised and are still practising shifting
cultivation, probably the earliest form of agriculture in which mankind was ever involved. The
methods are remarkably similar in different areas
of the tropics. After the trees have been felled
the area is burnt and the crop is planted, usually
with pointed sticks. After harvesting, the land is
generally abandoned and a new site is cleared.
Abandoned sites are left fallow for several years,
after which they are cleared again and a new cycle
starts. However, if the fallow period is too short,
crop production declines, as soils become impoverished. Indeed, to be sustainable, this form of
agriculture requires large areas of forest. It has
been estimated that, on average, a family needs at
least 200 ha of suitable forest land in order to
grow their subsistence food requirements and allow
for the proper regeneration of the forest. Traditionally, therefore, shifting cultivation was
practised by migratory groups moving through the
forest within clearly-defined territorial boundaries
which excluded outsiders[5].
    Much has been written on the subject of shift-
ing cultivation but conclusions are often contradictory. For some, as soon as agriculture begins in
the forest, even in its most primitive forms and
with very long fallow periods, primary forest is
destroyed and replaced by secondary formations for
a very long time. Thus, the forest ecosystem is
considerably damaged and its genetic diversity, in
particular, is seriously affected.
    For others, this form of land use is "widely
suited ecologically and socio-economically to the
simple needs of man and the potentialities of the
environment" in circumstances of relatively mild
population pressure and if enough land is available[6]. Indeed, under conditions that become increasingly difficult to meet nowadays, this type of

agriculture is certainly sustainable as it preserves essential life support systems, water and soil fertility. But this is only true of the stable forms of shifting agriculture as practised by traditional societies. Unstable forms, unfortunately, tend to predominate today, as landless farmers, unbound by territorial limits, settle on forested slopes on soils which rapidly lose their fertility. As a result, many of the remaining tropical forests are now threatened.

Pastoralism. Pastoral economics developed in the old world in open arid regions unsuitable for agriculture. Traditional pastoralism, often associated with hunting and gathering, has for a long time been a stable and sustainable means of subsistence. Nomad herders drove their livestock over large territories, the boundaries of which were usually determined by custom. Herds often supplied all needs, as essential products such as salt were obtained by exchange or barter. Hunting provided game meat, especially in times of scarcity. As long as the carrying capacity of the ecosystem was not exceeded, a situation of equilibrium with the environment prevailed. Fodder reserves, where grazing was prohibited in periods of drought, were often established. These reserves were collectively owned by a tribe or a village and trespassers were penalized. The hema system of the Arabian peninsula described by Omaz Draz is a good example of efficient management of an arid land ecosystem[7]. Another example, which must be typical of the past situation over large areas of Africa and Asia, is the pastoralist economy of the Jebel Qara in Oman, where a small population of some 20,000 inhabitants and 100,000 head of cattle still remain in equilibrium with the natural environment in an area of about 2,000 sq km[8].

This state of equilibrium was possible to achieve, as long as natural controls maintained the number of animals at a level consistent with the carrying capacity of the land. "In the absence of overgrazing, stock was healthy, damage caused by disease not very great, but enough to control growth. Ecosystems were in equilibrium until the beginning of the present century. Population did not increase or increased very little in tropical countries during the 18th and 19th centuries."[9] But with the disruption of territorial boundaries, the gradual disappearance of customs and the increase in human and livestock populations, caused primarily by improved medical and veterinarian care, carrying capabilities became rapidly exceeded and erosion started to spread. The example of Mauritania given by Gritzner is, in this respect, particularly striking[10].

Sedentary agriculture. Traditional methods of sedentary agriculture, including gardening, irrigation and terracing have constituted for many centuries stable forms of land use. The construction of terraces, in particular, has been practised with considerable skill and success by many mountain dwelling societies, especially in Asia. Examples are the terraces built by some of the Naga tribes to grow rice in north-eastern India or the terraces and watering aqueducts of the grain-growing Hunzas in the Pamir. In western Europe, the bocage with its criss-crossing network of hedges is another example of a stable system which provided territorial boundaries and preserved the soils against run-off and erosion[11].

These traditional methods of cultivation often constitute an optimum form of land use in the type of ecosystem in which they are practised. Their importance for sustainable development is therefore very great. Yet they are gradually vanishing under the pressure of modern agriculture. An example of the value of traditional methods in our modern world is the Chinampas system, a form of irrigated agriculture, which was used by pre-Columbian peoples throughout tropical America and which has now been revived in Mexico under the Man and Biosphere Programme of Unesco.

CHARACTERISTICS OF TRADITIONAL SYSTEMS

Ecological

Most traditional systems had many points in common and they generally met all three objectives of the World Conservation Strategy. Life support systems were preserved because sustainable forms of land use such as terracing, stable shifting cultivation and moderate pastoralism were usually practised. The harvesting of wild animals and plants was governed by religious beliefs and customary rules that made it sustainable. Genetic diversity was maintained as a result of the low pressure exercised over natural systems and by the imposition of religious taboos or the existence of sacred groves or ponds. Although not necessarily always intended as conservation instruments, these rules were generally effective in maintaining population in equilibrium with the environment.

Admittedly, certain species have been hunted to extinction in prehistorical or historical times. This may well have been the case of some of the larger European mammals. It is certainly true of the giant flightless birds of Madagascar (Aepyornis) and New Zealand (Dinornis). One must recognize that certain cultures were less conservation minded than others. As an example, certain Australian hunting tribes have caused erosion by an excessive use of fire in the dry season[12]. Conversely, certain cultures were perhaps more conservation prone than the average. The example of the Bishnois of western India, a religious sect that enjoins its followers never to cut a green tree or kill any animal is a good example of that kind[13].

It would seem, however, that traditional cultures that have succeeded in surviving did so because they were able to adapt themselves to stringent ecological conditions. Human and live-stock populations were maintained at low levels, probably not deliberately but as a result of warfare, disease and limited supplies of food. Whenever the carrying capacity was exceeded, the balance was probably restored by famine or emigration. Some of the ancient migration of peoples may well be due to this cause. If the balance could not be restored, it is very likely that cultures merely disappeared in a process of natural selection. The demise of the Mayan and Khmer empires may be examples of such a process. Countless un-named traditional cultures have probably gone the same way.

Ethological
Territorialism is a feature of many animal species, including man. Its purpose is to prevent over crowding of suitable habitats and to ensure a sufficient supply of food to the individual, family or group. As we have seen, traditional societies were strongly territorial. Individual groups or clans of hunters, fishermen, herders or shifting culti-vators all lived within clearly-determined bound-aries which they were not allowed to cross except for social purposes. In this way, wasteful com-petition for the same resources was avoided and the environment preserved. Territorialism may well be

the single feature that has contributed the most to the preservation of native cultures and of their resource base.

The opening of closed systems by conquest or invasion is certainly as old as mankind and has probably resulted in the extermination of many unique cultures. But many also survived or evolved anew after they had assimilated their conquerors. In our modern world however, completely closed systems have become very rare. The Jebel Qara in Oman may be a very unique exception. The island of Siberut in Indonesia has now been opened to development and the conservation of its culture, ecosystem and endemic species will be at best, the subject of a compromise[14]. Even the Pygmies in their tropical rain forests are now supplied with fire-arms by neighbouring farmers in exchange for game meat. Once opened, an ecosystem may soon become over-exploited and its carrying capacity exceeded. Formerly self-sufficient populations may then undergo a process of cultural disintegration and become increasingly dependent for their survival on famine relief. Irreversible ecological and cultural damage may then occur.

THE LEGAL RECOGNITION OF TRADITIONAL CUSTOMARY RIGHTS

Several legislations recognize that traditional societies, because of their specific lifestyles, must be allowed to continue to take from the wild the resources that are indispensable to the daily sustenance of their members. This recognition has even been embodied in a number or treaties dealing with the conservation and management of living resources, not least by the International Whaling Convention. In the United States, Canada and Australia, for instance, where there subsist traditional societies which have remained semi-closed, partly because of their inaccessibility, Indians, Inuit, Aleuts, and Australian Aborigines are exempted from the harvesting restrictions which are otherwise imposed on commercial or sport hunters or gatherers. To avoid over-exploitation, however, hunting is usually only allowed if it is performed by traditional means and to meet human needs for food and clothing. As an example, Alaskan natives may take endangered species if the taking is primarily for subsistence purposes. Edible portions of such species may only be sold in native villages for

native consumption, whereas non-edible by-products
may only be sold in inter-state commerce when made
into authentic native articles of handicraft and
clothing (Code of federal regulations vol. 50,
17.5). This should usually limit the risk of over-
exploitation, at least for species, the taking of
which by non-natives is prohibited. There may be
however, some exceptions where the regulations of
native harvesting is required. A "cause célèbre"
is that of the Bowhead whale (Balaena mysticetus).
This species was hunted almost to extinction in the
19th century. It has now been protected for more
than 50 years and is recovering very slowly.

The International Whaling Convention, however,
exempted the native subsistence harvest of this
species from its otherwise total prohibition. This
exemption was removed in 1977 as increased native
catch was threatening the recovery of the Bowhead.
This was unacceptable to the coastal whaling com-
mnunities of Alaska. The International Whaling
Commission eventually decided to allow a yearly
quota. The U.S. Government subsequently entered
into a co-operative agreement for Bowhead management
with the Alaska Eskimo Whaling Commission with a
view to providing for more Eskimo participation
and, as a result, obtain a better acceptance by the
Eskimos of management decisions and enforcement
measures.

With regard to competition between native subsistence harvesters and other users, many conflicts
have arisen in the recent past with commercial or
sport hunters and especially fishermen. The recognition of native rights may, indeed, if harvesting
is to be sustainable, result in a decrease in the
catch allowed to the other users. These conflicts
may not be easy to resolve. There is, however, a
marked trend towards granting a certain degree of
priority to subsistence users over other users of
the resources. Thus, the Alaska National Interests
Lands Conservation Act provides that, "... non
wasteful subsistence uses of fish and wildlife and
other renewable resources shall be the priority
consumptive uses of all such resources on the public
lands of Alaska..." (16 USCA 3112/2/). Another trend
is to increasingly involve users in the development
of regulations through formal participation in
local advisory committees and regional councils
such as those that have been established by the
Alaska Boards of Fisheries and Game. Also in
Alaska, local resource users have created organizations to facilitate their participation in manage-

ment. Examples are the Alaska Eskimo Whaling Commission mentioned above, the Eskimo Walrus Commission or the joint U.S. Canada International Porcupine Caribou Commission. Participation of subsistence users in the management and decision making process could provide a means to overcome resistance to regulations which too often attempt to impose unfamiliar forms of harvesting controls which conflict with traditional local mechanisms[15].

Within the boundaries of a tribal territory, customary rules often provided the means to avoid wasteful competition among individuals. Collective ownership of land and natural resources was widespread but the equitable apportionment of nature's products to all members of the group or clan made competition unnecessary.

As a result of the existence of territorial boundaries and customary rules, unlimited and free access to natural resources was prevented and as conservation was of importance to the community as a whole the "tragedy of the commons" which is inevitably the consequence of open systems was avoided. A good example is the vicuña in the Andes which was exploited on a sustainable basis for its wool in the times of the Inca Empire. After the vicuña became almost extinct through overexploitation, it was decided to try to restore this ancient system: local responsibilities for the culling and proportional distribution of the benefits[16].

The recognition of the rights of indigenous communities over the living resources of their territory, and the recent acceptance of their participation in the management of these resources, are important steps towards a further recognition of the rights and responsibilities of these peoples over the ecosystem in which they live. The protection of critical habitats, migration routes, and life support systems, in general, indeed requires their specialized knowledge, and development of the land cannot be achieved without their participation, or in defiance of their interests. The research project carried out among the Inuit of northern Quebec[17] and the Lancaster Sound Regional Study[18] which included an extended public review, with Inuit participation, of all issues involved in the future development of this sub-Arctic area, are important steps in this direction.

To take now the example of another continent and different conditions, customary hunting in Africa, for a long time a sustainable harvesting activity, was not affected by the prohibitions or restrictions imposed by colonial powers. Article 8.2 of the London Convention on the Preservation of Fauna and Flora in Africa gave international recognition to that exemption as early as 1933. Soon, however, with the decline of traditional customs, hunting became almost unrestricted[19]. The protection of native rights under such conditions meant little more than an official acceptance of the tragedy of the commons. In 1968, a new Convention for the Conservation of Nature and Natural Resources in Africa was concluded in Algiers. Article XI of that Convention provides that "the Contracting States shall take all necessary legislative measures to reconcile customary rights with the provisions of the Convention". This laid down the legal basis to reinstate the authority of states over uncontrolled hunting. Many national legislations, however, continue to authorize subsistence hunting, without a game licence, provided only traditional weapons or methods are used.

THE REVIVAL OF TERRITORIALISM

Cultural disruption and environmental degradation are generally the consequence of the opening of closed systems. It would seem therefore that the maintenance or re-establishment of closed or semi-closed systems could go a long way towards preserving traditional societies together with the natural resources which are essential for their livelihood. Moreover, as territorialism remains one of the deepest and most ingrained traits of the human species, it stands to reason that conservation measures which would be founded on that feature would have fair chances to succeed.

Several methods of territorial control of natural resources could be investigated.

Protected Areas
In the increasingly rare cases where man remains an integral component of a natural ecosystem, the establishment of protected areas may be the only means to ensure the survival of certain traditional societies. Protected areas of that type are listed as Category VII in the IUCN classification[20]. They have been given the name of Natural Biotic Areas or Anthropological Reserves. Their purpose is "to allow the way of life of societies living in harmony

with the environment to continue undisturbed by modern technology", and, therefore, to preserve both natural and cultural values at the same time.

Proposals to establish protected areas belonging to that category have been made by R. Dasmann[21] and by L. Brownrigg[21]. These proposals are extremely attractive. Both authors, however, recognize that many important conditions will have to be fulfilled if they are to be effectively implemented. The consent, co-operation and participation of the peoples concerned will be required; protected areas should prevent the settlement of outsiders but should not be prisons for insiders who should always be free to leave; neither should they be zoos, museums or tourist parks; they should be managed as much as possible by the peoples that inhabit them.

It will not be sufficient, however, to preserve the protected area from outside influences. Reserves of this type may well be destroyed from the inside if factors such as over-population, the exploitation and exportation of reserve resources for gain and the introduction of non-traditional methods and weapons are not adequately controlled. If exploitation is to remain sustainable, management plans, to be drawn up in co-operation with the reserve inhabitants, should provide for accepted measures of control and possibly for incentives to leave the protected area if it appears that its carrying capacity is likely to be exceeded.

Anthropological reserves are a relatively new concept and it is difficult to ascertain whether there has been sufficient field experience to provide material for the carrying out of a comparative study of the experience acquired so far and of the potentialities of that type of protected area for the future. A survey of existing literature, in particular from Australia and Brazil, where such reserves are known to exist would be particularly useful.

Closed User Groups
Competition among individuals or groups for the same natural resources soon result in a "tragedy of the commons" situation. The solution, therefore, should consist in granting a monopoly on the use of a resource to a group of users, such as an association or a co-operative, whose interest would then obviously be to exploit it on a sustainable basis as they would not be threatened to lose to the benefit of outsiders the product of their investments or

the results of their self-restraint. Within such closed groups the revival of traditional customs, with regard to both exploitation methods and sharing of the benefits among members, could provide ef-fective management tools. The establishment of close user groups would seem to be of particular value for three types of users: fishermen, hunters, and pastoralists.

Fishermen. The recent creation by the new Conven-tion on the Law of the Sea of a 200 miles Exclusive Economic Zone is in fact a decision to close, to the benefit of the coastal state, marine areas which had previously been fully open to international competition. Provided they can be effectively enforced, these new rules represent considerable progress as compared to the earlier situation. But now that national fishermen are protected from the inroads of foreign fishing fleets, there remains to find ways and means to protect them against them-selves, that is to say against wasteful over-exploitation induced by free competition and free access to the resources. This can be achieved by the establishment of coastal co-operatives with ex-clusive rights over certain areas, certain species, or both. Co-operatives would then adopt their own management plans and objectives, control access to the fisheries, enforce conservation regulations and allocate the catch among their members. The revival of traditional conservation-based management methods should then be easy. Fishing co-operatives of this kind exist in Japan where they seem to operate very satisfactorily[22]. The problem of the preser-vation of fish critical habitats over which fisher-men's co-operatives may have no control will have, however, to be taken into consideration.

Hunters. The regrouping of all hunters in a par-ticular area into a hunting association for the purpose of developing and implementing game manage-ment plans is an idea which is gaining momentum in certain developed countries. In many developing countries, on the other hand, the decline of custom-ary rules and the disruption of clanic territorial boundaries have resulted in unfettered competition and the depletion of populations of game animals and, therefore, of an important source of proteins. A possible solution could be to try to reinstate a sufficient degree of territorialism among hunters' groups to prevent unauthorized outsiders from hunting on the group's territory. This could be achieved by village co-operatives or associations which would, preferably on the basis of former customary rules, manage game populations, control poachers, preserve critical habitats, lay down harvesting regulations and apportion game meat among their members. The experience acquired in Tanzania with hunter's associations under the Wildlife Conservation Act of 1974 could provide interesting insights on the practical implementation of such an institution. Under sections 26 and 27 of that Act, authorized associations, including villages, may be granted game licences for the hunting of specified animals provided the meat is made available for consumption to all members of the association.

<u>Pastoralists</u>. Nomadic pastoral systems are almost everywhere threatened by overstocking and consequent desertification. Where, however, population pressure is still at a fairly low level, or if it is possible to reduce it, the hema system of grazing reserves could provide a means of achieving sustainable exploitation of the pastoral ecosystem. This will require the formation of co-operatives with limited access, territorial boundaries and collective management procedures. Again, customary rules applying to nomadic grazing could be revived and enforced.

<u>Protected Landscapes</u>
Traditional forms of sedentary agriculture, including land races and primitive cultivars of domesticated animals and cultivated plants are rapidly disappearing. Yet their preservation may be of great importance in view of their great potential usefulness for future agricultural developments. Their conservation, however, may be difficult to justify unless the national community is prepared to compensate farmers for the loss of income they incur as a result of conservation measures.

The experience of a few European countries in preserving certain man-made landscapes through institutions such as the British National Parks or the French Parcs Naturels Régionaux could constitute an interesting starting base for a study of the legal and financial requirements that could make conservation measures reasonably effective. The extent to which certain types of landscapes, such as the Bocage, could be sufficiently well represented in protected landscapes to constitute at least benchmark areas against which ecological changes occurring in modified areas could be measured, remains to be seen.

CONCLUSIONS

Over-exploitation of natural resources and ecosystem degradation are now progressing throughout the earth at an alarming rate. From a world which was mostly composed of closed, stable and regulated systems we are rapidly moving into one of open, unstable and unregulated systems whose carrying capacities are, therefore, easily exceeded. The opening, by force or otherwise, of closed systems has lead to the disappearance of territorial boundaries, competition with outsiders and disruption of conservation-oriented traditions. In many cases the opening of closed systems has also resulted in considerable increases in the size of human and livestock populations.

It can, however, be argued that the continuation of traditional lifestyles cannot be imposed against the will of the peoples concerned or that the benefits of development cannot be denied to these peoples for the sake of preserving the environment or vanishing cultures. Does this then mean that all traditional cultures are doomed? Perhaps not, as societies throughout the world become increasingly aware of their cultural identities and realize that maintaining them may not always be an obstacle to their development. In this lies hopes for the future.

PROPOSED SUBJECTS FOR FURTHER RESEARCH

1. Review anthropological work for books and papers that bring together anthropology and ecology and assess the state-of-the-art in such integrated work.
2. Try to promote further integrated research in the field. Select priority targets on the basis of known conservation priorities and national conservation strategies.
3. Review historic work for books that provide at least ecological theories to explain invasions or the fall of certain civilizations. Many historians seem to be unaware of potential ecological causes for important events or eco-

logical reasons for certain behaviours.

4. Review present legislation, including treaties, recognizing particular rights to indigenous peoples. Study the evolution of this legislation, gaps, prospects for the future, and enforcement.
5. Review present and future possibilities of global ecosystem management with the participation of indigenous peoples.
6. Review experience already acquired in anthropological reserves, successes and failures and try to establish conditions for success.
7. Review experience already acquired with local closed groups, such as co-operatives, that have been granted a monopoly for the exploitation of a renewable resource. Examine successes and failures and try to establish conditions for success.
8. Review the extent to which the protected landscape concept has been successful in preserving traditional activities and land races or primitive cultivars. Try to establish conditions for success.
9. Review incentives or disincentives, if any, used to promote conservation of particular forms of farming, animal husbandry, etc.
10. Excess human population and overstocking are often a major cause of the degradation of natural systems and traditional cultures. The subject is difficult and may be politically sensitive. Most of the papers reviewed tend to ignore it. If certain areas are to be saved and their productivity restored, solutions will have to be found. Is there any experience of population reductions induced by incentives or other means?

NOTES

1. See for instance Sale "The Importance and Values of Wild Plants and Animals in Africa". IUCN 1981.
2. P. Eaton "Customary Land Tenure and Conservation in Papua New Guinea".
3. G. Klee "Traditional Marine Resource Management in the Pacific".
4. M. Gadgil "Social Restraints and Resource Utilization: The Indian Experience".
5. W.S.A. Payne "The Role of Domestic Livestock in the Humid Tropics", in "The Use of Eco-

logical Guidelines for Development in the American Humid Tropics" - Proceedings of an International Meeting held at Caracas, Venezuela, 20-22 February 1974 - IUCN Publications New Series No. 31, 1975.

6. J. Phillips: "Shifting Cultivation"; in "The Ecology of Man in the Tropical Environment"; Proceedings of IUCN Ninth Technical Meeting, Nairobi 1963; IUCN Publications New Series No. 4, 1964.

7. O. Draz: "The Hema System of Range Reserves in the Arabian Peninsula, its Possibilities in Range Improvement and Conservation Projects in the Near East".

8. H.F. Lamprey: "Preliminary Proposals for the Conservation and Management of the Jebel Qara Region".

9. B. Abeywickrama: "Pastoralism"; in Proceedings of IUCN 9th Technical Meeting, Nairobi, 1963, IUCN Publication New Series No. 4. 1964.

10. J.A. Gritzner: "Environmental Degradation in Mauritania".

11. F. Terrasson: "Les valeurs écologiques des systèmes ruraux traditionnels et les bases culturelles d'une intervention : le cas des bocages à haies vives dans le centre de l'ouest de la France".

12. M.J. Meggit: "Aboriginal Food-Gatherers of Tropical Australia" in Proceedings of IUCN 9th Technical Meeting, Nairobi, 1963, IUCN Publication New Series No. 4. 1964.

13. M. Gadgil: "Social Restraint in Resource Utilization: The Indian Experience".

14. Saving Siberut, a Conservation Master Plan.

15. See Kelso "Subsistence Use of Fish and Game Resources in Alaska": Considerations in Formulating Effective Management Policies in Transactions of the 47th North American Wildlife and National Reserves Conference, 1982.

16. C. Ponce del Prado, "Inca Technology and Ecodevelopment, Conservation of the Vicuñas in Pampas Galeras"; paper presented at the Bali Congress.

17. W. Kemp: Inuit Land and Ecological Knowledge.

18. See Green Paper: Indian and Northern Affairs Canada 1982. The Lancaster Sound Region 1980-2000; and P. Jacobs: People, resources and the environment, perspectives on the use and management of the Lancaster Sound Region; Indian and Northern Affairs Canada, 1981.

19. See report of the Bukavu Conference, 1953.

20. IUCN: Commission on National Parks and

Protected Areas, Categories, Objectives and Criteria
for Protected Areas.

21. R. Dasmann: The Relationship between Protected Areas and Indigenous Peoples; L. Brownrigg:
Native Cultures and Protected Areas: Management
Options. Invited papers, World National Parks Congress, Bali, Indonesia, 1982.
22. J.P. Troadec: Le développement et l'aménagement des pêches mondiales d'un régime juridique
à l'autre - Colloque Objectif Mer - Paris, 1983.

Chapter Eighteen

ETHNOBOTANY AND ANTHROPOLOGY AS TOOLS FOR
A CULTURAL CONSERVATION STRATEGY

By

Enrique Leff
200 E. 72nd St.
Ap. 26-A
New York, NY 10021, USATwo

ABSTRACT

Much of the present situation is characterized by
planning policies and social structures which both
neglect local cultures and exploit the environment.
An alternative approach is suggested based not
simply on a return to tradition but rather an ethnically based productive system which embodies some
relevant traditional elements. Both ethnobotany and
anthropology have a prime role in developing the
theoretical tools to study scientifically this situation and provide a better base for planning.

As a general rule, planning policies for the conservation of nature and natural resources have
proved difficult whenever there are compulsory elements and inadequate attention to the cultural context. The respect for cultural diversity and its
conservation should be an important part of an overall conservation strategy, and may be the only practical means of attaining these goals. Through traditional practices and its ethnical style of appropriation of natural resources, every culture has
assimilated certain basic conditions for the regeneration of its ecosystems. The application of its
productive techniques thus induces a social process
of conservation and transformation of the environment that guarantees a sustained use of its resources. Nevertheless, the predominant economic
strategy, based on the maximization of profits and
wrapped in the ideology of human progress, has imposed a strong tendency towards the technological
unification of the cultural diversity of the human
race, displacing their traditional practices, de-
pleting their natural resources and degrading their

quality of life.

In our present historical and economic conditions, the alternative strategy to counteract the current ecological and cultural destructive process, cannot be based simply on the conservation of the landscape and the return to ancient cultural styles. Emergence and evolution define every living organization, as well as innovation as characteristic of human societies. Every culture, although identified by its traditions, is transformed through an historical process of influences from external social systems. Our historical option is to conceptualize an alternative strategy of development, based on the articulation of nature and culture and on a new paradigm of ecotechnological productivity, that would promote a sustained and diversified process of production of the means of well being for different human societies, while preserving their fundamental ecological structures and cultural traits for the reproduction of their natural resources.

The role of traditional practices in this eco-development strategy appears to be more complex than a simple historical return to the precapitalistic or "primitive" societies. In the first place, not all of their techniques and productive practices had a conservation impact on their environment. Moreover, the conservation qualities of those traditional practices do not simply arise from their technical properties, but in most cases are the effect of the social conditions of the application of such techniques, in the way that the productive practices are interlinked with the rest of the cultural behaviour of the people, their patterns of consumption, the socially sanctioned access to their resources, their religious beliefs. This is why the application of those traditional techniques will have its advantages only through a specific ethnical style of productive organization. The social and productive role of every individual within a culture, the deployment of his technical abilities, his knowledge of the environment, his attachment to his natal land, are all important elements of his personal identity and cultural integration. That is why the self-defence of the traditions of any community is the most efficient political action towards the preservation of its natural resources.

Even so, traditional practices cannot be preserved as such in an ecodevelopment strategy. Most of their productive techniques can become more productive through ecological and technological innovations, and some of them induce transformations of the whole productive organization of a community. Even culture will face these changes with different degrees of resistance and different attitudes and potentials of assimilation for these innovations. In other cases, especially in the more recent colonization projects, but also in communities strongly disrupted by their incorporation to the market economy, their actual productive practices and their technical means of exploitation of resources can already be ecologically inappropriate. In these cases, some of the unconscious conservation practices that in the traditional cultures were manifestations of their social and religious behaviour, now have to be replaced by an educational process and a conscious assimilation of some ecological and technological principles for the rational management of their resources[1].

In any case, not all the traditional practices that constitute an ethnical style of management of their resources can or should be preserved unchanged in an ecodevelopment strategy. It is therefore important to know the historical process of cultural assimilation of the ecosystems, as well as the historical transformation of the environment and the basic cultural traits that constitute the ethnical identity of a community and its principles of integrity. Nature and culture are complex inter-related processes that undergo ecological and historical transformations. Planners and scientists should participate in those processes not to try to reproduce their phenomenological manifestations, but to help preserve certain fundamental natural and cultural structures on which the productive potential of the ecosystems and the cultural integrity of a human society rely.

The above demands a scientific knowledge about the articulation between natural and social processes[2]. The inter-determination between nature and society cannot be fully understood through the effects induced by the international accumulation of capital on the exploitation of natural resources and the transformation of the ecosystemic structure and functions. These effects of the international economic system are always mediated by the cultural organization of the social formations living within a certain region. From there arises the importance of knowing the rationality of the peasant's society and of the so called "primitive" societies, as they generate the "laws" of exploitation and use of their resources, the conditions of reproduction-conservation or of exploitation-depletion of their environment.

Chayanov[3]/ has thus stated a law of equilibrium between the individual efforts and the consumption of the people in the community as the fundamental rationality of the peasant's economic unit. This law is constructed upon "demographic determinations" emerging from the family structure, and on a culturally-defined subjectivity of its individuals. These conditions would establish the balance and limits between the drive for consumption and the efforts to obtain it. The study of such cultural processes is important for a conservation strategy, as they help us to understand the rationality of the peasant's self-exploitation in relation to the satisfaction of their physiological and cultural needs, in a combined process of subsistence production and of commercial exchange with other communities and with the national and international economic systems. As the peasants' economies become inserted in the market system, the prices of their raw materials and foreign consumers' goods generally tend to rise in relation to the prices of their commerciable surplus. The rural worker tends then to increase the time he devotes to generate that surplus, as well as the rhythm and intensity of exploitation of its natural resources, often exceeding the capacity of the environment to regenerate those resources and destroying the conservation mechanisms of the soils against its degradation and irreversible erosion. This trend is increased by the intensification of the drive of consumption of the community through external propaganda, which generates a growing demand for the exploitation of a commerciable surplus and results in a continuous rise in the transfer of value from the peasant's economic unit to the external economic system. Nevertheless, the inexistence of an internal tendency in the rural societies towards a maximization of profits or of an economic surplus, acts as a balancing mechanism for the destructive effects upon the natural resources imposed by the capital accumulation process.

The use of some traditional techniques (whenever they have not been replaced by modern inappropriate technologies) helps to preserve the environment, even through a more intense exploitation of its resources. But these "buffer" effects disappear whenever the integrity of the culture is destroyed, and the peasant transformed into a wage-worker for the exploitation of the natural resources of the

region; it is worsened whenever inappropriate technological means of production are imposed upon the
traditional social organization and productive practices to maximize the profits of cash crops in the
short term.

Studies of pre-capitalist societies show as
well these conflicting and clearly differentiable
productive rationalities. There are those where
cultural practices are integrated with the conditions of equilibrium and conservation of the ecosystem; these seem to condition the social division
of labour and the productive roles of the community.
The productive process is mainly oriented to satisfy
the internal needs of the population, which balances
the carrying capacity of the ecosystem[4/]. In
contrast to this, other social formations tend to
maximize the commercial benefits of the exchange
value of their products; their traditional practices
and their traditional knowledge are more easily
transformed through the effects of the external
demands drawn upon their natural resources; the
production of such economic surplus often generates
an over-exploitation process of their ecosystems.

We have stressed the importance of understanding the cultural processes that mediate the articulation between the dominant historical and economic
processes, and the transformation of the natural
ecosystems. Nevertheless, the specificity of such
mediation can only emerge from the knowledge of the
structure of every culture, from the rationality of
its productive organization. The mediating character
of a traditional society over the effects of the
capitalist system on the environment, must then be
specified far beyond the economic determinations of
the commercial exchange between these social formations and the national and international economic
systems. On the other side, the demographic conditions of a peasant economic unit cannot simply be
derived from their genetic determinations, nor can
the division of labour of the pre-capitalist societies be explained with a framework of ecological
rationality. From the moment that language emerges
in human history, generating symbolic and ideological processes, it is impossible to understand a cultural organization as an emergence from its underlying biological structures. The symbolic effects
of language in history over-determine the genetic
determinations of human populations through their
effects on kinship structure, the production of
meaning in their religious beliefs and their social
roles. The productive notions taken by the people

do not simply respond to an ecological rationality, but the symbolization of the environment, the social meaning of their resources is articulated with the whole social organization and acts in return towards the process of transformation of the ecosystem through the productive practices of the culture. The forms of domination of a national and inter- national economic system over these different social formations depends upon the materiality of their cultural organization, generating differentiable forms of accumulation, of technical specialization and of exploitation of their resources.

Ethnology and Anthropology are fundamental theoretical tools to grasp this complex core of cul- tural organization and to reconstruct the ethnical styles of appropriation of the environment. At the same time they appear as practical disciplines to conduct a strategy of ecodevelopment, as the tra- ditional practices of pre-capitalist societies can serve as a starting point for the implementation of more efficient modes of management of the ecosystems under the principle of preserving its basic eco- logical structures and the cultural integrity of the people. In this sense, the theoretical function of these scientific fields, inasmuch as they help to reconstruct the historical process of articu- lation of culture and nature, serve the practical purpose of promoting a more harmonic structuration between ecosystems and sociosystems. Especially useful for the historiographic reconstruction of the interactions of different cultures with their natural resources is the study of ethnobotanics, and the analysis of its object of research deserves some attention.

Jacques Barrau places the origins of ethno- botanics even before the botanic taxonomy of Linneo. One of its precursors, Georg Everard Rumph, called Rumphius, already describes in his <u>Herbarium Amboinense</u> (1741-56) the popular nomenclature and taxonomy of the plants known to that culture. Nevertheless, the term "ethnobotanics" was invented by the American botanist Harschberger in 1895 for a scientific field of which the object would be to "show the cultural perspective of the tribes that used the plants or its products... determine the 'antique distribution' of the useful plants, and define the traces of the paths followed long time ago for the exchange of products of vegetal origin". The field of ethnobotanics was then enlarged with the findings of vegetal archaeology and the eth- nography of "primitive societies". Nevertheless, the ethnobotanic interests were oriented primarily towards the study of rare vegetals, with less enthusiasm for the more useful plants in general, and the domestic ones in particular. This retarded the botanic knowledge of plants of economic interest and the history of the social relations that determined the ecological and geographical transformations of the environment of different cultures. More recently, the field of ethnobotanics has included the "study of systems of ideas, notions and attitudes of an ethnical group with regard to their vegetal environment".

Barrau defines the enterprise of the ethnobotanist as one responding to three fundamental questions: 1) How men... see, understand and use their vegetal environment; how do they participate and how they recognize, name and classify their elements? 2) What is the cultural significance of the vegetals? 3) What are the origins, the uses, the properties and the economic value of these plants[5]?

Thus, ethnobotanics is the scientific study of the historical connections between different cultures and their vegetal environment. The specificity of these inter-relations arises from a double condition: from the natural one, the properties of the different plants determines its uses and the structure and functions of the ecosystem determines the evolution of its biologic populations; from the natural side, every cultural formation generates an ethnical style of appropriation of its environment that conditions the transformation of its ecosystems. From these inter-relations the productive functions of the community and its social division of labour take form, their technical means and abilities, their mythical representations, their patterns of consumption. But these cultural traits are also constituted through processes of transculturation that affect the social organization of an ethnical group and its actions towards their environment. The practical knowledge and the ideological formations of traditional societies emerge from the articulation of such ecological, cultural and historical processes.

Ethnobotanic enquiries are necessary to recover the traditional practices of today's and ancient cultures, and to unveil their historical process of constitution, conservation and destruction. Evidence and traces of these cultural processes can be found in the language and technology of these ethnical groups, as they emerge as structural tendencies[6] that sometimes survive to the actual traditional practices that made them emerge. Ethnolinguistics and ethnotechnology become then associated fields of an ethnological research. But inasmuch as the ethnobotanic study deals with the cultural significance and religious beliefs of the community, it should be supported by an anthropological study about the mythical representations of the people, as much of the rationality in their perception and use of their resources is "hidden" in their ideological formations[7].

In some cases the underlying values of the traditional societies in their unconscious behaviour towards nature and in the symbolism of their social practices will not be manifested in their cultural productions, technology, language or myths. A psycho-anthropologic inquiry on the cultural unconscious of the people (whose theoretical and methodological principles are yet to be developed) would then complete the study on the ethnical style of appropriation of the environment, and of the ideological formations of the community.

Anthropology, ethnobotanics and ecology thus become closely inter-related fields of knowledge, necessary to understand the traditional practices and the cultural management of natural resources. From a structural approach to the mythical representations, religious beliefs and unconscious behaviour, anthropology contributes to the analysis of the ideological formations of a culture[8]. This is important, as those formations do not simply reflect a natural economic rationality based upon a process of biological adaptation and assimilation to the environment through long periods of practical experimentation. This ideological conditioning of the peoples' actions determines their specific ethnical style of appropriation of their resources. From the perspective of the articulations of the traditional social formations with the national and international economy, the overall structure and rationality of a culture is a key factor in understanding the impact and resistance that the people and the environment will have on the demand for resources generated from the external economic system. Anthropological knowledge will also be necessary to re-establish some cultural traits of the population whenever they have been disrupted through the imposition of foreign modes of production and technological patterns, to rescue their cultural integrity and regenerate the productive capacity of their ecosystems.

From a spacial and physico-biological perspective, ecological research is necessary to understand the geographical conditioning of the environment on the cultural productive practices. It is an essential discipline as well for the planning of an ecodevelopment strategy. Only a well supported knowledge of the structure and functions of the different ecosystems can give us the clues for the transformations and selective regeneration that an ecosystem can assimilate, to maximize the productivity of the more useful species without disrupting the capacity of regeneration of the ecosystem. Ecological anthropology would then give us a closer view of the ecological conditions of a cultural organization and its rationality of resources' management.

From this articulated theoretical approach, ecological regeneration and cultural integration become inter-related processes. Biocenosis and history, evolution and social change are linked together. The research in the fields of ethnobotanics, ethnolinguistics and ethnotechnology will serve to rescue some traditional practices and the means of production of a culture, and to assess the ecological and historical viability of different modes of management of the natural resources[9/]. This traditional knowledge can then be fertilized by modern science and technology to generate an increasing ecotechnological productivity from the ecosystems while preserving the basic cultural traits of the people and conserving the essential ecological structures for the regeneration of their natural resources. This can only occur through a process of cultural assimilation for the generation of a new productive organization with more efficient means of production; from a participative action of the people in the defence of their resources and the management of their productive process in order to improve their living standards.

REFERENCES

1. Cf. E. Leff, "Hacia un Proyecto de Eco-desarrollo", in <u>Comercio Exterior</u>, Vol XXV, No. 1, Mexico, 1975.
2. Cf. E. Leff, "Sobre la Articulación de las Ciencias en la Relación Naturaleza-Sociedad", en E. Leff (Ed.), <u>Biosociologia y Articulación de las Ciencias</u>, UNAM, México, 1981.

Ethnobotany and Anthropology

3. A.V. Chayanov, La Organización de la Unidad Económica Campesina, Nueva Visión Ed., Buenos Aires, 1974.

4. Cf. M. Godelier, Antropología y Biología, Ed. Anagrama, Barcelona 1976; C. Meillassoux, Terrains et Théories, Ed. Anthropos, Paris, 1977.

5. J. Barrau, "L'Ethnobotanique au Carrefour des Sciences Naturelles et des Sciences Humaines", Bull. Soc. Bot. Fr. Num. 118, 1971, pp. 238 y ss.; "Plantes et Comportements des Hommes qui les Cultivent, l'Oeuvre Ethnobotanique d'André Haudricourt", La Pensée, 171, pp. 37-46.

6. Cf. A. Leroi-Gourhan, Le Geste et la Parole, 2 Vols. Albin Michel, Paris, 1964-1965.

7. Cf. M. Godelier, Economía, Fetichismo y Religión en las Sociedades Primitivas, Siglo XXI Eds., Mexico, 1974; C. Lévi-Strauss, "Structuralism and Ecology", in Social Science Information, Vol 12, No. 1, 1972, pp. 7-23.

8. Cf. C. Lévi-Strauss, Structural Anthropology, Allen Lane, The Penguin Press, London, 1968.

9. Cf. A.G. Haudricourt, "Domestication des Animaux, Culture des Plantes et Traitement d'Autrui", L'Homme, Vol 2, Num. 1, 1962; and "Nature et Culture dans la Civilization de l'Ingame: L'Origine des Clones et des Clans", L'Homme, Vol. 4, Num. 1, 1964. P. Gourou, "La Civilisation du Végétal", Indonésie, Vol 1, No. 5, 1948, pp 387-392.

268

Chapter Nineteen

CULTURAL ECOLOGY AND "MANAGEMENT" OF NATURAL
RESOURCES OR KNOWING WHEN NOT TO MEDDLE

By

P. Nowicki
9, rue de Collégiale
59800 Lille, France

ABSTRACT

In reviewing the literature including contributions
to this volume, the "noble savage" idea can only be
understood in relation to specific examples empirically observed. There are many difficulties too in
making planners appreciate cultural realities and
even more in letting the people communicate. But
"management" is also a sacrosanct concept, and may
be even more insidious than the "noble savage" idea.
And what is most lacking is discretion, leaving a
tendency to meddle which can have quite adverse
results.

The concept of the noble savage refuses to disappear, and perhaps rightly so. But let us understand this concept in terms of "noblesse oblige",
in that the rights to a certain title imply a structure of obligations within which that right is exercised.
     This structure of obligations is the axis of
our analysis which reflects our interest in cultural
adaptation to ecological reality. This structure
of obligations in the sense of cultural ecology is
no more and no less than the fit or misfit of human
land-use practices with regard to the carrying capacity of a given ecological system.
     The ideal of a symbiotic relationship between
man and nature seems to be demonstrated by one historical analysis, that of Gadgil concerning pre-
Colonial India, in which man is capable of behaving
as a "prudent predator". His model of the traditional distribution of resource use has a striking
resemblance to the model of different species of
the same genus (such as the birds in our garden)

which have overlapping niches. The analogy between the development of the caste system and the phenomenon of niche specialization according to the ecological models is not difficult to arrive at, and is intellectually very satisfying.

The debate on the validity of the noble savage concept can not be settled ex cathedra, however, but by empirical observation. Thus, as we shall see shortly we shall find nuances which are extremely important in the development of management strategies for the conservation of the world's resources, both biological and cultural!

The historical analysis of Mauritanian ecological evolution and cultural adaptive mechanisms by Gritzner[1] is fascinating in that we see an initial adaptation to an environmental system that with time changed because of climatic shifts. Resource use no longer being adequate to the constraints of the environmental situation produces degradation of the ecological system. Successive cultural changes in land-use practices seem to attempt to find a new equilibrium, but each time the weakness of the perturbed ecological system causes it to degrade even further before a new equilibrium with the carrying capacity can be attained. The degradation accelerates with intemperate incursion of new cultural elements from the outside, be they Berbers, Arabs, or Europeans, and land-use practices totally incompatible with long-term resource utilization completely decimate what potential there was in a sustainable relationship between local indigenous populations and their environment.

History repeats itself, cruelly and unrelentlessly, as we see in the Sudan, through the exposé given by Omar Draz regarding the inability in official circles, in the promulgation and application of a Decree in 1953, to recognize the ecological importance of the Hema system of range reserves in the Arabian Peninsula. That these lands were opened to free grazing went against the inherent sense of the social organization of grazing rights (and their control!), which even found expression in codified form in the Koran. It is a pity that his conclusion is recognized only after the fact that precious resources have been wasted.

> Groups of people met in the various countries where hema have been maintained, are of the opinion that if previously practised rights of usufruct were restored or allowed to be given, subject to fulfil-

ment of certain requirements, regeneration
of vast areas or ranges of forest land
could be achieved.

So it is that, even in contemporary times, the continued survival of important land areas in which
indigineous people have retained land-use practices
compatible with the ecological potential of their
site induces almost awesome respect, as in the case
of the Jebali people in the Jebel Qara Region of
South Oman, as described by Lamprey, or also certain
native populations in Latin America studied by
Leslie A. Brownrigg. This discovery of the apparently harmonious relationship between man and his
environment leads to a statement by the latter
author that,

> Native people possess an exact knowledge
> of the environment, including the species
> and ecological relations among them. Hunt-
> ing, gathering and fishing under native
> regimes apply knowledge of the natural
> history of each species to sustain yields
> through managed harvesting.

This thesis is the subject of Wilkes' presentation
of the Gitksan and Carrier Indians of north-west
British Columbia, Canada, but in a strikingly different context. For these Canadian Indians are
claiming the restoration of rights to manage the
catch of salmon, on the basis that their traditional
management has been more suitable to maintain sustainable yields, as was practised before the Federal
Government of Canada intervened on the question of
fishing rights. The two authors mentioned just
before, however, are regarding man-nature relationships which have not yet been submitted to the influence of outside management.

So is it the "native" in reality the epitome
of homo ecologicus, towards whom we should be turn-
ing for instruction on resource management? The
question is not posed (entirely) tongue-in-cheek!
We have to clarify our thinking towards indigineous
cultures, and the cultural ontology of their resource management, in order to better appreciate the
basis for our own motives in proposing management
plans.

This aspect of native mentality, a symbiotic
relationship between cultural and natural forces,
is in fact the reasoning behind the enigmatic postulates of François Terrasson.

> En explorant alors le domaine symbolique d'une culture on obtient en décriptant les symboles la véritable image de la nature qui fait fonctionner la société et prendre les décisions relatives aux zones naturelles du territoire.
>   Le symbolisme de la vie quotidienne ... nous dira également une foule de choses qui nous permettra de savoir si la société en question est un terrain favorable pour les mesures de conservation.

The text of Vayda et al. gives us good insights about the cultural reality relative to conservation, and by extension to natural resource management as a planning exercise. But before going further, we must put ourselves in the right state of mind by recalling that the consideration of "wealth" in non-economic terms is difficult in benefit-optimization paradigms which characterize planning. (An indication of the extent to which "The greatest good for the greatest number" concept of Bellamy pervades our cultural ontology regarding resource use.) In addition, benefit-optimization paradigms ignore that people confronted by the necessity to live will often take the path of least resistance.

> So far, most of the people we have been studying have been found responsive to economic opportunity. Being responsive does not mean, however, that they are ready to consider all the possible alternative uses of their labor, land, or capital, and then chose from them those likely to be most profitable. If there is an opportunity to gain profit in a particular way, the people frequently respond to that without necessarily considering whether or not there might be other ways even more profitable.

In fact, the basic problem of planning when confronting cultural reality is that plans are unresponsive to unprogrammed variables. Cultural reality is the day-to-day effort to survive with an end in mind that is other than wealth itself, be it purification by a pilgrimage to Mecca, or whatever. So instead of being astonished, we can understand the following reflection.

Some observers have concluded that a lack of obvious long-term planning by people in some areas implies an absence of decision-making capabilities. But the people we are observing in this project repeatedly demonstrate their willingness to use their minds actively rather than slavishly following a plan. Indeed, one can argue that in the absence of a firm, comprehensive plan, more, not less, decision-making is required.

In addition to the cultural ontology with regard to resource use governing human activity, the economic bias of planning may equally ignore the ecological reality in which the cultural reality is imbedded. In a rather concrete fashion, the "best" of plans fail because of basic ignorance in this domain. Piously, one can exhort planners to bring their data base to the people, to be verified and completed by them; but it may be difficult to obtain a rational exposé of local knowledge of the environment, in that a culture will have already translated the ecological reality into symbols which are totally incompatible with the "economic" reasoning regarding resource exploitation. The native, however, is not "dupe", and he will <u>not</u> interact with his ecological context in a way which will not give at least minimal results. This much, at least, the resource manager can observe, so as not to propose an objective which defies the common sense of local knowledge.

Communication with regard to the ecological basis for the cultural ontology of resource use is of course possible, but within certain limits that the outsider must be aware of. In order for a dialogue to be established, both parties must be able to transform their symbolic perception of ecological reality into a common lexicon. Some symbols may be very easy to reconstruct, by a substitution of elements which reflect the common lexicon, but others may not be. Why? Perhaps because it is difficult to substitute elements,

a) either fundamentally;
b) or because no replacement elements are readily perceived.

In such a situation, there are two possibilities. Either that one cultural ontology with regard to resource use substitutes itself for another - the classic process of westernized development - or the potentially dominant culture has to interpret by itself, the second culture to understand the symbolic construction of its physical universe. Untying the Gordion knot of a culture/environment relationship is perhaps the best contribution which cultural ecology can make to a conservation-oriented management plan.

To arrive at such an analytical result, the best may be again to take a clue from Terrasson, this time his examination of hedgerows, and to look at the landscape as a cultural manifestation. By this we mean that it is necessary to study the landscape, as modified by the man-nature interaction, to know which aspects have a functional role, in addition to the more political attributes in a cultural sense.

As much as hedgerows reinforce, in effect, agricultural productivity, therefore they must be understood not so much as boundaries demarcating land-tenure rights but as mechanisms to insure water retention and temperature control. So it is in general that, through the analysis of landscape attributes for meeting particular management objectives, and which to retain in order to maintain basic natural equilibria.

This leads us to make a distinction between natural resource management programmes per se, and the necessary prerequisite cultural conditioning so that a management programme will succeed.

For it should be evident by now, with all due respect to the concept of the noble savage, that a particular cultural group may or may not respect the constraints on resource use stemming from the theoretical carrying capacity of the land. This we see through several of the texts referred to so far, and again in the account of traditional marine resource management in the Pacific by Gary A. Klee. We can also remark from this example of Oceanic peoples among others, quite interestingly reflected as well by Polunin's examination of the maritime people of Indonesia, that direct responsibility for resources promotes resource use practices compatible with resource sustainability.

Continuing this line of reflection, in the case of the Lebali and the Latin American Indians, why is it necessary to institute management plans in areas where the people live harmoniously, to all apparent purposes, with their environment? What are the motivations of management, let alone development... and to this question the only answer lies in an analysis of which groups in the social context gain by such measures (and by how much), and which groups lose. The sceptic will have an a priori intuition that the loser is our protagonist, the noble savage, and his kinsmen.

With regard to any development project it is important to be able to know, to identify, who gains, who loses. That is, which social groups are concerned at each end of the stick: who have long-term interests, who have short-term.

There is a difference in making a punctual investment which increases the overall productive capacity of an ecological system, which supports itself, and the investment which changes initial circumstances so that the system is no longer self-supporting... then continued input from outside the system is necessary to maintain those who depend upon it, and internal productivity never equals the need for outside input.

Thus, as much as a cultural ecologist can presume to be a planner, there is an argument to be advanced for least compromising land-use planning, holding as many options open for the future as possible, by choosing land-use options which pose the least constraints on other possible uses... To do nothing may mean that everything still remains possible.

Let us take a closer look at what it means to feel responsible for the long-term use of sustainable resources, in particular from the angle of "who wins/who loses". Then, and only then, can we turn with some lucidity to the whole concept of "management" of natural resources.

It is too tempting to pass by the occasion to let the "natives" speak for themselves on this subject, so let us not resist temptation, and we shall recite a series of quotations from the text of Kemp regarding the perspective of management of the Inuit territories in Canada. For precisely in this context can we appreciate "the logic of social responsibility that sped the process of territorial acquisition and cultural displacement" which Kemp so justly puts into the limelight[2].

Perhaps this general attitude gives rise to more specific interpretations of the future role of native people, such as that stated by an investment banker in Montreal on May 8, 1974.

"... That the north will be developed and the resources utilized for the con-

> tinuation of the industrial sector of
> Canadian, and when warranted, Western
> Society, is no longer a question. The
> millions living in the developed regions
> of Canada cannot be held captive by a
> handful of people wishing to hunt rab-
> bits".

This logic finds itself in opposition
to another, that of the Inuit, as expressed by one of the rabbit hunters' himself.

> Please try to fathom our great desire
> to survive in a way somewhat different
> than yours. We do not dislike Western or
> Whiteman. We simply treasure our young
> and our culture. It is our belief that
> both (you and we) can live together side
> by side, but not necessarily eating out
> of the same bowl.

It must be underlined, when reflecting on these on-
tological statements, that the idea itself of management has some inherently rather biased connotations. For it we regard the question from the
perspective of our noble savage, again an Inuit; we
may find that his opinion on the matter is radically
different from our own.

> There is no group which has a greater
> interest in protecting fish and game re-
> sources than the village people who depend
> upon them for subsistence.

What is most insidious is the concept of management
itself. Whereas it is not so difficult to ridicule
the concept of the "noble savage", on the contrary
the concept of "management" has such sacrosanct
overtones that we are blind to the fact that, as a
concept (at least from the Western way of perceiving
it), it might be the more ridiculous of the two.

If for no other reason, the collection of texts
which are under our consideration is capital for a
serious reflection on the very meaning of management. What an occasion to demonstrate that management, if nothing else, should imply great discretion
before acting.

Thus we arrive at an appropriate stage to look
at the concept of management itself. Elsewhere
beforehand we have raised the question of why we
should want to manage anything at all, and yet we
realize that our noble savage may or may not be able

to do the job for us... and even if he can, as we
take up more than our fair share of space on this
planet, he will sooner or later be confronted with
a management problem which goes way beyond his capacities for coping: the continuous breaking down
of one link in the ecological chain after another,
a seemingly implacable process set in, motion by the
not-so-noble civilized society (of all epochs, for
that matter).

Management is a way of restoring a certain
virginity which has been lost. We wish to do now
what others may have been doing already before we
came along. Simply, the scale of the operation has
changed, as has that of the use of natural resources. We talk, in fact, about assuming responsibility. But as we are "sharing" the resources of
others, we are more or less constrained to share
responsibility for management with them. So, in
passing, let us incorporate in a theoretical construction of management another observation of Kemp,
that "responsibility, however, cannot be super-
imposed from the outside, nor can assumptions and
information upon which problems are identified and
decisions are made, ignore the local concerns and
points of view..." There we are! We are in the
position of calling the tune after having expro-
priated the fiddle.

It is important, when we shall try to conceive
of management from the perspective of cultural ecology, to realize the incongruity of the situation.
To illustrate this situation, no better expression
can be found than in this last passage extracted
from Kemp[3]/, which is remarkable for its poignant
clarity.

The potential explosiveness of the situation must be realized, and programs and
action must reflect the lack of Inuit
feelings about their lack of ability to
make changes. The Inuit feel themselves
to be victimized at many levels. Victims
of a political system that forces them to
negotiate for land that they already know
is theirs; victims of a bureaucracy that
does not recognize their desire for an
effective voice in decision making; victims of a funding system that does not
provide assistance for resource problems
viewed as important by local people; victims of a system of economic priorities
that allows for development to take place

at the expense of native values and life style; victims of having to justify their harvesting practices while development can make massive, long-term impacts on the environment and ecology; victims of a system of scientific enquiry which does not facilitate their access to sources of expertise who are actually willing to transfer their expertise, not sell it, to native people.

The contribution which cultural ecology can make to the development of management strategies - once we have passed the psycho-analytical phase of determining our real motivations for wanting to manage for someone else when we have not made such a brilliant effort for ourselves - is to elucidate how to understand "traditional" cultures as management systems. It is necessary to discern the keys for success... or failure... of a management process already engaged on a small scale, confronting the very ecological dynamic which we wish to manage on a larger, "comprehensive" level.

The problem, for the cultural ecologist in any case, is to understand why traditional practices developed. This will reveal a number of things, not the least of which is the theoretical carrying capacity of the land. The methodology, broadly speaking but sufficient for our purpose of illustration, is to discern what has been the evolution of the environment, because of,

a) either the influences ("impacts" for the moderns) of traditional practices,
b) or the natural changes (especially in climate, or species migration or degradation).

Obviously the influence of one might set in process a modification of the other, but it is usually possible to understand which is the independent, and which the dependent variable.

As fine examples of this, we have the texts of Klee and Gritzner. What is most significant is to determine under which "management regimes", in face of which ecological conditions, an equilibrium between social and natural forces has been achieved. No better example of this, and the corollary argument which follows, is the text regarding "Saving Siberut, A Conservation Master Plan". To continue, continual degradation historically can only imply that either the existing culture is not "condition", or rather adapted to the ecological dynamic with which it interacts, or that political power systems have become imposed on resource exploitation systems (implicitly, as an extraneous influence on a local culture). In either case, one encounters inertia with regard to experimenting with new "management" techniques as the physical environment changes.

It is necessary to remain lucid when considering the matter. Zero-sum games have existed long before Morgenstern explained them; and many societies have unwittingly played them, if one will allow the hyperbole. Cultural ecology can identify this situation, and explain it, which is far more important if it is necessary to "condition" the culture before implementing a management programme for it to succeed. After all, human nature might be responsible - for many things - but as Clifford Geertz has so succinctly put it, "There is no such thing as human nature independent of culture".

Historically, by a process of feed-back between proto-man's physical capacities, the natural parameters of his environment, the development of his neurological potential, and thus, finally, his increasing faculty to create a symbolic construction of both natural and social reality (and their interactions!), the biological entity "homonoid" became the cultural entity homo sapiens.

There are certain security mechanisms in this process of acculturation, or the whole process would have been dashed against the rocks the first time the wind changed direction. This metaphor explains human resistance to a whole series of natural calamities, be they long-term droughts or basic climatic shifts. The following passage is witness to the remarkable fact that a culture, once having achieved a symbiotic relationship with its natural environment, is resistant to change in itself. Alas for our pretentions for "conditioning" a culture to successfully become integrated into the functioning of a management plan! Gritzner notes "the environmental consequences of the removal of perennial grasses by grazing livestock..."

> It is perhaps somewhat ironic that historical use pressure and the traditional focus of developers upon increased agricultural and pastoral production have largely destroyed the very resources that sustained Mauritanian populations during periods of scarcity. Geographers, anthropologists, and botanists active in the

Sahel have long realized that when drought, disease, warfare, or other mishaps result in agricultural failure (requirements in excess of crop yield and storage) or sharply reduced livestock populations, these peoples were sustained by coping strategies based upon the availability of diverse native plants and animals.

Many of these species, as well as literally hundreds of other useful species recorded in the various biogeographical surveys... prior to Mauritanian independence (1960) are now either regionally extinct or occur in numbers so modest that they are no longer capable of guaranteeing the survival of needy populations.

While admiring the beauty of adaptive mechanisms, all of this is understandably discouraging for both the environmental and cultural manipulators, to call a spade a spade and thus name planners for what they really are. Not that we should not wish them success, but it is fair to say that this review, and all of the texts so ably by themselves, seek to remind the reader of the necessity to know very well why a management plan is necessary in the first place. The fact that there are good examples of management plans, as for Siberut in Indonesia, should not offset our incredulity in certain cases that a management plan is really necessary.

If cultural ecology demonstrates anything, it is that it is all too easy to meddle, either with cultures or with their natural environments, but it is very difficult to propose a management strategy better than their own. After all, these very cultures have been meddling with their own environments for quite some time, and the moral of the story is that they succeed as often as they do not to adapt in a symbiotic way.

We would like to end where others might have thought it appropriate to begin... True to a certain reputation for understatement characteristic of its culture, the Concise Oxford Dictionary gives meddle as v.i., busy oneself unduly (with), interfere (in).

If humans are anything, they are meddlesome, a., fond of meddling.

Finally, we will do well to keep in mind, when conceiving of a management plan for others, that culture is far more than a model of behaviour: it is an "ensemble" of reasons for a certain type of behaviour.

This point of view of cultural ecology has also philosophical overtones; and, to the extent that this point of view can "condition" the cultural bias of those involved in natural resource management, I have found no better credo than the following passage of Tabayiwa.

I do believe our purpose is to generate enthusiasm in conservation. I believe we are searching for meaningful tools. I believe we are all aware that sheer need to live on our natural resources is our biggest obstacle. I also believe those who live near virgin forests, in a way the trustees of our wildlife heritage, are also so poor that they need the harvest of the forests the most. I also believe that those who derive ornaments and pleasure from plunging into the wilderness are in the long run a force to reckon with. I believe we are aware that nature appreciation is not governed by a universal attitude. People interact with animals in different ways and for different reasons. The balance of nature as a scientific concept does not appeal to the man whose fields are devastated by monkeys, kudus and baboons. It is enough here to say that the totem system in Shona society was developed through observation and profound appreciation of nature. Times have changed and collective benefit from the wilderness has to be reciprocated by collective responsibility over what we all and each must have. An effort has to be made to induce a collective understanding that the wilderness cannot provide forever without a caretaker. Education thus becomes an essential dimension in conservation. To be effective, it is necessary to be sensitive to the already existing experiences and outlooks. The conservation theme must stretch further to include rebuilding of what we have already lost.

NOTES

1. In Commission for Environmental Planning (IUCN). Working Paper No. 13.
2. Op. cit. IUCN/CEP Working Paper, No. 13.
3. Op. cit. IUCN/CEP Working Paper, No. 13.

Chapter Twenty

TOWARDS ETHNOCONSERVATION

By

David Pitt
IUCN/CEP
CH-1196 Gland, Switzerland

ABSTRACT

A new synthetic discipline is called for uniting
the anthropological and ethnological sciences,
oriented specifically towards conservation goals
working through popular level initiatives including
traditional ideas. In such a folk ecology qualitative methods and improved communications would play
an important role.

INTRODUCTION

The most important feature of the papers in this
volume is probably the emergence or potential of a
new synthetic discipline uniting anthropology and
the ecological sciences which we might call - Ethnoconservation. This kind of combination is not of
course new. In an important essay on shifting agriculture, first published in 1954, Conklin develops
what he calls an ethno-ecological approach (Conklin
in Vayda, 1969) the use of ethnography, or participant observation to look at environmental attitudes
and behaviour. And of course without being called
ethno-something, there were similar unnamed approaches amongst earlier generations of anthropologists interested in ecology (e.g. again Vayda,
1969). Charles Winick in his 1968 Dictionary of
Anthropology mentions Ethnobiology. Ethnobotany
and ethnozoology generally have now well established
networks of interested specialists. Ethno in these
groups means both cultural and historical aspects
related to specific social groups which claim a
common descent or other close affinities. Recent
social anthropology has been much interested in
culture, indeed the subject has been called cultural

anthropology in some countries. Here again the recent emphasis has not been on the material culture itself, or on behaviour (as in Unesco's Encyclopedia of Social Science, 1964) which was in any case very often observations by outsiders of what it was thought people were doing. Culture has been seen rather as a set of ideas, symbols and models which penetrate all levels of society and which define in fact that society, and mark it off as a sub-culture. Language is important in culture in this sense and local religion, philosophy, arts and so on (CEP, 1983).

But the conservation angle, or more precisely linkages to conservation strategies, environmental planning and the larger problems of socio-economic development planning are still in an early stage of theoretical formulation and incorporation in pragmatic policies and programmes. The purpose of this paper, is to build on the contributions in this volume by suggesting the roles that anthropology can play in the creation of ethnoconservation, as an action oriented discipline. These contributions may be summarized under five major headings: social remoteness, alternative models, folk ecology, populist thrust and qualitative models.

THE EMPHASIS ON SOCIAL REMOTENESS

Modern social or cultural anthropology has had a long-standing interest in the tribal and indigenous peoples who are the focus of this volume. This interest partly stems from the history of a discipline which was once very closely linked to the bones and stones subjects, physical anthropology and archaeology. The break with these disciplines was not only a division of labour but of ideological dimensions too. An evolutionary premise underlay physical anthropology and archaeology. There was an assumption that the people today who lived subsistence lives were like the predecessors of the agricultural and ultimately, the modern industrial urban world. Modern social anthropology has taken a comparative rather than an evolutionary stance. Subsistence socio-economic systems were seen to be different, part often of social groups who were socially remote, rather than inferior in any sense. Whilst it may have been accurate to describe these societies as apparently traditional, resisting outside incursions of ideas, political power, this appearance could be deceptive. Tradition was often

an amalgam of new and old ideas, beliefs and behaviours flexible enough (Pitt, 1970 and 1976) to adapt
where necessary to situations of so-called "modern-
ism", industrialization, urbanization etc, as demonstrated by successful production systems with or
without capitalist infrastructures and the vast
numbers of migrants to urban areas.

The question of subsistence level was relevant
only in that it reflected social, political and
economic distance. For this reason anthropologists
have also been interested in those minorities who
are not at a subsistence level, but still outcast,
cut off from the majority society, by processes of
exclusion within that society or separated by a
deliberate "policy" amongst the people themselves.

The interest in these socially remote people
was undoubtedly in part due to pressures within and
between the different social science disciplines.
Social anthropologists are a minority themselves in
academe and even more in the development agencies.
Known as people who are prepared to spend their
lives in remote corners of the globe in quite intimate contact with what are thought to be strange
customs they are often suspected by their western
colleagues. As independence movements have replaced the colonial structures their reception at a
national level had been, with some exceptions,
hardly more cordial. The interest in the tribal
dimension, or in social exclusion was seen as a
political threat, especially when the anthropologists were indigenous, from the disposessed groups
themselves. Social anthropology had been pushed
more and more towards the peripheral social groups,
in some cases to serve as witnesses to their extinction (as amongst the Ik of Uganda) (Turnbull, 1972)
or their dispersal (it is rumoured that the anthropologist is the last person left on some Tokelau
Islands).

Social distance may be argued to be of fundamental significance to ethnoconservation. We have
seen in this volume that tribal and indigenous
people are the poorest of the poor, to use the World
Bank's phrase (Goodland, 1982). If they do number
200 million (though there are also estimates of 300
million) they constitute the largest single group
of the world's absolute poor. They are also the
people who inhabit the most fragile ecosystems,
where there are greatest numbers of endangered
species. In some cases the tribal peoples themselves are endangered, and there is still a massive
population decline, not only through migration but

Towards Ethnoconservation

through the ravages of diseases, seen in high mortality, especially infant mortality rates. The
argument that these peoples should be the first to
receive any help and protection seems at first sight
irrefutable. But the anthropologists have been able
to show that help in the past, even when well intentioned, has sometimes hurt the people. The unique
role and challenge for anthropology is to show how
the maximum of local identity can be preserved in a
world where development comes habitually from outside. Ethnoconservation and any anthropological
contribution to it, has to be part of "development
from below" (Pitt, 1976) where there is first of
all an understanding of the alternative nature of
many tribal societies.

ALTERNATIVE MODELS OF CLASSIFICATION

Edmund Leach (1976) has recently distinguished
between two types of social anthropology. An empirical anthropology, where there is direct observation of behaviour, and what he calls a rationalist
anthropology where there is an emphasis on categories of thought and ideology. Empirical anthropology has been important in providing studies of
observations about behaviour in environmental matters. But rationalist anthropology may have even
more potential . The latter which was pioneered by
Sir Edward Evans-Pritchard (e.g. 1940 studies of
the nomadic Nuer), showed the importance of ideas,
social values etc, in ecological behaviour. Such
an anthropology shows also that there are alternative approaches both to classifying the animal world
and man's relationships to it. Tambiah (1969) in
Thailand for example, showed how the classification
of animals is related to the social structure
through dietary prohibitions and this is well described in a number of studies of so called totemic
systems (Douglas, 1973). Bulmer in his New Guinea
studies (1967) showed for example why the Cassowry
is "not" a bird.
        The practical importance of these alternative
systems is enormous. Too often there are assumptions
about the relative value of different fauna and
flora and that the choice on the relative preservation of species and economic development goals
can be relatively easily resolved. The work of the
ethno-anthropologists have shown the complexity of
this situation and the inappropriate nature of many
outside views. A conservation strategy for example

286

elaborated by a person from a tribal and indigenous people might favour radically different species and different goals from that produced in Gland or the capital cities of the countries.

FOLK ECOLOGY

Anthropologists, rationialist and empirical, have been interested not only, in fact, not mainly, in dry taxonomies and classifications, but in the holistic models which people hold and the wide range of relationships which link them with their environment. What has been called a "folk-ecology" literature (e.g. Richards, 1975; Brokensha, 1980) has emerged. Here anthropology has a major contribution to make because the major thrust of this literature is to argue that traditional belief systems and practices are indeed alternative, possibly superior modes of managing environments. It has been clearly shown that such systems, even if based on what appear to be magical notions, are most often not at all irrational and may actively promote development goals.

There is a good deal of evidence to show that grass roots goals are not the same as those that predominate in orthodox western development or environmental theory. The accent may not be so much on economic goals, increases in productivity or income etc, but rather social goals, the preservation of certain valued ways and certain qualities of life, the resolution of local social conflicts and problems and above all, self reliance (Self Reliance, 1982). One can say that such goals are being increasingly recognized and increasingly incorporated in the new thinking on development. For example, in the international system, there has been a recognition that quality of life indicators (like PQLI) may be more important targets to aim at, rather than say goals such as GNP per capita. A critical argument from the point of view of environmental planning is that many traditional societies exist in fragile ecosystems that are easily and often degraded by outside influences after centuries of stability under traditional systems. It has been said for example that the dry ecosystems in which people like the Masai live have puzzled western ecologists but may represent the only method of existing in this difficult environment.

An important aspect of folk ecology has been folk demography (Ardener, 1974), indeed the revival

of interest by anthropologists in the environment
from the late sixties was stimulated mainly by the
great population - resources debate (e.g. Vayda,
1969; McFarlane, 1976). There are a number of anthropological studies which have shown the different
types of demographic attitudes that exist in traditional societies. Much of the great debate on
population, resources and conservation would be
better informed if these anthropological materials
were taken into account. It is not simply a question
of understanding why some groups favour larger families and then blaming environmental and development
problems on this. Anthropological studies have
shown that there are a range of demographic behaviours amongst traditional societies. In some cases,
(the Micronesian Yap Islands being the best docu-
mented case where the resource base was very limited) there were well-developed forms of birth control as well as social constraints on population
growth well before any modern family planning experts arrived (Pitt, 1977). Elsewhere it was shown
(e.g. Nepal, McFarlane, 1976) that population growth
or decline had a logic of its own, understandable
only in terms of the specific culture and situation.
    However, it is true that many societies do
place a different value on children than many
western societies, whether there are resource difficulties or not. Children are seen as a means of
providing essential labour or income, in situations
where machinery is either too expensive or presents
often insuperable logistical problems. Children are
an essential form of security, for care in old age
and sickness in those societies, the vast majority
of which do not have effective welfare state systems. This economic and social logic might be
argued to underlie pronatalist religions or similar
cultural values and structures rather than vice
versa.

THE POPULIST THRUST

Much social anthropology has then been concerned in
understanding, describing and analyzing the nature
of tribal societies. Characteristically such analyses have ended up in weighty tomes which line the
bookshelves of western libraries and museums. But
understanding has in recent years extended from
sympathy to promotion of what the peoples themselves
actually want. In international development strategies this is an important departure. Most of the

literature and action programmes since the mid-1970s
have been concerned with what Emmerj (1978) first
called basic needs. These were the elemental needs
which any group of people should have: health, safe
water, shelter, food and so on. But these needs
were characteristically defined most often by outside experts. They were needs which it was assumed
poor people needed. This was not necessarily the
same thing as what the people wanted. Although of
course there are quantitative minima which apply to
many basic needs, like calorific intake of food
etc., most have a cultural component (e.g. the type
of food) and local priorities. Also there are many
wants which are not material, particularly related
to human rights, identity and independence.

Many anthropologists in these situations have
not hesitated to present, espouse and advocate the
local cause. In some cases the anthropologist has
been an ombudsman (Salisbury in Pitt, 1976a).
Anthropologists have been particularly active in
the formation and running of non-governmental organizations which seek to protect and promote the
cause of exploited tribal peoples whose rights,
notably in land and resources, are threatened.
Groups like Survival International or Cultural
Survival have been dominated by anthropologists,
though the profession has also been used by those
who seek to control or exploit more effectively.

QUALITATIVE MODELS

Part of the alternative approach which has emerged
in recent social anthropology relates to a qualitative approach to conservation and environmental planning. Qualitative planning may itself be a cultural
phenomenon and it is also in some cases an impedi-
ment to planning either because such planning is
too top down (notably when planning becomes a self-
fulfilling prophecy) or not responsive enough to the
often rapid and volatile changes in environmental
and development situations. There is a saying from
Africa which says that you can only measure the toad
when it is dead.

Social anthropology has derived its data from
a close participant observation (or exceptionally
an intimacy with detailed historical records). From
such data it is possible to build up a picture of
local culture and wants and aspirations following
the French proverb that the truth is in the nuances.
From the outside such a qualitative approach has

been seen as the antithesis of the quantitative. But this is a misconception. The qualitative is an alternative method of measurement, relative not absolute. It may be equally pragmatic, near enough may be good enough for many purposes and the best may be often the enemy of the good. Striving to reach let us say World Health Organization's standards of water purity may be impossible and of marginal utility over lesser but adequate achievement.

But more important perhaps is that a qualitative approach can reflect more readily both the reality of life and the cultural context. Modern applied mathematics is in fact discovering the utility of qualitative mathematics, of topology, of catastrophe theory (Zeeman, 1977). The utility of such theories is that they are more flexible, but also are able to accommodate to a fundamental error in much quantitative modelling. Simply, many events of critical importance occur randomly. For example recent projections of world food capacities by the FAO and other international agencies have carried tne riders that their scenarios are dependent on the absence of any untoward events, like war, economic recessions etc. Such remoteness from reality may explain why so much planning and projection is as Peter Hall (1982) called it - a disaster.

The argument is not only that relatively simple quantification is often sufficient (computers work after all with two numbers) but that the cultural dimension is very often what is of significance to people. The Australian Aborigines count, one, two, many. But the many, be they animals, birds or whatever are identified individually, in terms of differentiation features relevant to the culture. In a sense, aboriginal mathematics are much more subtle than the Euclidian variety, as well as being humanized. Certainly many social, and with them environmental problems arise from the anomic alienating statistical processes that do not take into account the human factor.

What we have said about quantification might also be extended to questions of time and space. One of the most important sets of data to emerge from anthropological fieldwork has been the demonstration of alternative systems of time. Evans-Pritchard (1940) showed for example amongst the Nilotic Nuer how time was structured around significant social and economic events, and this has been well demonstrated in other fieldwork monographs. This different conception of time is often a fundamental obstacle to many environmental and development programmes. Again many strategies contain orderly progressions in time but these do not match with the perodic intensity of life amongst tribal peoples. Very often key economic activities amongst indigenous people (and associated ceremonial and ritual) are sporadic. This often unappreciated fact may result in disaster when for example migrant labour is recruited at these key times, or programmes are introduced without reference to cultural rhythms which characteristically take a long time to absorb new, possibly threatening, cultural items. Many programmes labelled as failures may have been successful if the slower cycle was understood. The time problems of environmental planning are, as Jacobs (1981) has argued, a priority area for action and research.

Similar comments could be made about space boundaries where much planning has missed the point of flexibility, so confining peoples to given pieces of land when their essential movements were nomadic, or deprived them of land which was central to their cultural heritage. More fundamentally, the rigid classifications of populations for administrative purposes has often frozen a structure where different peoples may have mixed and merged (Leach, 1970) so encouraging conflict resolutions and exchanges.

However, lest this essay be seen as an uncritical partisan claim for anthropology to be the lead science in ethnoconservation, it is necessary also to list the failings that much modern social anthropology has exhibited. These may be summarized under four headings: splendid isolation, lack of application, softness and naivety.

SPLENDID ISOLATION

We have stressed that ethnoconservation needs to be a hybrid discipline. Anthropologists certainly have worked in interdisciplinary teams but attitudes have not been basically co-operative. Anthropology has tended to view itself as a superior self-contained discipline, holistic and therefore not needing other disciplines. Perhaps not a professional guild like medicine, there is still a good deal of ethnocentrism. This isolation is increased by the reluctance of some other disciplines, especially outside the social sciences, to accept anthropology. Certainly ecology, zoology, botany etc. and anthropology will need to join hands more often for ethnoconservation to be effective. As a small example, the anthropological monographs we have talked about may give local names for species but not accepted taxonomic names.

LACK OF APPLICATION

Applied anthropology has had a chequered history. Until the Second World War it might be argued that anthropology was too applied. Many early studies, at least in Britain and France, were connected with social problems that arose in the colonial system. In some newly independent nations anthropology became something of a dirty word and there was a shift of resources to sociology or other social sciences. There were certainly some newly independent countries where anthropology retained both its reputation and a pragmatic orientation, notably India, whilst individual anthropologists pushed on with applied work, notably Fei Xiao Tong in China. In America and Europe anthropologists continued to be used (and some times abused) by agencies with developement interests, though there was much less work done in the environmental sector than for example in agricultural development. Certainly too there was a professional group, the Society for Applied Anthropology whose membership was mainly American and in 1981 similar groups were created in Europe. But the main thrust was still academic, a continuing involvement in what critics called "kinship algebra", the finicky details of marriage and descent systems. Even the work that involved fauna and flora, like the magisterial tomes of Levi Strauss (1970) and his followers on totemism and Amazonian myths, though rich in ethnographic detail was largely framed in terms of longstanding European philosophical debates rather than practical development problems.

SOFTNESS

Many "physical" or "natural" scientists regard social anthropology as the softest of what are regarded as all soft social sciences. Certainly, going back to Leach's (1976) distinction, the rationalist social anthropologists who claim a leading role for ideas and ideology, do not use much quantification. This is much less true of the empirical anthropologists who went through a very definite phase of counting everything. Demographic/ anthropological studies have certainly been laden with hard numbers. It might be argued too that the movement against positivism which had its roots in a reaction against the overly deterministic 19th century search for "laws" is potentially well adapted to conservation/development situations which are often fragile, volatile and flexible. Put crudely, it is not easy, perhaps impossible, to predict social events from even the most sophisticated quantative analysis and of more value may be a series of alternatives and contingencies which add up to different scenarios. The most serious effect of the hard/soft argument may be the way it prevents dialogue between physical and social scientists who each have a stereotype of each other and a block to communication.

The real point about the hard and soft argument, (and probably a necessary precondition for future work) is not so much that one side is right or wrong but that the issue is to some degree irrelevant. A common ground may be found in the so called qualitative or topological mathematics, which few anthropologists (a notable exception being Edmund Leach) have attempted to utilize. A significant application of topological ideas may be Thomian catastrophe theory. In many ethnoconservation situations the object of environmental planning may be to identify critical threats or risks and to set up preventive mechanisms. There may often be a critical mass in the conservation of species and something similar may apply to endangered human populations and their cultural traits as well, and probably the two are interdependent. At a given point the spiral may go either way, viciously down or virtuously up, to borrow Myrdahl's phrase. Few anthropologists (apart from those who are hybrid historian anthropologists) have really attacked these problems of criticality and causality.

NAIVETY

Most anthropologists have worked in situations of participant observation in direct contact with the people and often in most contact with certain elite groups. The "Take me to your chief" syndrome remained important after the colonial period, contact with women, young people or lower castes within the fieldwork area were rarer. Whatever its virtues the grass roots perspectives approach had some de-

fects too. There was a tendency, for instance, to
sometimes idealize the village community in the
manner of Rousseau and this may explain the cases
of contradictory analyses e.g. Oscar Lewis after
Robert Redfield in Tepotzlan, Mexico, or Derek
Freeman after Margaret Mead in Samoa. There was a
tendency too, to avoid policy issues, and documentary evidence, both a vital part of an action
oriented ethnoconservation.

CONCLUSION

The main reason why anthropology is of interest in
conservation and development is its concern with
both the ideas embodied in culture and the often
minority cultures of the world. The difficulties
of incorporating anthropology more fully into conservation activities is common to most interdisciplinary, intersectoral work. The structures
of the universities and their curricular have tended
to defend existing territories and the economic
crisis has further prevented boundary crossing.
Government agencies, and also international
agencies, have too many vested interests in the
top-down philosophy. There is then a leading role
to be played by NGOs like IUCN in creating genuinely
interdisciplinary teams and projects in the closest
touch and the deepest co-operation with local communities, and in this way giving a reality to ethnoconservation.

REFERENCES

Ardener, E. 1974. in Parry H. B. (Ed). Population
    and its Problems. Oxford University Press.
Brokensha, D. et al. 1980. Indigenous Knowledge
    Systems. Lanham, University Press of America.
Bulmer, R. 1967. Why the Cassowry is Not a Bird.
    Man n.s. V. 2 n. 1, pp. 5-25.
CEP (Commission for Environmental Planning, IUCN).
    1983. Culture and Conservation - An Action-
    Research Plan. Gland.
Defence for Children. 1982. Self Reliance. Mouton.
    Berlin.
Douglas, M. 1973. Rules and Meanings. Penguin,
    Harmondsworth.
Emmers, L. 1978. Facts and Fallacies Concerning
    Basic Needs Approach. Cahiers de l'Enfance.
    V. 41 pp. 28-40.

Evans-Pritchard, E. 1940. The Nuer. Oxford University Press.

Goodland, R. 1982. Tribal Peoples and Economic Development. World Bank, Washington.

Hall, P. 1982. Planning Disasters. Penguin.

Jacobs, P. 1981. Environmental Strategy and Action. University of British Columbia Press.

Leach, E. 1970. Political Systems of Highland Burma. Boston, Beacon.

Leach, E. 1976. Culture and Communication. Cambridge University Press.

McFarlane, A. 1976. Resources and Population. Cambridge University Press

Pitt, D.C. 1970. Tradition and Economic Progress. Oxford University Press.

Pitt, D.C. 1976. Social Dynamics of Development. Permagon Oxford.

Pitt, D.C. 1976a. (Ed) Development From Below. Mouten, The Hague.

Pitt, D.C. 1977. Population and Development. University of Auckland.

Richards, P. (Ed) 1975. African Environment. International African Institute, London.

Tambiah, S.J. 1969. Animals are Good to Think and Good to Prohibit - Ethnology. V. 8. n. 4. pp. 4241-459.

Turnbull, C. 1972. The Mountain People. London. Cape.

Vayda, A.P. (Ed) 1969. Environment and Cultural Behaviour. Natural History Press, New York.

Winick, C. 1968. Dictionary of Anthropology. Littlefield, Totawa, NJ.

Zeeman, E. 1977. Catastrophe Theory. Addisen-Wesley Reading, Mass.

Chapter Twenty-One

THE IMAGE OF NATURE IN THE URBAN ENVIRONMENT

By

F. Terrasson
Muséum National d'Histoire Naturelle
Service de la Conservation de la Nature
36, rue Geoffrey St.-Hilaire
Maison de Buffon
75231 Paris Cedex 05, France

ABSTRACT

A very important factor in understanding reality is mental images. We need to know what lies behind the image of nature. A series of methodological considerations are suggested, by which this dynamic image can be understood. Then there is a discussion of the images that urban societies hold of nature. These images, mythical and fantastic, whether positive or negative, are totally unrealistic, and often destructive.

UNCERTAINTY

Disparities in the access to certain assets are easy to describe. Identifying the basis of the claim to equality is however more difficult to achieve, especially in the case of nature. When we talk of the things that are lacking, that have been denied to some of us, do we refer to snow, to winter sports, to swimming at an overcrowded beach; or are we talking about a walk in a peaceful park, making contact with what is left of rural civilization?

When we talk about a yearning for nature, we imply that we have a precise image of what nature is, both objectively as a reality, and subjectively, in the fantasy of the dreamer.

At the scientific level, the natural environment is the sum of all biological and physical elements of our ecological systems. But this definition throws absolutely no light on our problem. What brings about a decision, the answer to the yearning, the need for being in nature, does not in any way correspond to a cold and objective evaluation of the reality, but rather to an intuitive and emotional response.

It is well known, and our advertising people never let us forget it, that what really matters is the mental image of a product. This image conforms in varying degrees to the reality, or may not, in fact, relate to it at all.

What then is the image projected by this product "Nature"? There lies the question, even if we do not place ourselves in the marketing perspective of supply and demand. Let us summarize the principles of the method to be used in order to understand the mental images involved. Improvisation and approximations have caused considerable damage to the concept, since each of us assumes that his vision of nature is shared by all.

METHODOLOGY

Although it is impossible to list all the rules of behaviour that apply to a psycho-sociological survey, it is possible to make some specific points in connection with the analysis of the perception of nature.

The Question Must not Influence the Answer

Many studies dealing with the motivation of access to a natural environment were carried out by people (associations, administrations, professional tourist groups, etc.) who had not really come to grips with their own mental image of nature; they were not "deconditioned" in terms of what it represents and therefore communicated their own image through the unconscious manner in which they phrased their questions.

This complexity can also apply to psychosociological study groups and, in spite of the current familiarity with the more obvious traps of interviews, the emotional character of the relationship with nature creates many biases. These pitfalls produce and reinforce another problem, which will be dealt with further on, that of the interpretation of the answer. Influencing the interviewee by the way the question is posed, leads him to answer what he thinks is expected of him.

Consideration of the Fluctuations
of the Rules of Communication

It is not enough to issue a message; it must be done correctly. And it is not enough to issue it correctly; it must be received. Moreover, receiving it does not necessarily mean perceiving it correctly. It is essential to remember that when two people talk, the message is never strictly verbal. Tone of voice, facial expressions, body language, all add up to create a non-verbal language, the power and significance of which might be a determining factor. This type of non-verbal communication is especially relevant when emotions come into play, as they do with the concept of nature.

The above applies both to the questions asked and to the answers given.

No Literal Interpretations

The answers given during an interview are not really significant in themselves, for the following reasons:

- the bias of the question;
- the image that the interviewee tries to project (give the correct answer), in terms of the cultural models of the times;
- the very presence of a person whose opinion (in fact or by assumption) is valued by the interviewee;
- not knowing one's own mind. Many people have not given any thought to the question they are about to answer;
- dichotomy between conscious thought and the reality of unconscious drives;
- lying, pure and simple; and
- answers that conform with the super-ego and not with a behavioural reality.

When confronted by a tangle of interpretations, it is possible to turn to other techniques. Dynamic mental images are revealed more accurately through behaviour than through words. The ethological study of effective attitudes towards the natural environment indirectly makes it possible to return to their source in the fantasy of the inquirer and also to prove that yearnings and real behaviour patterns are often far removed from what has been said.

A combination of several methods is recommended because it makes cross-checking possible. It is, for instance, possible to recount dreams pertaining to nature, or spontaneous adventure stories in beautiful or terrifying natural environments.

GENERAL PATTERNS PERTAINING TO NATURE'S IMAGE

When carrying out a motivation study, it is important to consider the background of the theory of communication. But when we talk about the natural environment, this becomes the top priority as motives function at communication levels which are especially hard to study because they deal with emotions, instincts, drives and the unconscious mind.

This statement stems from the comparative study of what is the image of nature and the power it carries within different societies. It is easy to observe that on all sides, the first reaction to the universe is an emotional one and even when it is couched in rationalization, it is this emotional current which dominates and eventually takes over all decisions.

Recognized rules of behaviour in various societies are often communicated emotionally, rather than intellectually and through reason: music, ritualistic myths, fairy tales and, in our contemporary world, advertising, films and ideologies are examples.

In this context, societies depict nature as being a giant entity, which embodies everything that is not man-made. Nature, in fact, represents everything that has escaped our will, all that is not built or controlled.

When absolutely necessary, it also includes things that were built by man but in communion with Nature (for instance the bows and arrows of the so-called primitive societies, rural architecture, etc.). And mostly, all that is part of us but escapes our will our instincts and our drive, things that we tend to perceive as being part of nature within mankind.

This identification of the status of nature and emotional response, this kinship between the unconscious and the virgin forest will especially be relevant to the way in which the urban mind perceives wilderness.

BASIC MENTAL IMAGES OF NATURE AMONG CITY DWELLERS

Within the general background that we have just described, every culture has developed its own motives, on the basis of a few themes which are constantly being updated:

- Is nature good or bad; is it not, in fact,
  part of a concept that transcends these dis-
  tinctions?
- Are we part of nature?
- Should we fight it, or join it?
- Do we own nature, or is it an independent
  entity?
- Do we belong to nature?

Based on the answers to these questions, important
patterns have emerged in connection with the natural
milieu. Most people conform to these patterns in
their respective societies. The presence of individual deviations, of categories stressing certain
nuances, does not preclude the fact that these patterns influence the majority of people.
Evaluating the status of the city dweller in
terms of his yearning for nature thus only becomes
possible when we define the dominant cultural pattern pertaining to nature in our major occidental
cities. It is also useful to remember that this
emotionally charged model might be as unconscious
for our repressed and controlled societies, as the
very emotions they stem from.
What goes through our minds is a complex ima-
gery which embodies contradictions, myths, concrete
or imaginary facts, references to several phases of
life, on the basis of a status comparable to that
of nature itself.
A complete account is impossible. But it is
most useful to have a checklist to verify this ima-
gery when attempting to establish policies dealing
with nature.

The Good Nature
"Nature has made us. It has given us life. It
grows our food. Nature is our Mother. We must be
faithful, go back to her, since she is the source
of life".
It thus follows that "Everything in nature is
good for us. It suffices to be in nature to heal,
to be well". This good nature is easy to wander
through, it is forever sunny and warm. There may

be snow but "it is still sunny". Snow never falls,
it is simply there, a permanent gift.
The man of nature is good, a hard worker. Nowadays, the peasant is the latest version of the
noble savage. We can and we must consume nature's
products.
This idyllic vision was created and is being
nurtured by several factors:

- The release of different concepts dealing
  with the protection of nature. Even if the
  organizations responsible for releasing the
  information have not said in so many words
  that nature is always good, this is the message that the public has perceived, since why
  would one wish to protect something that is
  not fundamentally good?
- Movements that might be called "fundamental
  ecology", which extoll the merits of natural
  foods, refuse vaccination, reject medicine,
  etc.
- Advertising by travel agencies, publicizing
  nature forever beautiful, attractive and
  safe.
- A general indoctrination towards a thought
  process which is simple and manichean:
  things are good or bad, black or white, no
  shades of grey.

It is obviously not necessary that a large section
of our population really adheres to all these images, created by these groups. A mere inculcation
is sufficient. Without refusing vaccinations directly, the impression is left that nature is good,
nature is best... One might perhaps learn on reading the newspaper that bilharzia is rampant in
Africa, but this fact will be absorbed by the intellectual portion of the brain and will not eliminate
the emotional image created by the tourist folder
in which Africa is warm, radiant and bare under the
sun.
The images consequently produced are easily
revealed, they stay close to consciousness. However,
the following theme tells a different story.

The Bad Nature
Somewhere lies a disappointing sub-nature, not the
good nature, but a nature which greatly disturbs us.
All the things that wallow in slime, all the
organic creatures like toads, snakes, octopi...

And within our own human nature, all the organic phenomena, digestion, decay of bodies, blood and secretions, even our sexuality, all these items display a repugnance which reminds the city dweller that he himself is an organic animal. All that sticks, that oozes, that crawls or slithers is bad and must be destroyed. "It is hard to understand why nature produces such things. So much, in nature, is beautiful, why not rather protect those elements?" Thorns, quagmires, puddles, brambles, what an abundance of hostile, nasty nature.

Those characteristics are not qualified as natural. They are even perceived as being against nature, abnormal in fact.

Since it has been decided that all that was natural was good, all that is not pleasant and friendly to man shall not be accepted as being part of nature. Many elements that are part of the ecological reality are not part of nature for the city dweller and when he destroys them, he does not feel that he goes against the preservation of nature.

It is thus hardly a contradiction to say that nature is good and bad at the same time. What is bad simply does not have the right to exist.

The principal causes of this situation are likely to be as follows:

- the deficiency or poor quality of the teaching of natural science;
- the predominance in our daily lives of an overprotected environment, characterized by insufficient biological parameters;
- the ideological influence of a group of decision-makers and technicians who deal with biological factors as if they were dealing with industry; and
- the identification within a society of repressed instincts, swinging between the savagery and the organic quality of nature on the one hand, and the driving impulses of thwarted instincts on the other, a situation which produces both guilt and terror. The rejection of the animal elements of man leads us to reject that which reminds us of it in open nature or which represents it symbolically.

Nature the Liberator
The revenge of the repressed. We vaguely know that we have ignored the part of ourselves related to

nature.

We therefore imagine that these unconscious censures, that we both desire and fear, will automatically be eliminated at the very contact of fields and forests.

"Nature means the end of all constraints, it is our blossoming. It is the place which imposes no rules, where we may finally be ourselves. In nature, all is permitted". In nature, we also find this elusive "elsewhere", this fairy kingdom where you can have your cake and eat it too, a place which is always different from the famous "here and now" that we all know. In effect, the emotional impact created by nature can destroy the barriers erected by conscious thought and build a really wild natural milieu: deep forests, caves, desert, virgin forests, or simply narrow milieu.

In this case, fear of the unconscious thought which emerges can provoke a fear of the nature that produced it. Thus there is a desire to transform the wilderness into a cultural mould (neon signs and fences), so that the mind can cling to what is familiar and does not open towards its own depths, made terrifying by the absence of emotional education in our societies. Going towards nature that is perceived as liberating, and sometimes rightly so, we then make an abrupt come about fearing the problems inherent to freedom. And so we proceed towards an artificial state of freedom, which involves breaking down fences, rolling in fields of hay ready to be harvested, littering, making noise and loudly demanding more control and more development.

I Compensate - I Consume
The nature rush is thus largely the search for a mythical paradise, as opposed to an inferior daily routine. The dichotomy between nature and city is parallel to that between work and leisure and these oppositions are black and white.

The motor is therefore the compensation, and its necessary corollary is consumption.

Any durable emotional void tends to create compensation, which is occasionally a palliative measure, but it is always a temporary one, and the basic problem just goes on and on.

What is compensated by a flight into nature is an existentialist dissatisfaction, a state of affairs which is very general everywhere and at all times.

Even those who live in nature, and often in full harmony with nature, dream of far-off paradises.

It would thus be mistaken to believe that a flight into nature comes only from the lack of biological surroundings. However, the poor adaptation of our primate physiology to living and working in a large city reinforces this process, and leads one to dream of heavenly lands. Stress needs a paradise.

This paradise has been depicted as a wild natural environment. When it disappoints us, we attempt to transform it, but it mostly sustains the idea that compensation is a good way to solve problems, a concept which is indefencible on the psychiatric level.

Compensate through nature, consume from nature, that is the model through which the city dweller nurtures his dissatisfaction and his neurosis.

Nature Enhances Me

An important enhancing factor is "Keep up with the Jones's".

Today, it is fashionable to go into nature. Everybody is doing it. It's in. It is an integration rite. To go where everyone else is going, that really shows that I am accepted, that I am one of them, that I behave in a way that society has deemed as being worthy.

Then there is another factor. Going into nature means doing what everyone else is doing, but "everybody else" is perceived as a type of elite. They who have grasped the value of nature before anyone else did.

This worthy natural milieu is not actually related to its ecological worth, but rather to a transfer of worth upon the nature lover.

"I am among those who understand"! Running parallel is another component of worth, which deals with a nature that is hostile, difficult, a nature to be beaten. A certain macho attitude is evoked, based on the old relationship between nature and female. We therefore wear the costumes and various attributes likely to project the image of dynamic virility, and that of belonging to an avant-garde where one feels superior and integrated.

The general cultural fabric of our societies constantly supports this state of mind, with its concepts of domination, of control, of transformation, of battles and fights, as soon as we talk about the elements of the natural environment.

Nature in the Urban Environment

A GLOBAL MODEL; VARIABLES AND DEVIATIONS

Such mental images appear to dominate. This does
not mean that no one can escape them. They may only
partially exist among some people, and with more or
less intensity. They may or may not co-exist with
other more rational images.
Their power shall be considerably influenced
according to the type of nature involved. Both
mountain climbing and deep sea diving are enhancing
activities. Lolling about on a beach is much less
so.
The contact with a highly humanized nature, in
dreamy parks or leisure developments, will never
provoke an image of a terrifying nature. A rural
environment will often project the image of the
"Good Nature", more so than does a wild forest.
It is therefore important to adjust the above
information according to different places, the
nature of activities and also, according to the
psychological profile of the individuals involved.
This will require additional study for each
category.
In the framework of the general policy applying
to those who habitually seek out nature, such nuances will not be necessary. They become locally
operational when studying various tourist developments. At the national level, it is the attitude
of the masses that count.
This is the reason why the images carried by
minority groups, which possibly project a more objective vision, are not analyzed in this study: we
are talking about the amateur naturalists, artists,
regular practitioners of outdoor activities,
hunters, fishermen, etc.
Nor has anyone developed the differences of the
attraction between an officially protected natural
environment that carried a label, and "normal"
nature, places that are frequented less or for different reasons. The image of "protected" nature is
quite complicated and in order to analyse it, one
would have to draw up some extensive psycho-
sociological preliminaries.
Let us just say that this image conforms to
the above characteristics with a special regularity
and at a most powerful register, magnifying the
various phenomena$\underline{1}/$.

CONCLUSION: A DANGEROUS MYTHICAL UNREALISM

For most of us who like to be, or would like to be, in nature, it is a mythical place, the promotion of fantasies of power, of evasion, of motherly support or, in a negative vein, of distress or aggression. To this end, we use some objective facts, which we later integrate into a comprehensive image, an image which is totally unrealistic.

The gap between the image projected by the "product" we expect and the reality leads us to request modifications of this image, the transformation of the populations involved, the "artificialization" of the landscapes visited.

The yearning for nature presently expressed by most people is doomed to remain forever unsatisfied, as it corresponds to a reality which does not really exist. It leads to activities that dress up a so-called desired nature with the signs which would hopefully make it look like the mythical image. Thus the pseudo-rural, the peasant of the olden days, the artificial handicrafts and the so-sophisticated folklore. Education and information methods, applied to tourism, have, until now, under-played the importance of these mythical components. Starting from the concept that placing man in nature enhances him, they have not yet adopted the idea that, on the contrary, it is the city man who modifies nature, in his desperate attempt to make it into a disembodied and neurotic conception.

The axes of another policy that we do not intend to develop here must be subject to some harsh statements:

- The yearning for nature is not what we thought.
- In its present form, it is practically impossible to fulfil.
- It is destructive in terms of civilizations and environments.
- It is not knowledge, rest or thought oriented, but leans to a passive consumption, the anti-educational impact of which is a great source of concern.

Nature in the Urban Environment

NOTE

1. Please refer to Jean-Paul ZUANON's study:
"La protection de la Montagne, des discours aux politiques, des mythes aux réalités." (Protection of
the mountain, from speeches to policies, from myth
to reality). Institut d'études politiques. Université des sciences de Grenoble, juillet 1980.